A WINE TOUR OF FRANCE

A WINE TOUR OF FRANCE

A convivial Wine Guide
& Travel Guide
to French vintages & vineyards

Updated Edition

Frederick S. Wildman, Jr.

Vintage Books
A Division of Random House
New York

FIRST VINTAGE BOOKS EDITION, May 1976

The greater part of the contents of this book has appeared as separate articles in *Gourmet Magazine*.

Library of Congress Cataloging in Publication Data

Wildman, Frederick S
    A wine tour of France.
    1. Wine and wine making—France. 2. France—
Description and travel. I. Title.
[TP553.W55 1976]   641.2′2′0944   75–37822
ISBN 0–394–71755–4

Maps by Joan Maestro

Cover photograph: Marvin Newman—DPI

Manufactured in the United States of America

To my father, Frederick S. Wildman,
who early in my life taught me to love wine
and to Earle MacAusland,
who encouraged me to write about it

Preface

Wine is one of man's oldest, pleasantest, and most consoling companions. Its myriad nuances add dimension to our sense of beauty. It also has a magical quality—noted by such diverse men and organizations as François Rabelais and many Christian sects —and this is its inherent sociability, its capacity to change the most splintered group into a communal whole. The simple drawing of a cork can transform a dreary supper into something alive and warm. Like a candle at the center of a darkened table, wine's glow fuses those within its ambit into a convivial brotherhood. In this era of mass communications, but of private isolation, that is no small boon.

Wine is a pleasure and a friend. The drinking of it can be an uplifting aesthetic experience; it certainly generates an ambience of conviviality at table and elsewhere. I have had the good fortune of being born into a very winey family and so found all this out early. I also discovered, the first time at the age of six, the delights of touring through the world's greatest vineyard— France. A few years ago, when I was still a rather tremulous neophyte as a writer, Earle MacAusland, the editor and publisher of GOURMET, encouraged me to convert my random scribblings into articles for his magazine, and out of these this book was born.

For the armchair traveler, it is hoped that the book will be informative and amusing, giving him the savor of France and an understanding of those of her wines he finds available from his local merchant. But better yet if the book succeeds in goading him from his comfortable retreat to explore the pretty French countryside and to indulge for a few weeks in unbridled bibulous pleasure. For A WINE TOUR OF FRANCE is designed to be of practical use to the actual as well as to the vicarious traveler.

At the beginning is a map of France with a suggested twenty-one-day itinerary circling the country by way of her finest vineyard regions. Therefore, the tour is divided into four trips—to Champagne and Alsace; through Burgundy and the Rhône; to Armagnac, Bordeaux, and Cognac; and down the valley of the Loire and to the Normandy coast. If all four trips are to be taken consecutively, breaks of a week or so between them are certainly recommended—to get off the road for a bit and to let one's gastronomic ballast settle. There are approximately 60 *Michelin* stars scattered throughout the itinerary. These combined with the multitude of *caves* and tasting sheds along the way would make the most heroic gastronaut whimper and reach for his Eno's Fruit Salts. And even apart from the physical liability in taking such a marathon all at once, aesthetically speaking it would be a pity. France is, after all, a gourmet's paradise, and paradise should be savored slowly, not sprinted through.

It must be assumed, too, that not everyone—alas, probably all too few—will have the time to space out the twenty-one-day tour to the ideal six or eight weeks. If one has but a short vacation, any one of the four trips can be undertaken handily—with a leisurely pause in a resort area or a stay in Paris at the end—within the paltry two or three weeks American custom decrees is an adequate holiday. Indeed, one can pick up the tour anywhere along the twenty-one-day road that may be convenient, as each day is planned to link with the next in a continuous circle, with driving distances, restaurants, and hotels carefully considered, so that those who are pressed for time can make the most of the portion of the journey they take.

There are other good reasons to take this tour in as leisurely a manner as possible. A tour becomes more than just a question of sightseeing when it has a point of focus. In France, where taste is a fine art, no more fitting one could be found than her wines. There is something about wine that seems to encourage the muses. Where good wines are made, there, too, architecture, literature, music, poetry, and certainly the cuisine, have flourished. The Burgundian-Flemish roofs of Beaune, the paintings of Van Gogh done at a stone's throw from Châteauneuf-du-Pape and Tavel, the writings of Ronsard and Rabelais on the banks of the Loire, of Montaigne and Montesquieu in Bordeaux, the glorious cuisine of the late Fernand Point at Vienne in the Rhône valley—all were touched with a vinous grace. Such great works should be enjoyed at one's leisure, on the spot, with a bottle of what their creators savored.

Here, then, is the book, which covers a lot of this. It is not just a treatise on the vineyards of France, but also a ramble through its legends, history, art, architecture, literature, and gastronomy—all from a Bacchic point of view, or, to mix Saint Paul's metaphor slightly, "seen through a wine glass clearly." Writing this was something of a labor of love, and I can only hope that it will give as much pleasure in the reading of it as there was in its writing.

F. S. WILDMAN, JR.
February, 1972

Contents

List of Maps

Lists of Major Vintages

A WINE TOUR OF FRANCE

A Brief History of French Wines

& *Diverse Information on Storage,* *Service & Tasting*

France is *the* great nation of wine. Others on this planet provide excellent vintages. Some even make unique ones. But no other country produces such superb wines in anything like France's profusion. To ignore her contributions would be as unthinkable as failing to mention the Bible in a survey of Western religion.

Wine, of course, has been around much longer than France; it has been with us at least since the dawn of recorded history. In those thousands of years before the advent of the icebox and the tin can, wine was one of the earliest preserved foods and one of the easiest to prepare. The problem of fresh food and drink was a considerable one. Few things kept, and if they were liquid they were likely to be unhealthy even when fresh. Primitive man learned to smoke, salt, and dry solid foods. Liquids in some instances could be converted into solids, such as milk into cheese, but almost every other pleasant or nutritious fluid turned or became dangerous. The juice of the grape, however, was an exception. It not only tasted good but improved with age. It was healthful and harbored no nasty bacilli, and its mildly alcoholic content produced an exhilarating effect. Small wonder that such a beverage was considered fit libation for the gods.

The Athenians, who were great tipplers, probably brought the wine grape to France. Marseille was one of their earliest trading posts in the western Mediterranean, and though the resident

Greeks doubtless preferred their own vintages of Chios and Lesbos, they probably planted vineyards nearby to provide their day-to-day needs. A rather chauvinistic school of French wine writers maintains that there were vineyards in the Rhône valley and in Burgundy even before the Greeks arrived. To back the theory, there is evidence of vines in French soil that go back into prehistory. That the ancient Gauls had deliberately cultivated these is not beyond possibility. Far from being the rude barbarians depicted by Latin-influenced historians, the truth is that the Gauls developed an advanced agrarian society, with towns and trading places, complicated metallurgy, and an intricate religion based on abstruse astrological patterns.

In the first century B.C., the legions of Rome swept through Gaul. Wherever the Romans went, vineyards sprang up behind. Under them, Gaul grew green with the vine, to such an extent that it began to rival the vineyards of Italy.

The perennial problem of Rome was a shortage of wheat; Italy's craggy soil served well for vineyards but could not supply enough wheat for her daily bread. Gaul, on the other hand, with its great broad plains of Beauce, Narbonne, and Champagne, was ideal wheat country. As wheat was what was needed, in 92 A.D., the Emperor Domitian decreed that no more Gallic land was to be planted with vines. Though the edict, like Prohibition in twentieth-century America, was imaginatively interpreted, it was not revoked until 280, by the Emperor Probus. It was a great day for the Gauls, who returned enthusiastically to their destined vocation.

By the fourth century, vines had been planted in nearly every area now known in north European viticulture. Burgundy, Bordeaux, the Rhône valley, and even the Moselle were under cultivation. The wine trade, which because of ease of water-borne transportation followed the great river valleys, thrived. Shortly thereafter the Roman Empire collapsed, as a mass of German tribes spilled over the frontiers. The Empire embraced Christianity as disaster overwhelmed it, and the Church became the island on which the flotsam of that magnificent wreck was gathered and preserved. Monasteries were created and became centers of music, architecture, literature, and religious speculation—places of calm in an angry sea of barbarism. Wine, of course, has always been a companion of the muses. Moreover, it was and is an integral part of the Mass, the very blood of Christ. So wherever the Church went, wine had to be available. The Roman viticultural methods the monks studied were advanced, and as these monks, ideally, had no higher goal than to strive toward perfection for the glory of God, it is not surprising that the Church became the discoverer and developer of many of France's finest vineyards.

Up until the seventh and eighth centuries, the pull of trade, communication, and culture was southward. But when the Moslems stormed across the Mediterranean world, that sea gradually changed from being the focus and highway of civilization to a stagnant pond. Consequently, Europe turned to the north where, under a Germanic tribe, the Franks, a new Empire was forming. For a moment, under its great emperor Charlemagne, western Europe basked in the false dawn of a new civilization. The shift in cultural direction affected wine, too. Charlemagne encouraged vineyards in his domains; the Rhine and Burgundy particularly bore the mark of his enthusiasm, and the great classic southern French vineyard areas of Narbonne and Provence began to be eclipsed by those closer to the stirrings of new wealth. Burgundy was within easy portage of the burgeoning Low Countries and Flanders, and its vineyards prospered. This historical taste is reflected to this day. Belgium and Holland have a penchant for good Burgundy, their per capita consumption being far above the European average.

Bordeaux moved in a different direction, largely because of a twelfth-century scandal. Eleanor of Aquitaine, married to Louis VII of France, grew tired of her husband's religiosity and love of Crusades, and an annulment was arranged. Then, to the great shock of the French, Eleanor married Louis' arch-enemy, the future Henry II of England. As a result, her domains in southwestern France passed to the English crown. Bordeaux thus became an English possession, and a great maritime wine trade sprang up. Britain's three centuries' domination of Bordeaux has influenced English taste ever since.

By the end of the fifteenth century, the English had been expelled from French soil, and Burgundy had been annexed. From then on, except for two upheavals, France developed steadily into the world's foremost vineyard.

The first upheaval was the French Revolution. All Church property was secularized, and the great ecclesiastic vineyards that had been so carefully tended for more than a thousand years were broken up and sold on the block. In many ways this was a tragedy. Great estates, such as the Clos de Vougeot, were split into small plots and sold to dozens of owners. Some new owners maintained the high standards the monks had held; others, alas, simply used their plots to advertise their other commercial holdings. However, in general a high standard was kept, and so thé millennium of monkish effort has been passed down through the new owners as a patrimony for the appreciative oenophile.

Then, a series of blights and diseases struck the vineyards of France during the nineteenth century, culminating in the last half with the dreaded phylloxera. The phylloxera, a plant louse native to vines of the eastern United States, was brought to Europe accidentally in a shipment of experimental rootstocks, and it ravaged European vineyards, killing the roots of the vines. It took years of struggle against this pest to find a solution. Finally, by grafting European cuttings to American rootstocks, which were immune to the phylloxera, Europe saved its vineyards. The resultant wine produced was much the same, with one marked difference. Wines made from the old, pure vines often lived seventy or eighty years; those from the new plantings were lucky to last half that long.

As the nineteenth century progressed and transportation improved, wines were shipped farther away, and the possibility of fraud increased. Of course, with the great château-bottled clarets there was less chance of dishonesty than with a bottle from some *négociant* who had bought and blended wines from dozens of small growers. The temptation to "stretch" a wine with a cheaper one, and undercut rivals, was a very strong one, and some firms succumbed. As each firm lowered its standards and prices, its commercial competitors were obliged to do the same. Adulteration of wines became widespread, and the reputation of French wines as a whole began to suffer.

Consequently, it was a red-letter day when, in 1935, French Senator Joseph Capus, after years of hard work, managed to have passed the founding law for the *Institut National des Appellations d'Origine des Vins et Eaux-de-Vie*. The wine lover now knows with reasonable certitude that any wine bottled in France under Appellation Contrôlée or V.D.Q.S. standards is guaranteed by law to be what the label says it is. The honor of French wines was saved, and for that we may be eternally thankful.

French wines today may be summarized in five general categories:

VIN ORDINAIRE

This is the lowest in the hierarchy of French wines, sold in all French grocery stores and supermarkets, and its price is based on its alcoholic content. It is made usually from a blend of North African wines and perhaps cheap wines from the Iberian peninsula or the Midi. Unless one is almost penniless, it is not to be sought after.

VIN DE MARQUE

This is a "trademark" wine that a specific *négociant-éleveur* (a person who buys wines and then blends and matures them under his control—literally "raises" them) has established as his brand. Depending on the firm that made it, a *vin de marque* may be quite good in a commercial sort of way. It is usually a blend of several wines, not necessarily all French unless so stated. A level higher than *vin ordinaire*, it is the usual table wine in French bourgeois households. Never great, but usually inoffensive and sometimes very pleasant. It is not expensive.

VIN DE PAYS

This is a cover-all term, not legally guaranteed. It simply means a wine of the countryside, and, depending on where you are, it may be good or awful. One often finds *vins de pays* in French country towns, sometimes right out of the barrel. Occasionally, though rarely, it will be a real find, for there are pockets of good wine produced in areas too small to go through the bother of registering for a V.D.Q.S. or Appellation Contrôlée commission. As these wines are generally consumed right in the locale, all the rigamarole would hardly be worth it.

On the other hand, as the wine is not legally protected, it may be simply a mixture an unscrupulous innkeeper is trying to foist off on an unwary drinker. However, if you like the man, and he looks honest, try his wine. It may be a very pleasant, and certainly inexpensive, experience.

V.D.Q.S. (VIN DÉLIMITÉ DE QUALITÉ SUPÈRIEURE.)

This term is a legal guaranty covering a sizable section of good French table wine. Though wines in this category are not generally as distinguished as those under Appellation Contrôlée, V.D.Q.S. covers areas that produce good, sound wines of pronounced regional characteristics. They are often bottled without a vintage date, but have to pass quite strict regulations as to how they were made—examinations of taste by knowledgeable, impartial juries, chemical analyses, and so forth—before they are allowed to carry the V.D.Q.S. seal.

APPELLATION CONTRÔLÉE

Appellation Contrôlée is a legal guaranty that covers nearly all French wines aspiring to excellence. The one major exception has been the wines of Alsace, which, because of their German roots, have been difficult to codify under a French system. However, codification was finally achieved in 1970 and all of Alsace is now under Appellation Contrôlée regulation.

A label with the words "Appellation Contrôlée" does not necessarily mean that the wine is good. Its primary function is to say that it is honest: what is on the label is, by law, in the bottle. There are other factors that intervene—mediocre vintages, or mistreatment of the wine by shipper, importer, or store owner, among others. Still, as Appellation Contrôlée covers only the better vineyard regions, it is safe to assume that the wine will be above average. If the vineyard is known to be good, the vintage a memorable one, the importer knowledgeable, and the storekeeper careful, the result will probably be excellent.

The system of Appellation Contrôlée, as set up by Senator Capus and since modified, is necessarily complicated. Each region has its own historical traditions which manifest themselves in many forms. Some regions use a single variety of grape to make their great wines. Others use a blend. Some kinds of grapes thrive in one kind of climate or soil, others in different ones. These are just the beginnings of the nuances and variations in which each region takes pride and which mark its wines with a distinct flavor and bouquet.

To bring order to this anarchy of wine types, semiautonomous Appellation Contrôlée committees, directed by wine notables of each locale, had to be established. Their task was to organize a system that would best guard and encourage the unique qualities of the local wine. As a result, each area has its own rules and classifications, which are constantly being modified to correct oversights and abuses, or just to reflect changes, as some vineyards of hallowed reputation sink and others start to swim.

For the amateur, unless he is a gentleman of leisure with large and independent means, keeping up with this mass of information is impossible. It has to be left to the professionals, the shipper or the importer.

How Wine Is Made

Red Wine is usually made from dark grapes, though occasionally a small percentage of white grapes is added to give the resultant wine delicacy and finesse. After the grapes are picked, they are placed in enormous, open-topped barrels called *cuves*. They are mashed to break their skins, and as the sweet grape juice seeps out it comes in contact with natural yeast on the grape skins. The action of yeast on the sugar in the grape juice causes fermentation.

Fermentation is the process whereby two elements of sugar are broken down roughly into one element of alcohol and one of carbon dioxide. Thus grape juice with a twenty-four percent sugar content will produce a wine with an alcoholic content of approximately twelve percent. The carbon dioxide dissipates into the air, causing a boiling effect as its bubbles float to the surface of the wine and break. The alcohol, of course, remains. (In the making of sparkling wines such as Champagne, a second fermentation is encouraged in a tightly wired-down bottle, and the carbon dioxide produced is trapped inside and forced down into the wine itself. Hence the bubbles.)

The color of red wines comes from allowing the grapes to

ferment for several days with their skins and often their stalks. The juice, or must, as fermenting juice is called, absorbs their flavor, tannin, and color.

Vin Rosé may be made of dark grapes or a blend of dark and light. A rosé ferments on the grape skins usually for about twenty-four hours; thus its color and flavor are not as deep as that of red wine. After their short period in the *cuve*, the skins are pressed dry, and the juice is added to the free-run juice that was pressed from the grapes by their own weight. The result is a pale red wine —*vin rosé*.

White Wine may be made from either dark or light grapes or a mixture of both. In all cases the grapes are pressed immediately, before their skins can lend their flavor, color, or tannin to the wine.

Chaptalization is a device used in wine making to guarantee an adequate alcohol content. Named after one of Napoleon's ministers, Jean Antoine Chaptal, Comte de Chanteloup, who popularized it, the process consists of adding sugar to the juice of grapes that have not received enough sunlight to have sufficient natural sugar. Sugaring is somewhat frowned upon by wine purists, and certainly a wine that is chaptalized will rarely achieve the marriage of ingredients that marks a great natural vintage. Still, the process has made a great many poor wines mediocre and several mediocre ones palatable, and one must count one's blessings. It is a pity, however, that chaptalization is sometimes overdone by those vintners who want to produce wines high in alcohol. In such cases there is often a pronounced residual sugar taste.

Sulphur is used in the vineyard as an insecticide; in the *caves* to fumigate and sterilize casks; and in wine making to stop unnecessary oxidation. It is also sometimes used in lesser wines to stop fermentation and allow the natural sugar to remain. Sulphur in all cases, and especially the last, has to be used with a very light hand, or else an unpleasant aftertaste will remain. Used properly, it is one of the best weapons in the vintner's arsenal. Used badly, it is one of his worst enemies.

THE MATURING OF WINE

After fermenting, wine undergoes a rather complicated period of aging in a cask usually made of oak. From time to time it goes through what is known as a *soutirage*, or racking—the clear wine is drawn off the top, leaving behind the lees (the heavy, coarse sediment) the maturing wine has thrown. Before the wine is bottled it is "fined," often with albumin, such as egg white, which is whipped into the wine. As the albumin sinks it carries the particles of floating sediment with it to the bottom of the cask. Sometimes the wine is then filtered as well. After bottling, a normal red wine (but not a Beaujolais) is left for at least two years to mature in bottle. White wines and rosés require less time.

Once it is in the bottle, a wine sometimes throws a deposit; if it is old, it will almost certainly do so. This by no means indicates that the wine is bad. It may be difficult to handle and it will probably have to be carefully decanted, but the deposit is also a sign that the wine is alive—it hasn't been pasteurized, artificially preserved, or run through filters until it is numb. Drinking a pasteurized or overfiltered wine is like having a conversation with an anesthetized patient. The outside form may be the same, but the wine is lifeless and there is no response.

STORAGE AND TREATMENT OF WINE

A wine continues to mature once it is in a bottle. There is a first stage of bottle sickness, when the wine for a while tastes flat and listless. It then goes on to reach a peak, and finally declines. The timing and duration of that peak vary, though a great wine may take longer to develop and to be recognized than lesser and more facile types. A great wine, in fact, is likely to be unpleasant and hard when young, saving its Olympian qualities for those who can afford to wait for it. It does not condescend to quick, easy popularity, but when it finally does come forth, few can deny that it was worth waiting for.

For the modern city dweller, storing wines for any length of time creates a problem. Apartments nowadays seem to be designed by zealous pygmies equipped with micrometers, their sole desire being to use the last inch of an already cramped floor plan. In such a situation, the only place to put wine is in the bottom of a closet, first making sure that heating pipes don't pass through it. The ideal temperature for storing wine is cellar temperature, or about fifty degrees. However, if the wine is not going to be put away for a long period of time, any place of moderate and, most important, stable temperature will serve nicely. Unlike whiskey or other distilled spirits, wine is a living thing, and it should be treated in the same commonsensical way as living creatures. People become sick with abrupt changes of temperature; so does wine. After severe shaking or protracted voyaging a wine, like a person, needs a rest. Otherwise, it will arrive at your table tired, and taste so.

If possible, a bottle should be stored on its side, label up, so that the cork will stay wet and not shrink, which would admit deadly air. The bottle should be label up so that it will be easy to read and any sediment will fall on the opposite side of the bottle. If in transporting the wine from wine closet to table the label is kept top side up, the deposit will stay where it has fallen and will not have a chance to mix.

SERVICE OF WINE

Moderately young red wines that have a lot of tannin in them, specifically those of Médoc and Rhône, do best when opened and then decanted; or a glass can be poured off the top of the bottle, allowing the air to reach a broader surface of the wine than the inch diameter of the neck. Wines should be left in this manner for an hour or two, to give them a chance to "breathe." Air seems to soften the taste of tannin, allowing the wine to break through it and blossom. However, wines that have little tannin, such as some Burgundies and very old clarets, will begin to die as soon as they are exposed to a large quantity of air. To allow them to breathe too much is to give them pneumonia, and one can taste their tragic demise as one empties the bottle.

TEMPERATURE OF SERVICE

A red wine is normally served at low room temperature, 65° F., though a Beaujolais is sometimes cooler, 55° F.

Most rosés and whites should be cool, but not icy. About 45° F. is excellent. A Champagne or liqueur wine such as a Sauternes may be even a little cooler, let's say 40° F.

Overuse of the ice bucket kills bouquet and flavor. The only man who wants his wine ice-cold is one uninterested in its taste. He should stick to Martinis.

It is the abominable habit of thoughtless or lazy wine stewards to store their white wines and rosés permanently in the refrigerator, which ensures their being half dead from cold on arrival, and to place the bottle, after pouring the initial libation, in an ice bucket until it is freezing. In the former case, there is little one can do but try to warm the wine up gently and hope for the best. In the latter, the bottle should be rescued at all costs. Forget your cuffs. Grab it, by the neck if necessary, and pull it dripping wet up on the table.

GLASSES

A good wine glass has a stem and is of clear crystal. It is about the size of an orange, with a roundish bowl and a chimney that come together a little at the top. It has a capacity of ten to twelve ounces, and it should never be filled more than halfway.

The reasons for the design and service are quite logical. The glass has a stem so that one can hold it and not sully the brightness of the wine with the smear of fingerprints. It is clear crystal so that the color of the wine can be seen in its natural beauty, and—for those who are visually sensitive—a candle can project its flame in shimmering ruby or topaz on the tablecloth.

The design of the bowl allows the bouquet of the wine to concentrate at the lip of the glass—the point of rendezvous for it and the oenophile's appreciative nose.

The glass should never be filled more than halfway so that one has room to swirl the wine, coating the upper part of the glass with a thin winey film. As this evaporates, it creates a sublime vapor, which rises and concentrates in the glass's narrowing chimney.

For the collector of fine crystal, glassmanship is a most amusing pastime. Fine wine goblets are a pleasure to see and to hold, and if one wants to embark on a beautiful but expensive voyage through a good *cristallerie*, one will find a glass for nearly every type of wine. Some of these are legitimate shapes used in the locales from which wines come. Others are not. They are just lovely forms to titillate the eye and open the purse. For the long haul one needs a glass that is not too delicate and fragile, but is dependable, attractive, and easy to live with. The glass described above is such a one. It serves well for whites, rosés, and reds.

An ordinary bottle of wine, by the way, contains about twenty-five fluid ounces, which should serve between five and seven glasses—enough for one or two adults in good form, or three or four with dyspepsia.

THE ART OF TASTING WINE

To taste wine properly is, of course, mandatory if one is to recognize the shades, colorings, and nuances that make it great. A person who has not learned the trick of getting the taste of wine to the areas of maximum sensitivity must be bewildered and amused by all the talk of great wine vintages.

Most people taste with their tongues, useful but not very sophisticated sensory receptors. The tongue can taste sweet, bitter, acid, and salt, and thus is a good stage setter. It can help tell how old and how "ready" a wine is, and what its chemical constituents are. It can provide a bass harmony to the dozens of melodic variations that the symphony of great wine possesses. But in terms of sensory sensations it can't compare with the olfactory nerves that are in the nasal cavity above the mouth. This area is what most people improperly refer to as the palate. The palate, or the roof of the mouth, is actually quite insensitive to taste.

The problem is to get the fumes of the wine up into the nasal cavity without gagging. First, you examine the wine, letting light stream through it, or, if you are using a *tâte-vin*, letting the rays reflect back through the wine from the bottom of the little silver cup. Color gives an indication of age. Blood-red wines are likely to be younger than those with a russet hue. White wines with a golden color will be older than those of lighter color.

The wine should then be swirled in the glass and sniffed. The bouquet rising from the top gives a good idea of what will follow.

A small mouthful should then be taken and rinsed around the mouth and swallowed. This is known as "fixing the mouth"—cleaning it of previous flavors.

Another sip should then be taken and dandled a while on the tongue, teasing its zones of sweetness and acidity.

Finally, take a little wine and wash it all around your mouth, gargling a little if you wish. Then breathe air slowly through your mouth and the wine that is in it. Holding this wine-laden breath down in your lungs, swallow whatever residual wine remains in your mouth. Then shut your mouth and slowly and firmly breathe the fumes warmed in your lungs out through your nose. If the wine is a great one, a symphony of tastes will blossom in your head; for the olfactory nerves, which have been caressed by this trick, respond with far greater sensitivity to the nuances of taste than the tongue. This trick is the key to accurate winetasting.

However, a few words of warning. It takes a little practice to taste perfectly. The first few times, one is likely to breathe or swallow out of sequence. The result is a lusty cough and a deluge of wine. Once the trick is learned, it is easy to do, but it would be wise to practice the first few times near the kitchen sink.

One of the most appealing things about fine wine is that it runs directly counter to the acquisitive streak that seems to have infected so many other areas of pleasure. Unlike a painting or an uncut book, a mature wine cannot be bought for an "investment," it can be purchased only to be enjoyed. Like a flower in bloom it has its moment, then dies. To be enjoyed during this fleeting time, it must be opened and consumed; it cannot be kept.

So many traditional aesthetic pleasures have disappeared or become adulterated in this century. But wine remains a delight in good fortune, a comforter in adversity, a stimulator of conversation, and an inspirer of the senses. Man has had worse companions. We must be grateful that France continues to excel in the making of wines. To her and to those wines, then, let us raise a glass of her best, and set forth upon this tour of her vineyards and vintages.

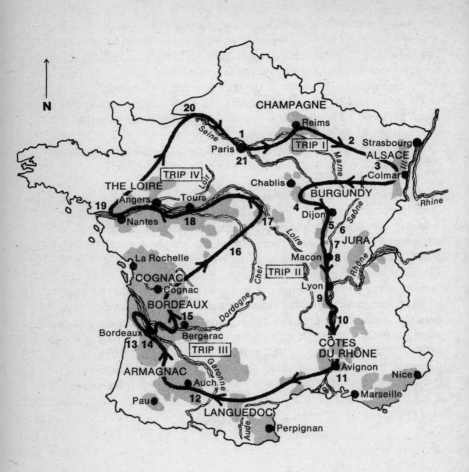

N

CHAMPAGNE

Reims

1 TRIP I 2 Strasbourg

Paris ALSACE

21 3

Colmar

THE LOIRE TRIP IV

Chablis BURGUNDY

Angers Tours 4 Dijon

19 5

Nantes 18 6 JURA

17 7

16 Macon 8

La Rochelle

COGNAC TRIP II

Cognac Lyon

BORDEAUX 9

15 Dordogne 10

Bordeaux Bergerac

13 14 TRIP III CÔTES
DU RHÔNE

ARMAGNAC Avignon Nice

Auch 11

Pau 12 Marseille

LANGUEDOC

Perpignan

Numbers on the map refer to days of the itinerary.

A Wine Tour of France

Itinerary

Indispensable to start out on any motor trip through France are: The over-all Michelin map, *France—Grandes Routes,* Number 989; the traditional *Guide Michelin* (the *guide "rouge"*); and the newer *Guide Kléber*. The two guides are extraordinary in their attention to detail and they are annually revised. Each has slightly different features—such as good maps of towns and cities in the *Michelin* and convenient, touristically annotated maps of every *département* in *Kléber*—and each makes slightly different epicurean judgment of restaurants. Above all, each has the exact up-to-date information on days of the week and times of the year when restaurants and hotels are closed. This WINE TOUR itinerary indicates for the months from March through October when the *restaurateurs* and *hôteliers* close down for their own holidays, but to travel off-season, or to plan on an important two- or three-star meal for a specific day, one should rely on the most recently published editions of the guides—not even editions of the previous year will be foolproof. It is worth noting, too, that the guides give the approximate prices you can currently expect to pay at restaurants and hotels; if the budget must be watched, they will tell you what you need to know. And, through ingenious systems of symbols, both guides require little knowledge of French to be understood.

Listed with each day of the itinerary are the Michelin regional maps for the area; these can be acquired as one goes along. With the proper map, one can confidently leave main highways and explore the countryside by pretty back roads—and, indeed, it will usually be along lesser roads that one finds the wine villages and their vineyards. Also listed are the Michelin *Guides Verts* for the French provinces. These are packed with intelligent touristic and historical information and some are published in English as well as in French.

For those making a leisurely tour or otherwise changing the itinerary, lists of additional restaurants and hotels are given near the beginning of each chapter of this book. Throughout, complete addresses and telephone numbers are given for the making of reservations. The name of the *département* (given in parentheses) must be used in all addresses and to make phone calls.

Finally, every lover of France and of wine would want to have —even if the luggage cannot hold them for the trip—two more books: *Bouquet de France* by Samuel Chamberlain (Gourmet Distributing Corporation, N.Y.) and Frank Schoonmaker's *Encyclopedia of Wine* (Hastings House Publishers, Inc., N.Y.).

TRIP I—Champagne & Alsace

DAY 1

Orly to Paris · 19 kms. or 12 miles · Michelin regional map 100 · Michelin Guide Vert *Paris* (in English) and *Environs de Paris* (in French)

Deplane at Orly, rent a car, drive to Paris. Lunch or supper at ***Lasserre** (17, avenue Franklin-D.-Roosevelt, Paris 8ᵉ; tel. 359.53.43—Host: M. Lasserre; closed Sundays and month of August) or at ***Maxim's** (3, rue Royale, Paris 8ᵉ; tel. 265.27.94 —Host: M. Vaudable; orchestra and dancing in the evening).

Hotels

Ritz: 15, place Vendôme, Paris 1ᵉʳ; tel. 073.28.30
Meurice: 228, rue de Rivoli, Paris 1ᵉʳ; tel. 073.32.40
Crillon: 10, place de la Concorde, Paris 8ᵉ; tel. 265.24.10
Plaza-Athénée: 25, avenue Montaigne, Paris 8ᵉ; tel. 359.85.23
Lancaster: 7, rue de Berri, Paris 8ᵉ; tel. 359.90.43

L'Hôtel: 13, rue des Beaux-Arts, Paris 6ᵉ; tel. MED.89.20
Pont Royal: 7, rue Montalembert, Paris 7ᵉ; tel. 548.42.50
Université: 22, rue de l'Universite, Paris 7ᵉ; tel. 548.45.62
Cayré: 4, boulevard Raspail, Paris 7ᵉ; tel. BAB.10.82
Saint Simon: 15, rue Saint-Simon, Paris 7ᵉ; tel. 548.35.66

Restaurants

See the excellently organized guides to Paris restaurants in both the *Guide Michelin* and the *Guide Kléber*.

DAY 2
Champagne (p. 31) · 320 kms. or 200 miles · Michelin regional maps
56 & 62 · Michelin Guide Vert *Nord de la France* (in French)

Morning: Leave Paris early by Porte de Pantin; take N. 3 to Épernay
(Marne)—140 kms. or 85 miles. Visit *caves* and taste Champagne.
Lunch at **Le Berceaux** (13, rue Berceaux; tel. 51.28.84—Hosts:
M. & Mme. Courgnaud); or, if country dining with a view is pre-
ferred, in Champillon (Marne) at the **Royale Champagne** (6 kms.
or 4 miles north of Épernay; tel. 3—Hosts: M. & Mme. Desvignes-
Dellinger).

Afternoon: From Épernay, take N. 3 eastbound to Chalon-sur-
Marne, switch to N. 44 to Vitry-le-François, then to N. 4 to Nancy
(Meurthe-et-Moselle), capital of Lorraine—distance from Épernay
is 180 kms. or 110 miles. Supper at **La Rôtisserie des Cordeliers**
(6, rue Bénit; tel. 24.33.38—Host: M. Maget). Spend night at the
Grand Hôtel Stanislas, on one of Europe's prettiest squares (2, place
Stanislas; tel. 52.83.62—Host: M. Pouchol).

DAY 3
Alsace (p. 43) · 180 kms. or 110 miles · Michelin regional map 87 ·
Michelin Guide Vert *Vosges* (in French)

Morning: From Nancy drive to Lunéville via N. 4, then to Sélestat
via N. 59; 13 kms. or 8 miles south along the river Ill is the town
of Illhaeusern (Haut-Rhin). Lunch at the charming and excellent
Auberge de l'Ill, one of the finest restaurants in France, with garden
on the riverside (tel. 47.83.23—Hosts: M. & Mme. Haeberlin).
Distance from Nancy to Illhaeusern—150 kms. or 95 miles.

Afternoon: Drive from Illhaeusern west 7 kms. or 4 miles to Ribeau-
villé, a charming Alsatian town, then south on the *route du vin* to
Riquewihr; sample Alsatian wines—Traminer, Gewürztraminer,
Riesling, and Sylvaner. For rustic and inexpensive evening, have
supper and spend night in Kaysersberg (Haut-Rhin) where Albert
Schweitzer was born and raised, at a charming country inn, the

Hôtel du Château (38, rue Général-de-Gaulle; tel. 47.12.72—Hosts: M. & Mme. Kohler). If luxury is essential, go on to Colmar (Haut-Rhin). Supper at the Maison des Têtes (19, rue des Têtes; tel. 41.21.10—Host: M. Edel; closed 1–20 July); spend night at Hôtel du Champ de Mars (2, avenue Marne; tel. 41.54.54—Host: M. Irrmann).

NB: Should you be taking this trip on the way to a vacation in Switzerland, see The Lesser Vineyards (p. 300) for vineyards of the Jura which lie southwest of Alsace, between Burgundy and the Swiss border. If you are going on to tour Burgundy, your next destination is the vineyards of Chablis.

TRIP II—Burgundy & The Rhône

DAY 4

Burgundy—Chablis (p. 66) · 380 kms. or 230 miles · Michelin regional maps 65 & 66 · Michelin Guide Vert Bourgogne (in French)

Morning: Leave early, taking N. 83 southwest from Colmar to Belfort, N. 19 to Vesoul and Langres, then N. 428 to Chatillon-sur-Seine (Côte-d'Or). Lunch at the excellent and charming country inn, the Hôtel de la Côte-d'Or (3, rue Charles-Ronot; tel. 31—Host: M. Richard). Distance from Colmar—275 kms. or 175 miles.

Afternoon: Drive west on N. 65 to Chablis (Yonne)—65 kms. or 40 miles. Taste wines, especially those of the Clos des Hospices, followed by Les Clos, Valmur, Grenouilles, Vandésir, and Blanchots; other interesting Chablis include Vaillon and Fourchaume. Then take D. 91 south of Chablis, cross Autoroute, take N. 444 to Avallon (Yonne)—40 kms. or 25 miles. Supper and spend night at excellent and lovely Hostellerie de la Poste (13, place Vauban; tel. 4.48—Host: M. Hure).

20 A WINE TOUR OF FRANCE

NB: To begin this Burgundy trip from Paris, get an early start and drive from Paris to Chatillon-sur-Seine in time for lunch—a distance of 245 kms. or 155 miles. Or, go directly from Paris to Chablis —180 kms. or 110 miles; lunch at the **Etoile-Bergerand,** visit the vineyards, and go on to Avallon for the night.

DAY 5
Burgundy—Côte de Nuits, Northern Section (p. 75) · 160 kms. or 100 miles · Michelin regional map 65 · Michelin Guide Vert *Bourgogne*

Morning: From Avallon drive via N. 6 and N. 454 through lovely village of Semur-en-Auxois. Drive on to Dijon, then southwest 8 kms. or 5 miles on N. 74 for lunch in Marsannay-la-Côte (Côte-d'Or) at **Les Gourmets** (tel. 23.41.87—Hosts: The brothers Gauthier & Mme. Gauthier). Or, drive 6 kms. or 4 miles farther down the *route du vin* to the famous wine village of Gevrey-Chambertin and lunch at the fine and charming restaurant **La Rôtisserie du Chambertin** (rue du Chambertin; tel. 34.33.20—Host: M. Menneveau; closed in August). Wines to sample here are Chambertin, Clos de Bèze, Charmes-Chambertin, Clos Saint-Jacques, Clos de la Roche, Clos Saint-Denis, and Bonnes Mares.

Afternoon: Continue on *route du vin* as far as Clos de Vougeot, then cut back onto N. 74 and go south 18 kms. or 11 miles to Beaune (Côte d'Or). Supper and spend night at a fine and comfortable restaurant-hotel known to generations of wine-lovers, the **Hôtel de la Poste** (3, boulevard Clémenceau; tel. 77—Hosts: M. & Mme. Marc Chevillot; closed from mid-November to first of April).

DAY 6
Côte de Nuits, Southern Section & Côte de Beaune, Northern Section (p. 86 & p. 100) · 40 kms. or 25 miles · Michelin regional maps 65 & 69 · Michelin Guide Vert *Bourgogne*

Morning: Visit Beaune, especially the wine museum and the astonishing Hôtel-Dieu, or "Hospice de Beaune," a medieval charity hospital for whose upkeep wine auctions are held every fall. Shortly after noon, return up N. 74 to Vosne-Romanée (Côte-d'Or) for lunch in a pleasant little roadside inn, **La Toute Petite Auberge** (Tel. 23.10.54—Host: M. Tupinier). Wines of the region include Romanée-Conti, La Tâche, Richebourg, Romanée-Saint-Vivant, La Romanée, Grands-Échézeaux, Clos de Vougeot, Musigny, and Échézeaux; also such curios as whites Blanc de Vougeot and Blanc de Musigny—quite a viniferous handful.

Afternoon: Visit town of Vosne-Romanée and Clos de Vougeot. Return toward Beaune, stopping off at town of Aloxe-Corton to visit vineyards of Corton and Corton-Charlemagne. Supper in Beaune at the **Hôtel du Marché** (12, place Carnot; tel. 4.23—Host: M. Croix). Wines to sample are reds, Corton or Corton-Grancey, and white, Corton-Charlemagne. Return for second night at **Hôtel de la Poste** in Beaune.

DAY 7
Burgundy—Côte de Beaune, Southern Section (p. 113) · 90 kms. or 55 miles · Michelin regional map 69 · Michelin Guide Vert *Bourgogne*

Morning: Leave Hôtel de la Poste in late morning, drive southward on N. 73 along Côte de Beaune via Pommard and Volnay to La Rochepot—17 kms. or 10 miles from Beaune. Visit Château de Rochepot and village; lunch at the **Relais du Château** (rustic, but very good).

Afternoon: Return to N. 73 to Meursault; taste wines. Turn south toward Puligny-Montrachet and Chassagne-Montrachet. Continue short way for supper and night in Chagny (Saône-et-Loire) at the pretty and very good **Hôtel Lameloise** (36, place d'Armes; tel. 49.02.10—Hosts: M. & Mme. Lameloise). Wines to try this day are reds, Pommard, Rugiens, Épenots, Volnay, Cailleret, and Santenots, and whites, Montrachet, Chevalier-Montrachet, Bâtard-Montrachet, Meursault-Perrières, and Meursault-Genevrières.

DAY 8

Burgundy—Chalonnais & Maconnais (p. 123) · 90 kms. or 55 miles ·
Michelin regional maps 69 & 73 · Michelin Guide Vert *Bourgogne*

Morning: Drive south from Chagny on N. 481 through wine villages
of Rully, Mercurey, and Givry to Cluny (Saône-et-Loire). Visit ruins
of the huge abbey. Lunch at the **Hôtel Moderne-Chanuet** (place
Pont-de-l'Etang; tel. 18—Host: M. Chanuet; closed early October
through mid-November). Or, lunch at another good restaurant,
the **Hôtel de Bourgogne** (place de l'Abbaye; tel. 14—Host: M.
Gosse). Red wines to try are those of Rully, Mercurey, and Givry;
whites, of Pouilly-Fuissé, Pouilly-Loché, and Pouilly-Vinzelles.

Afternoon: Drive past the prow-shaped rock of Solutré, through
Pouilly, then to Crêches-sur-Saône; cross the Saône River to east
bank and follow N. 433 southward to Thoissey (Ain). Supper and
spend night at the excellent and charming **Hôtel Chapon Fin** (tel.
49—Hosts: M. & Mme. Paul Blanc of the great culinary Blanc
family). Wines, same as above, plus reds of Beaujolais: Saint-
Amour, Chénas, Moulin-à-Vent, Juliénas, Fleury, Morgon, Brouilly
and Côte de Brouilly.

DAY 9

Beaujolais to Rhône, Northern Section (p. 133 & p. 145) · 100 kms. or
62 miles · Michelin regional map 73 · Michelin Guides Verts *Bourgogne* and *Vallée du Rhône* (in French)

Morning: Take D. 95 to Juliénas and follow *route de Beaujolais*
southward through Fleurie, Villié-Morgon, and Saint-Lager to Sal-
les-en-Beaujolais (all Rhône), stopping off at various village winetasting spots. Have simple lunch in Saint-Lager at **Au Goutillon**
(tel. Cercié 71—Hostess: Mme. Ruet) or in Salles at the attractive **Hostellerie Saint-Vincent** (tel. 4—Host: M. Favel). Or, for
lunch in one of France's finest restaurants, drive on to Villefranche-
sur-Saône and then south to Anse. Take left on D. 51 to Collonges-

au-Mont-d'Or (Rhône). Here is the great **Auberge Paul Bocuse** (50, quai Plage; tel. 47.00.14—Host: M. Paul Bocuse; closed 2 weeks in mid-August).

Afternoon: Drive to Lyon (Rhône), France's third largest city; sightsee and shop. Drive by Autoroute or by N. 6 to Vienne (Isère). Supper at **La Pyramide,** still one of France's great restaurants and shrine to the culinary genius of the late Fernand Point (boulevard Fernand-Point; tel. 85.00.96—Hostess: Mme. Fernand Point). Spend night next door at **La Résidence de la Pyramide** (40, quai Riondet; tel. 85.16.46).

DAY 10
The Rhône, Northern & Central Sections (p. 145 & p. 153) · 90 kms. or 55 miles · Michelin regional maps 74 & 77, or 93 · Michelin Guide Vert *Vallée du Rhône* (in French)

Morning: From Vienne, cross Rhône River to west bank and take N. 86 southward to Ampuis and Condrieu (Rhône). Above Ampuis are grown the wines of the Côte Rôtie, one of the Rhône's greatest reds. Condrieu itself produces, along with its neighbor, Château Grillet, an interesting and unusual white wine. There is an excellent and pretty restaurant in Condrieu, right on the bank of the Rhône, the **Hôtel Beau Rivage** (tel. 85.52.24—Host: M. Castaing). The cuisine is excellent, the wine list filled with the best local provender; it is a fine place to have lunch.

Afternoon: Proceed down-river to Tournon and cross to the east bank at Tain-l'Hermitage. Taste excellent Hermitages, both reds and whites, as well as Saint-Josephs, in Tain's central square. Then drive to Valence (Drôme) to have supper and spend night at the renowned **Hôtel-Restaurant Pic** (285, avenue Victor-Hugo; tel. 43.15.32—Hosts: the family Pic; closed in August). Here, sample white Hermitage, Chante-Alouette, red Hermitage and Crozes-Hermitage; also a white sparkling wine from across the river from Valence, Saint-Péray, different from Champagne but interesting.

DAY 11

The Rhône, Southern Section (p. 160) · 160 kms. or 100 miles · Michelin regional maps 93, 80 & 83 · Michelin Guide Vert *Provence* (in French)

Morning: From Valence take the Autoroute or N. 7 to Orange—100 kms. or 62 miles. Then take N. 576 in direction of Nîmes, turning left before the river Rhône to arrive at the pretty town of Châteauneuf-du-Pape (Vaucluse) for lunch at **La Mule du Pape** (place Fontaine; tel. 83.50.30—closed in August). It serves excellent Provençal specialties and has a fine cellar of wines of the locale.

Afternoon: Cross the river at Roquemaure, visit Tavel and Lirac, then head toward Avignon, stopping off at Villeneuve-lès-Avignon (Gard) to check in at the lovely **Hostellerie Le Prieuré** (place du Chapitre; tel. 81.76.31—Host: M. Mille). Spend remainder of the afternoon visiting Avignon (Vaucluse) which during the Middle Ages was the capital of Christendom. Dine at **Le Prieuré.** Wines to sample are Châteauneuf-du-Pape, both red and white, rosés of Tavel and Lirac, and wines of Gigondas.

NB: This regal trip through Burgundy and the Rhône could end conveniently with a seaside holiday on the Riviera. Distance from Avignon to Nice (Alpes-Maritimes) is 255 kms. or 160 miles.

TRIP III—Armagnac, Bordeaux & Cognac

DAY 12

Armagnac (p. 170) · see also The Lesser Vineyards (p. 300) · 420 kms. or 265 miles · Michelin regional maps 80, 83, 82 & 79 · Michelin Guide Vert *Pyrénées & Gorges du Tarn* (in French)

Morning: From Avignon, drive via Nîmes, Montpellier, Béziers and Narbonne to Carcassonne (Aude)—260 kms. or 165 miles. Explore medieval city and lunch at center of it at **Le Sénéchal** (6, rue Viollet-le-Duc; tel. 25.00.15—closed winter through March). Sample local wines of Minervois, Corbières, Rivesaltes, and Roussillon.

Afternoon: Drive on to Auch (Gers) at the center of Armagnac—
160 kms. or 100 miles. Supper and spend night at the excellent
Hôtel de France (place de la Libération; tel. 05.00.44—Host: M.
Daguin).

NB: Trip III can be taken independently of the others by flying to
Nice from Paris. Rent your car there, and take several days to explore the Mediterranean coast from the Italian border to Marseille
and Cassis, to go north to Avignon, and then to drive west, according to the itinerary above, to Auch and on to DAY 13 and the tour
through Bordeaux. Or, for a quick trip, fly to Bordeaux from Paris,
rent the car, and follow the itinerary, starting on DAY 13 with
lunch at Langon and a tour of the vineyards of Sauternes. You will
get back to Paris in six days (see DAY 16).

DAY 13

Bordeaux—Sauternes & Graves (p. 187 & p. 195) · 185 kms. or 115
miles · Michelin regional maps 82, 79 & 71 · Michelin Guide Vert
Côte de l'Atlantique (in French)

Morning: From Auch, take N. 130 northward to Nérac; from there,
N. 655 northwest to Grignols and Bazas. Lunch at Bazas at the
Relais de Fompeyre in the outskirts of the town on the Route de
Mont-de-Marsan, Bazas (Gironde) tel. 51. The host is M. Mora,
and the menu includes such regional *spécialités* as *Baudroie à la
Bordelaise,* one of the few denizens of the sea that is washed
down well with a good red wine, perhaps an interesting *vin de
Bourg* from the *Relais'* cellars. After lunch, Sauternes lies twelve
miles to the north. Distance 140 kms. or 85 miles.

Afternoon: Explore nearby vineyards of Sauternes, then drive approximately 50 kms. or 30-odd miles northwest to Pessac (Gironde),
just southwest of Bordeaux and not far from Château Haut-Brion.
Have supper and spend night at the pretty **La Réserve** (avenue
Bourgailh; tel. 45.13.28—Host: M. Flourens). Food and the wine
list are excellent. Wines to try are: dry whites, Châteaux Carbonnieux, Bouscaut, and Olivier; sweet whites, Châteaux d'Yquem,
La Tour-Blanche, Climens, and Coutet; reds, Châteaux Haut-
Brion, La Mission Haut-Brion, Pape-Clément, Haut-Bailly, Latour-Martillac, and Domaine de Chevalier.

DAY 14

Bordeaux—Médoc (p. 206, p. 215 & p. 222) · 150 kms. or 95 miles `·` Michelin regional map 71 · Michelin Guide Vert *Côte de l'Atlantique*

Morning: Drive north through the Médoc. At Pauillac, visit wine museum connected with Château Mouton-Rothschild. Lunch in Lesparre-Médoc (Gironde) at **La Mare aux Grenouilles** (tel. 3.46).

Afternoon: Drive back through Médoc to Bordeaux; spend rest of the day sightseeing and shopping in the city. Sup at the **Restaurant Dubern** (42, allées Tourny; tel. 48.03.44). Wines to try are Châteaux Latour, Lafite, Margaux, Mouton-Rothschild, and Pichon-Longueville, the three Léovilles, and Gruaud-Larose, Cos d'Estournel, Brane-Cantenac, and Palmer. Return for second night at **La Réserve.**

DAY 15

Bordeaux—Saint-Émilion & Pomerol (p. 233 & p. 244) · 80 kms. or 50 miles · Michelin regional map 71 · Michelin Guide Vert *Côte de l'Atlantique*

Morning: Leave Bordeaux eastbound by N. 136, driving through Entre-Deux-Mers. At Branne, turn right and go up the Dordogne River to Saint-Jean-de-Blaignac (Gironde). Here you will find, overlooking the river, the charming and very good **Auberge Saint-Jean** (on N. 670; tel. 51.51.06—Host: M. Male; closed last 2 weeks of September). Wines to try here are dry white Entre-Deux-Mers and Saint-Émilions and Pomerols.

Afternoon: Visit Saint-Émilion (Gironde), a charming old town, and the neighboring vineyards of Saint-Émilion and Pomerol. Have supper and spend night in Saint-Émilion at the **Hostellerie de Plaisance** (place du Clocher; tel. 51.72.32). Or drive to nearby Libourne for supper and the night at the **Hôtel Loubat** (28, rue Chanzy; tel. 51.17.58—Host: M. Ginisty). Wines to try are Châteaux Pétrus, Cheval-Blanc, and Ausone.

DAY 16

Cognac (p. 256) to Limoges · 240 kms. or 150 miles · Michelin regional map 72 · Michelin Guides Verts *Côte de l'Atlantique* and *Périgord* (in French)

Morning: From Saint-Émilion or Libourne, drive north to Guitres, and take N. 10 *bis* and N. 10 to Barbezieux. Then take N. 731 toward Cognac. Thirteen kms. or 8 miles south of Cognac, stop in Cierzac (Charente) for early lunch at a pretty inn, **Le Moulin de Cierzac** (tel. 32 at Saint-Fort-sur-le-Né—Hostess: Mme. Vignaud).

Afternoon: Visit Cognac and Jarnac and distilleries there in early afternoon. Then drive on N. 141 via Angoulême to Limoges, where one may shop for porcelain. Fourteen kms. or 8 miles northeast of Limoges at Saint-Martin-du-Faux (Haute-Vienne) is a good place to have supper and spend the night, the **Château-Hôtel La Chapelle Saint-Martin** (on D. 20; tel. 17 at Nieul—Host: M. Dudognon).

NB: Trip III can be ended by taking the route described next, for DAY 17, to Pouilly-sur-Loire and then returning the following day to Paris—Pouilly to Paris is a distance of 200 kms. or 125 miles.

TRIP IV—The Loire, Normandy & Calvados

DAY 17

Upper Loire (p. 267) · 240 kms. or 175 miles · Michelin regional maps 69 & 65 · Michelin Guide Vert *Châteaux de la Loire* (in English and in French)

Morning: From Saint-Martin, drive via N. 141 and N. 140 to the medieval city of Bourges (Cher) for lunch at the **Restaurant Jacques Coeur,** opposite the "palace" of the same name (3, place Jacques-Coeur; tel. 24.12.72—Host: M. Quilleriet; closed first 2 weeks of August). Wines to try are Quincy, Sancerre, and Reuilly.

Afternoon: Drive northwest via N. 455 to the lovely hilltop town of Sancerre, then go south a few kilometers and cross the Loire River to Pouilly-sur-Loire (Nièvre). Have supper and spend night at **L'Espérance** (17, rue R.-Courad; tel. 1.14—Host: M. Raveau). Wines to drink are Pouilly-Fumé and Sancerre.

NB: Starting Trip IV from Paris, the drive to Bourges for lunch is 225 kms. or 145 miles. Or, lunch in one of the several good restaurants in Pouilly-sur-Loire (p. 269).

DAY 18
Middle Loire (p. 277) · 220 kms. or 140 miles · Michelin regional maps 64 & 65 · Michelin Guide Vert *Châteaux de la Loire*

Morning: From Pouilly, drive down the west bank of the Loire on N. 751; stop to visit châteaux at Chambord and Blois. Lunch in Chaumont-sur-Loire (Loir-et-Cher) at the **Hostellerie du Château** (tel. 79.88.04—Host: M. Bonnigal). Wines to try are those of Vouvray and Amboise.

Afternoon: Visit châteaux at Chenonceaux and Amboise, then drive to Vouvray to visit *caves*. Have supper in Tours (Indre-et-Loire) at one of France's greatest restaurants, **Barrier** (101, avenue Tranchée; tel. 53.20.39—Host and chef is Monsieur Barrier himself; closed Wednesdays). Spend night in Montbazon (Indre-et-Loire) at the magnificent **Château d'Artigny** (south of Tours on D. 17; tel. 56.21.77).

DAY 19
Middle Loire to Lower Loire (p. 287) · 200 kms. or 125 miles · Michelin regional maps 64, 63 & 67 · Michelin Guides Verts *Châteaux de la Loire* and *Bretagne* (in English and in French)

Morning: From Montbazon, follow the Indre River on D. 17 to Azay-le-Rideau; visit the château. Then take N. 751 to Chinon, the fortified city where Joan of Arc forced the quaking king to recognize her and give her arms. Go on a short way past Saumur to Chêne-hutte-les-Tuffeaux (Maine-et-Loire) for lunch at the lovely inn, **Le Prieuré** (tel. 51.01.01—Hostess: Mme. Bernard). Wines to try are sparkling Saumur, reds of Bourgueil and Chinon, rosés and whites of Anjou.

Afternoon: Continue on N. 751 down the Loire to Basse-Goulaine (Loire-Atlantique)—8 kms. or 5 miles east of Nantes. Supper at the **Restaurant du Parc** (tel. 1—Host: M. Duteil; closed last 2 weeks of September). Wines to try are Muscadet and Gros Plant. Continue to Nantes (Loire-Atlantique) and spend night at the **Hôtel Central** (4, rue Couëdic; tel. 71.70.15—Host: M. Robert).

DAY 20
Normandy & Calvados (p. 295) · 400 kms. or 250 miles · Michelin regional maps 55, 59, 60 & 63 · Michelin Guides Verts *Bretagne* and *Normandie* (in English and in French)

Morning: Leave Nantes early, drive north via N. 178 to Château-briant. Take N. 775 and N. 178 *bis* to Laval, then N. 162 and N. 816 via Mayenne to Bagnoles-de-l'Orne (Orne). Lunch here at the very pretty **Hôtel Bois-Joli** (avenue Ph.-du-Rozier; tel. 33—Host: M. Guiral; closes at end of September for the winter).

Afternoon: Continue via Argentan and Lisieux to Pont-l'Évêque; here, visit Calvados distillery of Père Magloire. Then drive on to the ravishing Norman port of Honfleur (Calvados) at the mouth of the Seine. Supper and spend night at the charming **Ferme Saint-Siméon** (route de Trouville; tel. 3.47—Host: M. Goulet; closed winter through first 2 weeks of March). Sample Norman cider and Calvados brandy, and cheeses from local villages of Camembert, Livarot, and Pont-l'Évêque.

DAY 21

To Paris · 200 kms. or 125 miles · Michelin regional map 55 · Michelin Guides Verts *Normandie* and *Paris* (in English and in French) and *Environs de Paris* (in French)

Morning: From Honfleur, take N. 180 eastward to Bourg-Achard, N. 313 to Elbeuf, N. 321 to Pont-de-l'Arche, then D. 5A to Léry (Eure). Lunch at a fine country inn, the **Restaurant Beauséjour** (place de l'Eglise; tel. 8—Host: M. Nauwelaerts).

Afternoon: Drive back to Paris. Supper either at the *****Tour d'Argent** (15, quai Tournelle, Paris 5ᵉ; tel. 033.23.32—Host: M. Terrail; closed Mondays), or at the *****Grand Véfour** (17, rue Beaujolais, Paris 1ᵉʳ; tel. 742.58.97—Host: M. Oliver; closed most of August and Sundays).

Champagne

Flying the Atlantic is now merely a six-and-a-half-hour meal and snooze. Consequently, the cultural and time shocks are apt to be considerably greater than in the old days of a comfortable six-day crossing on the *Ile-de-France*. The cultural shock is of course not all that bad. Paris is a delight and there is no real pain in slipping off the plane into one's favorite restaurant to recoup with a good meal and a couple of choice vintages. The time shock is something else. Inside the body is a hidden clock; whatever the time is in France, it keeps ticking the hours that exist back home. It usually takes a few days before one gets hungry, sleepy, or awake at the right times.

The best way of changing the clock's rhythm is to have a splendid meal and go to bed early. With that one can get up at eight the next morning, French time—two o'clock in the morning in New York—without breaking stride. Any other system merely extends the period it will take to get used to the new time zone.

So, upon arrival, rent a car at Orly, drive to Paris, have a spectacular and well irrigated meal, go to bed, rise early the next morning, and set forth to the nearest of France's great viniferous provinces—Champagne.

It is ironic that the province of Champagne, the immemorial amphitheater of conflict between Europe's East and West, should provide the cool effervescence that has become the capstone for celebration and friendship. Champagne's rolling fields and bosky river bends periodically have been the site of man's bitterest and most dramatic struggles. Here Roman legionnaire fought with

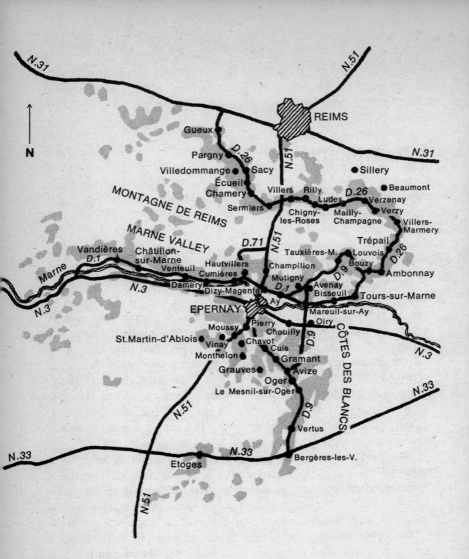

DAY 2
Itinerary p. 18

The Best Regions of Champagne

Michelin Regional Maps 56 & 62
Michelin Guide Vert *Nord de la France*

Gallic tribesman; here the bloody tide of Attila and his Huns was stopped by Theodoric, the Visigoth; here Poilu, Tommy, and Doughboy ground down the aspirations of imperial Germany after four years of ghastly deadlock.

It was also in Champagne, in 496, that Clovis, the warrior-chief of the Franks, was baptized and anointed by Saint Rémi, the bishop of Reims, in France's first official Christian ceremony. This started a custom that was to last nearly as long as France was a monarchy. The Reims cathedral became the French equivalent of Westminster Abbey, the holy spot on which her kings had to be anointed before they could validly wear the crown. It will be remembered that Joan of Arc's single driving ambition was to push the weak Charles VII to Reims so that France would again have a legitimate king around whom to rally and drive "Les Goddams," as the English were called, back beyond their Channel.

Joan was from Lorraine, but Champagne produced a host of its own men of arms. It was one of the great provinces of medieval France, and its counts and seneschals etched its name in steel and

---

RESTAURANT-HOTELS

Épernay (Marne)	*Le Berceaux p. 18, p. 37
Champillon (Marne)	*Le Royale Champagne p. 18, p. 38

RESTAURANTS

Reims (Marne)	**La Chaumière (184, av. Épernay; tel. 47.35.97—closed Aug.) p. 37
Reims (Marne)	*Le Florence (43, blvd. Foch; tel. 47.35.36—closed Aug.) p. 37
Nancy (Meurthe-et-Moselle)	*La Rôtisserie des Cordeliers p. 18

HOTELS

Reims	Lion d'Or (52, pl. Drouet-d'Erlon; tel. 47.54.28) p. 37
Nancy	Grand Hôtel Stanislas p. 18

blood from the Holy Land to the Bay of Biscay. The Crusades were ardently joined by the nobility of the province, as the chronicles of Joinville and Villehardouin attest. Both these crusaders, incidentally, were native Champenois.

The martial ardor of Champagne did not cease with the end of the Middle Ages; it was still apparent in the seventeenth century. During the Thirty Years' War, the Prince de Condé won his greatest victory at Rocroi, on Champagne's northern border. Here, in an all-day fight, the infantry of Spain, which had dominated the battlefield for a century and a half, was annihilated, ending that country's influence in northern Europe. Condé was a mere twenty-two at the time, but he was wise enough to celebrate his triumph with what every gourmet must admit is a perfect meal—a cheese of Brie and bottle of red wine.

Condé was to earn another gastronomic footnote at the end of his career. His cousin, Louis XIV, decided to drop in on Condé's delightful palace at Chantilly. Along with the king came his entourage of about two thousand courtiers and hangers-on. Condé's chef, Vatel, was reputedly not only the best cook in France, but also the most efficient, and so he naturally was expected to rise to the occasion. A well-ordered house, after all, should be able to put up a couple of thousand unexpected guests without too much trouble. But to Vatel's great chagrin, the necessary food could not be found on such short notice. The crowning blow came when he heard that the fish, which he was counting on as his *pièce de résistance*, had failed to arrive. Rather than face the mortification of disappointing his prince and king, he retired to his room, like the gentleman he was, and threw himself on his sword. When the news of this leaked out, it was treated as a national disaster. Even so self-centered a group as the Sun King's court was aghast that so great an artist would immolate himself and, even worse, his talent, rather than face their displeasure. The sorrowful irony reached a crescendo when it was discovered that the fish had indeed arrived on time. Vatel, in his nervousness, had simply misunderstood a sloppy carter's answer to his question. At any rate, between Rocroi with its Brie, and Vatel with his fish, the Prince de Condé earned his niche in the gastronomic pantheon.

During the past two centuries, Champagne has been invaded

time and again. Russians and Prussians, English and Americans, all have trampled over its fields and vineyards. After Napoleon's defeat at the Battle of Leipzig (when he was forced to abdicate and go to Elba), the Russians invaded France, and Champagne was occupied by the troops of the Tsar. As soldiers always do, they began "liberating" the glorious liquid they found tucked away in Champagne's enormous cellars. Slavic thirst has always had a heroic reputation, and here it had a chance to live up to it. The amount of Champagne tossed down the Cossack gullets was mind-boggling, but the Champenois didn't seem to mind. They felt that once a person had developed a taste for their lovely wine, nothing else would do, and this optimistic viewpoint proved quite correct. Until the Revolution, Russia was Champagne's largest customer.

Another result of the Russian occupation was the origin of what most believe to be the most Gallic of terms and institutions, *le bistrot*. When the Russians arrived in France in 1814, they discovered to their dismay that, though France had restaurants where one could sit down and muse over a meal and a bottle of wine, there was no place to get a quick drink. They soon rectified that situation. Striding into a restaurant, they would proceed to the serving shelf between the kitchen and the restaurant and, pounding their fists upon it, would demand a drink. The ever-thrifty French soon covered these counters with zinc to protect them from scars and wine stains. Finding that business was booming, they enlarged them. But what to call this new zinc counter? That was obvious: the word most frequently used by the Russians as they bawled for their drinks—"*bystro*," the Russian for "quick."

In the past hundred years, every generation of Champagne has seen a foreign army pouring through. In 1870 there was the stunning defeat of Napoleon III at Sedan and the subsequent Prussian occupation. But worse was to come. During the four years of World War I, Champagne, with its gently rolling woods, wheat fields, and vineyards, became an inferno of · exploding cordite, chattering machine guns, bilious gases, and lumbering iron hulks. All Champagne became a battlefield. The first and second battles of the Marne were fought over the pastures of Brie. Château-Thierry and Bois de Belleau, both focal points of the second battle, are names engraved alongside Gettysburg and

Saratoga on the escutcheon of America's arms. The great Champagne cellars of Reims and Épernay became dugouts to protect human as well as bottled life. When peace came at last in 1918, much of Champagne looked like a combination of hell and the surface of the moon. It would have taken a team of Bosch, Brueghel, Goya, Doré, and Bacon to depict it properly.

But nature heals, and within a few years the trenches and shell holes were little more than shallow indentations. Verdure masked the blackened stumps of trees. Only an occasional helmet or bayonet protruding through the grass served to remind that on Champagne's fields millions of soldiers had bled for causes that were soon all but forgotten.

World War II treated Champagne much more mercifully. The French defeat in 1940 was so precipitous that the fighting ended almost as soon as it had begun. The collapse of the German army in France in 1944 was equally rapid, and Champagne, though invaded and reinvaded, was scarcely touched. The province is now the epitome of peace.

Champagne is an odd-shaped area of about 120 miles east to west and 180 miles north to south, lying to the east of Paris. Brie, its westernmost section, starts almost at the gates of Paris. It is beloved by turophiles as the home of what many believe to be the world's most elegant cheese. Bounded on the north by the river Marne, Brie extends southward for about twenty miles, nearly to the Seine. East to west it runs sixty miles, from near Épernay to Paris. It is a delightful *pays,* pastoral, dotted with charming little villages, and crisscrossed with meandering streams. Despite its proximity to Paris, it is almost entirely untouched.

Each town in Brie makes its own variation of the splendid cheese. There is Brie de Meaux, Brie de Coulommiers, Brie de Montereau, and Brie de Melun, to name just a few. Which is the best is the basis of considerable local dispute, though it is generally accepted that farm-made Brie, called Brie *fermier,* is better than the Brie *laitier* made at a large creamery. However, as with so many good things of this world, Brie *fermier* is rather hard to come by.

Immediately to the east of Brie, the Champagne country begins. By "Champagne country" I mean the rolling hills covered with vines of Pinot Noir, Pinot Meunier, Pinot Blanc, and Pinot

Chardonnay. From these grapes, the same used to make the best Burgundies, comes that effervescent elixir that has made the province's name a byword wherever celebrants and lovers—indeed all the more amiable of humanity—gather.

It may seem ironic that Champagne's war-torn slopes should provide the classic potion for lovers and newlyweds, but perhaps it is not so odd at that. After all, Mars, the god of War, and Venus, goddess of Love, rocked Olympus with their tumultuous love affair.

The best vineyards of Champagne lie within a fifteen-mile radius of Épernay, a small city of about twenty-three thousand on the banks of the Marne. A number of great Champagne firms have their headquarters and their enormous *caves* there, and as it is only a little more than a two-hour drive from Paris, the questing oenophile can make an easy one-day tour to satisfy his curiosity and his thirst. Many of the great houses welcome visitors and take them on guided tours. Information about these tours can be obtained at the Syndicat d'Initiative, a small structure between the cathedral and the station on the place Thiers.

Épernay has a rather good little hotel-restaurant, Le Berceaux. The *Michelin* has recently given it a star, an overdue accolade, as the restaurant has long and rightfully been regarded as having one of the best cuisines in the region.

The only rival of Épernay as the headquarters of the Champagne trade is Reims, fifteen miles to the north. A semi-industrial town of just under 140,000, Reims is much bigger than Épernay. It is famous, of course, for its magnificent cathedral, and also as the spot where the generals of the Third Reich surrendered to the Allies on the seventh of May, 1945—VE Day. Since then no earthshaking events have taken place there. However, Reims does have a number of pleasant spots for the imbiber. The most comfortable hotel is probably the Lion d'Or. It has the added advantage of being a stone's throw from the Florence, the best restaurant in Reims. It is run by Monsieur Zoboli, and the specialties include *pâté de canard truffé* and *gratin de queues de langoustines au ratafia*. Closed in August.

Between Reims and Épernay are two other very good restaurants. One, with two *Michelin* stars, La Chaumière, is only a mile and a half south of Reims. The host is Monsieur Boyer.

About thirteen miles to the south, four miles north of Épernay at Champillon, is the Royal Champagne, a very pretty restaurant-hotel perched high on a hill overlooking the vineyards and the valley of the Marne. Its cuisine is very good, with many regional specialties including the light, red, still wines of Champagne.

The vineyards of Hautvilliers can be seen from the Royal Champagne. It was in this area that the nearly legendary Dom Pérignon made his wine and worked his art. It is almost impossible to separate Dom Pérignon fact from Dom Pérignon myth. We actually know very little about him apart from the fact that he was an excellent cellar master for the Abbey of Hautvilliers at the end of the seventeenth century. Legend, however, has garlanded him with the reputation of being the originator of a host of innovations and, in effect, the inventor of Champagne. Though this cannot be demonstrated by any documentary evidence, it nevertheless has been accepted by the folklore of the province, and so I shall repeat it.

The story goes that some time around 1660 the Dom was made cellar master of the Abbey of Hautvilliers. He was in charge of not only the cellars, but the wine making itself, a job that he took on with enthusiasm, as it was the love of his life. One facet of his character greatly influenced his work: the Dom was a putterer—one of that odd tribe usually judged as wastrels or dreamers by their contemporaries, but who have made most of the advances of history.

Mathematics had its Newton; cartography its Mercator. Wine, happily, had Dom Pérignon. The problem facing a seventeenth-century *vigneron* was one that had puzzled his ancestors for three thousand years. Air is the natural enemy of wine. After fermentation, how can a bottle be firmly sealed so that air will not enter and spoil the wine?

A number of methods, all partially successful, were then in use. One was to add to each bottle a few drops of olive oil, which rose to the surface and formed a protective slick. Another was to make a stopper of oil-soaked rags. A third was to jam a tightly rolled grape leaf in the bottle's mouth. None of these worked too well. At that time wine was bottled after its first fermentation. For a certain period during the following year there was a second "working" as the remaining yeast converted the sugar residue into alcohol. The by-product of this conversion, carbon dioxide, easily broke through the olive-oil film or rolled-up grape leaves and dissipated into the atmosphere.

In the lonely recesses of his *caves* the good Dom began experimenting to combat the problem of keeping air from the wine. First he tried wooden bungs and finally, working through the family of woods, he arrived at cork. Perfect! But by firmly sealing the wine after the first year's fermentation the Dom achieved an unforeseen result. The carbon dioxide that had hitherto escaped through the imperfect stoppers now had no place to go. And so it went down, into the wine itself. When the Dom opened his first bottle of dry white wine, the cork "popped," and the world had its first bottle of Champagne. He sipped it, beamed, and said, "I am drinking stars."

The main vineyards of Champagne lie in two blocks separated by about sixty miles of pastures and woodlands. The southernmost of these regions is centered around the twin towns of Bar-sur-Seine and Bar-sur-Aube. The northern area, which is much more famous, follows the valley of the Marne for about fifty miles from below Château-Thierry to above Épernay. At Épernay the vineyards mushroom out to cover the slopes south of the city—known as the Côte des Blancs—and the flanks of a hillside north of it on the road to Reims—called the Montagne de Reims. The soil in this northern region contains a high percentage of limestone or chalk, a characteristic common to many other white-wine producing areas of the world.

The wines from the Montagne de Reims are usually made from the Pinot Noir and Pinot Meunier, dark-skinned grapes. The grapes are pressed immediately so that none of their color is imparted to the wine. The characteristics of these wines are fullness of flavor and body.

The valley of the Marne around Épernay produces wines that are generally made from the Pinot Noir and the Pinot Vert Doré. The resultant wine is marked by an almost excessive roundness and softness.

South of Épernay on the Côte des Blancs the white Pinot Chardonnay is used. The resultant wine is light, elegant, delicate, and sometimes a little hard. As the French word for white is *blanc*, this Champagne is called Blanc de Blancs. To the anger and dismay of Champagne vintners, this name is widely copied by sparkling-wine makers in other parts of France and the world.

The process of making Champagne today is infinitely more complicated than the initial experiments of Dom Pérignon. The best Champagnes are *cuvées*, or blends, from several select vineyards around Épernay, the Montagne de Reims, and the Côte des Blancs, the proportion from each region being a determining factor in the end result. (Most of the great Champagne houses either own vineyards or have sources in all three regions.) The grapes are carefully chosen, pressed, tasted for texture and quality, and blended by master tasters into the characteristic flavor of whatever house is about to bottle them.

Better-than-average years are usually declared "vintage," and bottles bearing a date are made mostly from wines of that year. However, a nonvintage Champagne from a reputable house is likely to be nearly as good as all but the very best vintage Champagne. This is because the secret of making Champagne lies in the blending of wines of disparate types. Although a nonvintage Champagne may be made from wines of two or more years, the spectrum of taste may be just as complete as if it were made from wines of a single great vintage. The expertise and artistry of the blender combined with the quantity of good wines he uses determine the result. Thus, great firms with large stocks can produce excellent nonvintage wines.

As soon as the wine is fermented and blended, it is bottled and given a two percent shot of sugar. Often a little yeast is added. The bottle is then stoppered, and the cork firmly wired onto the bottle. The effect of the yeast on sugar is a second fermentation, and the by-product of this is carbon dioxide. Under ordinary circumstances this escapes into the air, but with the bottle so tightly sealed it cannot. It goes instead back into the wine and makes the myriad bubbles that are the hallmark of Champagne.

A less welcome by-product of fermentation is sediment, and its removal requires a great deal of time and trouble. Although mechanical means are being developed to take care of the problem, it still demands considerable and expensive manual labor. Bottles are put neck downward in sloping racks called *pupitres*. Every day for several months, each is given a slight twist and shake, and the angle of its mouth is gradually pushed toward the vertical. By the time the bottle is completely upside down, whatever sediment there is has firmly nestled against the cork. The neck of the bottle is then frozen, and the cork and an icy inch or so of sediment-laden wine are "popped." The wine in the bottle is now bone dry, as whatever sugar was once in it has been converted to alcohol and carbon dioxide. This dryness is a little too much for ordinary taste, so before the bottle is recorked a second dose of sugar syrup is usually added—allegedly in the following ratios: Nature, none; Brut, up to one and a half percent; Extra Dry, up to three percent; Dry, up to four percent. There are sweeter categories, but as these are rarely seen on the American or English markets, it would be academic to list them. It should perhaps be added that most major Champagne houses have noticed that though popular taste professes to like the driest Champagne, it actually prefers it somewhat sweeter. Consequently there is often a little more sugar syrup slipped into the wine than the ratios listed above indicate.

After the disgorging of the sediment and the second dosage of sugar, the wine is immediately recorked and prepared for shipment. By the time it is finally dressed and ready in its case, it is said to have passed through the hands of over a hundred artisans—one of the reasons, apart from tax, that a bottle of real Champagne is likely to be so expensive.

Some of the great Champagne houses whose products are found on the American market are: Moët et Chandon, Pommery-Greno, Veuve Clicquot, Roederer, Lanson, Henriot, Taittinger, Mumm, Bollinger, Perrier-Jouet, Heidsieck Monopole, Ayala-Montebello-Duminy, Krug, Veuve Laurent-Perrier, Saint-Laurent, Charles Heidsieck, Piper-Heidsieck, Mercier, de Castellane, Irroy, and Pol Roger. The Champagnes vary from house to house. Like femininity, some are lean, some full, some delicate, some round and soft. Which is the best is a question of taste.

But whichever Champagne is chosen, it seems to add an instant zest to a roomful of people. There is an almost visible thrill that surges through a group whenever the sound of a Champagne cork's pop is heard. It is a perfect apéritif, exhilarating without being annihilating. It goes with nearly every sort of food. And as an after-dinner libation to clear the palate, it knows no rival.

It is, apart from the drink of lovers, the cup par excellence of the Christmas-New Year's season. At that time of year, more than at any other, Champagne is the perfect drink. Its bubbles seem to breathe conviviality. A Christmas morning without Champagne would be a melancholy thing; New Year's without it would be unthinkable. Champagne has been so long associated with ushering in the New Year that the late Thomas Augustine Daly asserted that even Adam must have celebrated with it. In his poem "The First New Year's Eve" he wrote:

> *The Man, the One and Only One—*
> *First Gentleman on earth—*
> *Said: "How about a little fun?*
> *Come! Let us have some mirth!*
>
> *"To some swell Night Club we must roam,"*
> *Said he, "and drink Champagne,"*
> *But she said: "We can stay at home,*
> *And still be raising Cain."*

Alsace

On the easternmost fringe of France, abutting like a ship's prow into Germany, is the ancient province of Alsace, bordered by Switzerland to the south, Germany to the east and north, and the rolling hills of France to the west. Alsace is something of a country all to itself with definite natural frontiers—the Rhine and a low range of pine-covered mountains called the Vosges. Between the two is a flat, orchard-covered plain watered by a pretty, meandering stream named the Ill. When the Romans first arrived, they dubbed the region the "Land of the Ill"—in Latin *Ilsus*—and from this word Alsace gets its name.

No land could appear more peaceful. Orchards, vineyards, lovely half-timbered villages, cattle, swine, geese—all combine to present an aura of Graustarkian well-being. But it was not always so. Since Roman times Alsace has been the border state between warring powers on opposite banks of the Rhine. Nearly every Alsatian generation has witnessed the arrival of ravaging armies and seen the province forced over and over again to become attached to one or the other of its two neighboring giants. The region has been invaded four times in the past hundred years, each time marking a change of administration. The scars of these invasions, surprisingly, are not especially evident. The countryside remains green and placid, a seeming garden of peace. A hybrid civilization has sprung up, Germanic in base, but with its Teutonic heaviness mitigated by Gallic taste. Indicative of this are the language, the architecture, and even the cuisine.

Alsatians speak an argot similar to that of south Germany and

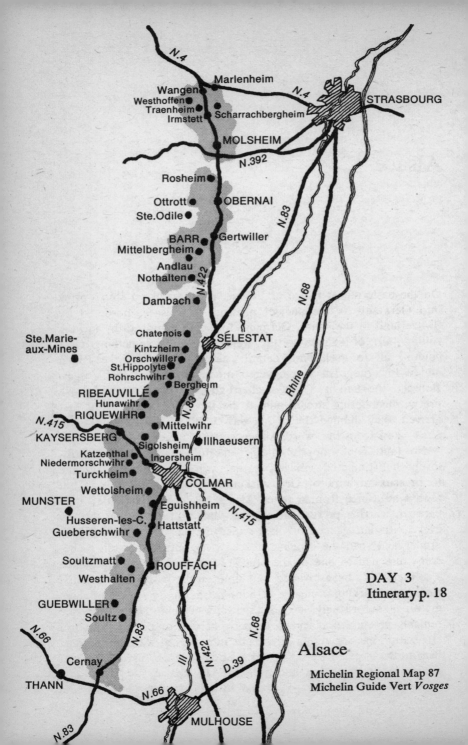

DAY 3
Itinerary p. 18

Alsace

Michelin Regional Map 87
Michelin Guide Vert *Vosges*

Switzerland, interlarded with a number of French words. The cuisine shows its German ancestry too, but the French influence has improved it miraculously. Alsace is really a trencherman's paradise. The food and wines are excellent, the servings huge, and the bill, which in other regions too often jolts one out of postprandial euphoria, is usually astonishingly small. Pigs and geese, pâtés and sausages made from their livers, cream, from which comes the whipped cream that tops Alsace's delicious fruit tarts, and such excellent cheeses as Münster are the bases of Alsatian cuisine. Compounding these delights are such mixtures as quiche, often considered a native of Lorraine, but just as much at home in Alsace. This delicious pie often contains the whole gamut of Alsatian richness—lard, flour, butter, ham, egg yolks, cream, and cheese.

Many an Alsatian specialty is made from another standard fare of central European cuisine, cabbage. The German sauerkraut, at best a rather acidulous mouthful, has been tamed into the Alsatian *choucroute*, a delicious and subtle confection served with piles of pork, sausages, salt pork, chunks of ham, and perhaps a piece of goose or two. This is considered a snack by an Alsatian in moderate health.

Various forms of liver pâtés have been made in Alsace since ancient times. The Romans knew and praised them. The idea of

---

RESTAURANT-HOTELS

Kaysersberg (Haut-Rhin)	Hôtel du Château p. 19, p. 52
Ottrott, nr. Obernai (Bas-Rhin)	*Hôtel Beau-Site (pl. de l'Eglise; tel. 95.80.61)
Ribeauvillé (Haut-Rhin)	*La Pépinière (3 miles NW of village; tel. 47.64.14)

RESTAURANTS

Illhaeusern (Haut-Rhin)	***Auberge de l'Ill p. 18, p. 53
Colmar (Haut-Rhin)	*Maison des Têtes p. 19, p. 53

HOTEL

Colmar	Hôtel du Champ de Mars p. 19

force-feeding the goose was yet to be developed, but they had another system for making its liver creamy and fat. Immediately after the goose was killed, its liver was put in a warm bowl of milk. The liver of a fresh-killed goose apparently absorbs like a sponge, and the result was a smooth, rich liver for the tables of the contemporaries of Lucullus. Geese have always been a great favorite in Germany, and so have liver pâtés and sausages. The apotheosis of liver pâté is the divine *pâté de foie gras*, perfected in Alsace in the late eighteenth century by Jean-Joseph Clause, pastry chef to the Marshal de Contades. Another splendid goose dish is *oie à l'alsacienne*, roast goose, served with *pâté de foie gras*, pork fat, and sausages, often on a bed of *choucroute*.

For the sausage lover, Alsace is a paradise. There is *Schnied-erspettel*, which is a lightly smoked pork-and-beef sausage, flavored with caraway seeds; cervelat, a smoked pork sausage; *boudin*, a blood sausage with tongue mixed in; and such classic German contributions as *Mettwurst*, *Leberwurst*, and *Bratwurst*. Other regional specialties include *Schifela*, shoulder of pork with turnips; *civet de porc,* a rich pork stew with a thick dark sauce; and *porcelet rôti,* or roast suckling pig. Chickens are plump and juicy, and constitute the major ingredient of the Alsatian *vol-au-vent* mixed with cream and a few mushrooms. Carp, trout, and salmon also abound in the mountain streams of the Vosges and the Rhine, and from the forests of the Vosges come such game as wild boar, venison, partridge, and pheasant.

As one can see from this short survey of the province's gustatory delights, the food is not light. To balance it Alsace produces delightful and refreshing wines, the perfect foil for the weighty cuisine.

The wines of Alsace have a long history. Though some maintain that wine grapes were brought by the Romans and planted during the time of the Empire, Alsatian grapes are native and have been there since before time began. The Romans did improve grape raising enormously, as they had a profound knowledge of the principles of horticulture. Wine making under their tutelage became much more of a science. The Alsatian, however, will point out that this improvement in wine-making procedures was something of a two-way street. Wood is the classic building material in the forest-clad part of the world, and the ancient

Gauls and Germans made nearly everything out of it. In the Mediterranean, where trees are in short supply, clay or masonry is the most used material. When the Romans arrived they substituted the north European wooden barrel for their clay amphora as the receptacle for maturing wine. The result was impressive. Wood, which is slightly porous and at the same time contains a certain amount of tannin, seems to be the perfect substance in which wine should start its life.

By the Middle Ages, Alsatian wines were known all over northern Europe. It was a period of great prosperity for the province. In medieval times the main sources of wealth were mines, timber, and agriculture, and Alsace had all three in abundance. Her port of Strasbourg on the Rhine allowed her to export her products, especially her wines, to Holland and Belgium, and from there they were trans-shipped to the English, Hanseatic, and Scandinavian markets. Alsace at this point was a part of the Holy Roman Empire, which, as Voltaire sarcastically observed, was "neither holy, nor Roman, nor an empire," but a loose confederation of German states with an elected emperor. Strasbourg was a great imperial center, its cathedral one of the best-known ecclesiastic masterpieces of Christendom, its steeple soaring over 450 feet above the thronging markets around it.

It was during that time that a strange, debt-ridden putterer arrived at Strasbourg from Mainz. He spent a number of years tinkering with an invention that he refused to let anyone see. He ran up considerable bills for lead and other odd substances, finally being hounded out of the city by his creditors. Thus Strasbourg just missed becoming the home of the invention of the movable-type printing press, the first and the most revolutionary of all the means of mass communication. Johann Gutenberg went back to Mainz, set up the machine that he had been perfecting, and produced the world's first printed Bible.

The Thirty Years' War was a great disaster for Alsace. The province became a perennial battlefield as Catholic and Protestant, German, Swede, Austrian, Spaniard, and Frenchman tramped through the orchards, killing cattle and burning villages. The countryside was devastated year after year, and commerce and agriculture came to a standstill. At the end, it fell under the sway of France, there to remain for two hundred years.

In 1870 the Prussians invaded France, quickly destroying the armies of Napoleon III. In the ensuing peace they demanded Alsace as a spoil of war. To their dismay the Alsatians found themselves under the autocratic control of the Kaiser. Though of odd ancestry, they became very ardent French patriots, longing for their return to their "mother country." At the end of World War I their prayers were answered. In 1919 Alsace was reincorporated into the French Republic. In 1940, after the Wehrmacht had overrun France, the Germans tried again to make Alsace a part of the Reich, but this attempt was of short duration. By 1944 French and American armies were back in the province, and the last Germans were finally ejected in 1945. Since then Alsace has been a land at peace, its villages reconstructed, its orchards and vineyards replanted.

The great vineyard area of Alsace lies along the eastern flank of the Vosges just as it comes down onto the plains of Alsace. It is a strip sixty miles long and rarely more than three miles wide. The best-known towns are Marlenheim, Ottrot, and Goxwiller near Strasbourg; Barr, Mittelbergheim, and Dambach north of Sélestat; and then a whole galaxy of delightful little wine villages between Sélestat and Colmar: Bergheim, Ribeauvillé, Hunawihr, Zellenberg, Beblenheim, Riquewihr, Mittelwihr, Ammerschwihr, Turckheim, and Kaysersberg. South of Colmar on the road to Belfort are a few other viniferous towns: Eguisheim, Husseren, Voegtlinshoffen, Soultzmatt, Guebwiller, and Thann.

During the war periods, the prosperity of Alsace fell off, as did the standards of viniculture that had made Alsatian wines so popular during the Middle Ages. When the Germans took Alsace in 1870, they did little to improve this sad decline. In fact, they established a law that refused to allow Alsatian wines to be named Rhine wines. They were labeled as mere "ordinary wines." Thus with no incentive and no monetary reward the Alsatian vintner had little reason to be proud of his vines or to improve his wines. Wine making fell into the doldrums.

In 1919, however, the picture changed. The Alsatians were delighted to be back within the French Republic. The French were quite willing to recognize Alsatian wines as being of a separate and unique type, as they were quite different from any other wine made in France. A certain pride returned to Alsatian wine growers, and they determined to elevate the quality by uprooting the vines producing large quantities of mediocre wines, and replacing them with "noble" vines. Alsatian wines have been growing in popularity ever since.

However, it must be remembered that Alsatian wines are really a branch of the Rhine wine family. As the German wine-making customs are quite different from the French, it was exceptionally difficult to write a French Appellation Contrôlée that would both cover Alsatian vineyards and allow them to make wines in their traditional way. Finally, in 1962, it was determined to accept Alsatian wine-making customs as the norm, and this was written into law. Nowadays over ninety-nine percent of the wines of Alsace are white. To be called Alsatian they must come from a certain delimited area within the province, be made of special grape types, have at least eight percent natural alcohol for ordinary wines, and eleven to be called Grand Cru or Grand Vin.

It is this emphasis on the grape types, rather than on the area, that makes the Alsatian classification unique in France. In other parts of the country, though each wine must be made of certain types of grapes, it is the specific vineyard that is stressed. But in Alsace, where many grape varietals are grown, the wine is judged by the characteristics of the grape itself.

Riesling, Pinot Blanc or Klevner, Pinot Gris or Tokay d'Alsace, Muscat, Traminer, Gewürztraminer, and Sylvaner are the seven grapes classed as *cépages nobles*. Any bottle with one of these names on the label must contain one hundred percent of the juice from the grape cited. In this respect, Alsatian laws are far more severe than those of almost any other part of the world. In Germany, for example, only sixty-six percent of the wine must be made from the grapes cited on the label. In California, the proportion must be only fifty-one percent.

If the wine is made from a mixture of grapes, it must be clearly stated on the label. If the grapes come exclusively from "noble" vines, the word *Edelzwicker*—Alsatian for noble mixture—must be used, following the words "Vin d'Alsace." If the wines are made from a mixture that contains any one of the three "acceptable" but not "noble" vines—the Knipperlé, Chasselas, or Goldriesling—then the word *Zwicker*, or mixture, must follow "Vin d'Alsace."

Occasionally, Alsatian wines will vaunt the names of their villages, sometimes even individual vineyards within the villages. However, this is seldom done, and is not guaranteed by law. If the vineyard is known and the shipper has a sound reputation, the name may have some validity. But, in most cases, it is little more than a trademark.

The quality to look for in most Alsatian wines is freshness and fruitiness. These are wines to be opened when young. A good Alsatian wine will be pleasant at a year and a half, perfect at two or three, and, with certain rare exceptions, begin to decline after five. During their youth they are lissome, fragrant without being too perfumed, and ideal for a picnic or with cold luncheons or suppers. And as has been mentioned before, any meal of roast fowl or pork, ham or sausage finds the Vins d'Alsace its natural irrigation.

To judge which wines of Alsace are the best implies a certain arrogant belief in one's own taste. In general, here as elsewhere, the Riesling is a splendid grape, producing an elegant, sophisticated, crisp, *nuancé* wine, which in my opinion is delicious. The Traminer and Gewürztraminer are very close relations, the Gewürztraminer producing a wine that is slightly spicy—*Gewürz* in German meaning spice. Both are great favorites in Alsace, but I find them a little heavy and overpowering. The Sylvaner is a light, agreeable, refreshing wine, not great, but ideal for picnics and such. It has the additional advantage of being reasonably inexpensive. The Muscat produces a very fruity and not very dry white that, I suppose, some people must like. The Chasselas and Pinot Gris are pleasant enough, but lack the finesse of the Riesling. All these wines are white, of course, but Alsace produces a few reds and rosés, too.

The reds of Alsace are in reality dark rosés made from the same Pinot Noir that is the noble grape of Burgundy. The Pinot Meunier, a close relative of the Pinot Noir, is also sometimes used. The result is what the Alsatians call by the old French name for a dark rosé, *"clairet."* It can be one of the finest rosés made in France. Altogether different from the excellent wines of Tavel, it is more reserved and subtle, with brooding currents of flavor. It is, alas, rather expensive, as the Pinot Noir is a shy bearer, especially this far north.

One cannot speak of the food and wine of Alsace without going on to her splendid after-dinner libations, the fruit brandies or *eaux-de-vie*. These, like the cuisine and the viniculture, are marked by both Teutonic and Gallic tradition. Fruit schnapps are a great favorite in Germany, and the best of them come from the Schwarzwald. The Swiss, too, love their fruit brandies, and their finest come from around Basel. In France, the best come from the orchards and fields of Alsace. Though the three regions that produce these brandies appear, because of political boundary lines, to be completely separate, this is not so. The Schwarzwald, Basel, and Alsace all lie cheek by jowl. Within a fifty-mile radius of the Alsatian town of Colmar lie all three of the finest fruit-brandy-producing areas of Europe.

The French word for brandy, *eau-de-vie*, or "water of life," is an indication of how highly the French people regard it. Nearly every province makes some kind of brandy, but most of it is quite ordinary stuff, good for *la grippe*. Sometimes when it is sampled in the romantic aura of the place where it was made, it seems good. However, when the same bottle appears in more mundane circumstances it never seems to taste quite as it did on the spot. An exception is the *eau-de-vie* of Alsace.

Alsatian fruit brandies are all, with the sometime exception of kirsch (which is made from cherries), called by the French names of the fruits from which they are made. Framboise is made from raspberries, Fraise from strawberries, Poire from pears, Cerise from cherries, Mirabelle from small yellow plums, Prune from ordinary plums, Quetsch from large, elongated, violet-colored plums, Prunelle from small, wild plums, and Pêche from peaches.

Methods of making these brandies vary by fruit and distiller. Unlike most of the other good brandies of France, they have not yet been put under Appellation Contrôlée, though it is to be hoped they soon will be. The best fruit brandy is made only from the fermented juice of the fruit involved, sometimes with a little of its crushed stones to add flavor. In taste the fruit brandies are likely to be a little sweet, blossoming with the pungency of the fruit from which they were made.

Alsace is one of the most pleasant provinces to tour. Apart from the towns destroyed during the war that have been rebuilt with a gray and uniform lack of style, the villages of Alsace are

romantic dreams, completely off the beaten track of the summer
hordes on their way for their four weeks of annual skin burning
on the Mediterranean's overcrowded shores. The countryside of
Alsace is filled with fruit trees and vines. Brooks bubble out from
clefts in the pine-covered Vosges. Villages are gems of medieval
architecture, filled with half-timbered houses and lovely wrought-
iron work.

When traveling in France, I follow two simple rules whenever
I have the time. I always take departmental roads, rather than
the great Routes Nationales, and I always try to stay outside the
cities in some agreeable country inn, where the food is inevitably
delicious if prepared by the *patron*, and the rooms are usually
spotless. Plumbing may be a little primitive in that only a shower
may be available, rather than a bath, but this can be remedied
by an occasional lapse into a hotel *grand luxe*. Inns are quieter,
and one gets a feel of the country, which is after all the reason
that one supposedly is traveling. Parking is no problem, thievery
in small towns almost nonexistent, service is interested and appreciative, and there is no chain of upturned palms as one makes
one's departure on the morrow. Country inns moreover are usually very inexpensive. Nowhere in France do my "two rules of
French traveling" bring a more immediate reward than in Alsace.

Colmar is the great center of the Alsatian wine trade, but
regrettably it was badly damaged during the war. However, running northwest out of Colmar is the wine road leading by Kaysersberg, Riquewihr, Hunawihr, and Ribeauvillé, all famous for their
beauty and their good wines. Of them Riquewihr has taken the
greatest pains to fix itself up. It is lovely, but in some ways almost
too cute, its natural beauty hidden somewhat by overly self-
conscious stressing of its charm. It is a little like a lovely girl
wearing too much makeup. Kaysersberg is more to my taste. It
is a natural, working little village, with a stream running through
it, a tower guarding the hillside behind it, and vineyards climbing
up the slope. It is from here that Albert Schweitzer came, and
one senses how such an environment would help in the formation
of the balanced, calm, humanistic spirit that was his.

Kaysersberg has just the sort of inn that I like to visit. It is
called the Hôtel du Château, a half-timbered delight facing the
fountain in the main square. The rooms are spotless, the food is

excellent and copious. Madame Joseph Kohler is the charming hostess, and her husband oversees the cuisine. Mademoiselle Kohler, the daughter of the house, waited on the tables on this occasion and spoke nearly flawless English—rather surprising as it was learned entirely in the local school. The bill for a stupendous supper, a room, and a breakfast for two was phenomenally inexpensive.

For those of more Olympian tastes Alsace has several gastronomic objectives of the first rank to offer. One of the prettiest, most elegant, and most expensive is the three-starred Auberge de l'Ill at Illhaeusern. Both the food and the site are divine. *Spécialités* include a *brioche de foie gras frais*, the likes of which one will seldom taste again, a salmon soufflé, and *noisettes de chevreuil Saint-Hubert*, a classic venison dish. The restaurant is right beside the river Ill, and there is a pleasant garden beside its flowing waters where one may imbibe the pleasures of nature and the wines simultaneously. The host has the fine Alsatian name of Monsieur Haeberlin. One must telephone for a table in advance.

Colmar, too, has a lovely restaurant, the Maison des Têtes, a charming old seventeenth-century town house. The *foie gras truffé* is excellent, the *choucroute garnie à l'alsacienne* superb. Excellent venison is served for those who find their appetite only whetted by the first two dishes. In the cellar is a good cross section of the best local wines. The host is Monsieur Edel.

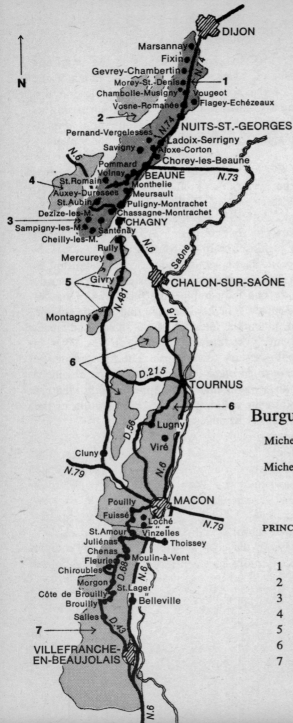

N

DIJON

Marsannay
Fixin
Gevrey-Chambertin
Morey-St.-Denis
Chambolle-Musigny
Vosne-Romanée

1

Vougeot
Flagey-Echézeaux

2

NUITS-ST.-GEORGES

Pernand-Vergelesses

Savigny

Ladoix-Serrigny
Aloxe-Corton
Chorey-les-Beaune

N.73

Pommard
Volnay
St.Romain
Auxey-Duresses
St.Aubin
Dezize-les-M.

BEAUNE
Monthelie
Meursault
Puligny-Montrachet
Chassagne-Montrachet

4

3

CHAGNY

Sampigny-les-M.
Cheilly-les-M.

Santenay

Rully

Mercurey

N.6

Saône

5

Givry

CHALON-SUR-SAÔNE

Montagny

N.481

N.6

DAYS 4–9
Itinerary pp. 19–22

6

D.215

TOURNUS

6

Burgundy

Lugny

Viré

Michelin Regional Maps 65,
66, 69 & 73
Michelin Guide Vert *Bourgogne*

D.56

Cluny

N.6

N.79

Pouilly
Fuissé

MACON

N.79

Loché
Vinzelles

PRINCIPAL REGIONS

St.Amour
Juliénas
Chénas
Fleurie
Chiroubles
Morgon
Côte de Brouilly
Brouilly
Salles

Thoissey

Moulin-à-Vent

St.Lager

Belleville

D.68

N.6

Chablis, p. 68

1   Côte de Nuits

2   Hautes Côtes de Nuits

3   Côte de Beaune

4   Hautes Côtes de Beaune

5   Chalonnais

6   Maconnais

7   Beaujolais

7

VILLEFRANCHE-
EN-BEAUJOLAIS

D.43

N.6

The Winelands of Burgundy

Burgundy—no longer a kingdom, no more a duchy, not even, for nearly two centuries, a political entity of any sort. Yet how many of the world's hundred-odd sovereign states are better known? Burgundy may be only a phantom of its former self, but, like Milton's "stubborn, unlaid ghost/That breaks his magic chains at curfew time," its spirit walks with us yet.

Burgundy as a province was slain, along with so many other noble creatures, during the French Revolution. Rationalism was very much in vogue then, as it still is, and the French government decided that such illogical, emotional, and dangerous units as the ancient provinces would have to be broken up. Consequently, Burgundy was divided into *départements*—the Yonne, Côte-d'Or, Saône-et-Loire, Ain, and part of the Rhône. This proved a bit complicated for all but the bureaucratic mind, so people continued to call the region Burgundy. Its shade proved too virile to be wished away by mere governmental decree.

In ordinary conversation, however, "the shade of Burgundy" does not refer to some ghostly reminder of a previous age. It signifies a rich tint of red, the color in fact of Burgundy's superlative wine. But there is more to the region than its magnificent

RESTAURANT-HOTELS

At Beaune, Changy, Thoissey, Tournus, Belleville, Cluny; see the following chapters on each region of Burgundy.

vintages—it is a salmagundi of things to delight the mind and senses. Its history, its countryside, its architecture, and, certainly not lowest on the totem of values, its cuisine, all conspire to titillate the man of more than *moyenne sensualité*.

Historically, Burgundy has been inhabited for over fifteen thousand years. Evidence of a large colony of Cro-Magnon men has been found beneath the prow-shaped rock shelter of Solutré, which dominates the vineyards of Pouilly-Fuissé. During the few thousand years before Christ, the Gauls of Burgundy evolved a rather sophisticated civilization with bronze and iron artifacts and even a few towns of moderate size. They were intelligent and bellicose, and they managed, in the early days of Rome, to ravage central Italy. They later tried a surprise attack on Rome itself, only to be foiled by the cackling of the famous Capitoline geese. The Romans invaded Gaul in 58 B.C. and for nearly a decade marched back and forth, beating its unruly inhabitants into submission. Their commander, as any schoolboy who has staggered through the ablative absolutes of the *Gallic Wars* knows, was Julius Caesar, shortly to be assassinated. Many is the student whose major regret is that this doleful act didn't take place a few years earlier.

The climax of Julius Caesar's campaign was the defeat of Vercingetorix at the siege of Alesia. Alesia is in the heart of Burgundy, only about thirty miles northwest of that slope beloved to oenophiles, the Côte d'Or.

The Romans were absolutists in more than ablatives, as the Gauls were to discover. A hard but equable system of Roman law was imposed and enforced by the powerful, superbly trained legions. Anarchy and disorder, the endemic characteristics of the Celt, were replaced by peace and burgeoning wealth. Fun, in short, by good works.

However, there were some advantages to this new regime. The vine, probably brought to Gaul by the Greeks, prospered, and in spite of imperial edicts to the contrary, spread. And the area later to be called Burgundy gained critical importance in Roman north-south communications. A glance at a topographical map of the area will show why. Italy and most of the Mediterranean world are cut off from northern Europe by a series of natural obstructions. To the north and east lies the barrier of the Alps. To the west is France, also far from flat, for in its center is a great bulk of mountains, steep hills, and zigzagging valleys that lead nowhere. It is called the Massif Central and even now is difficult to cross, a fact that has so far saved it from the blessings of carbon-monoxide culture.

The only hole in this dam of mountains is a river valley that runs between the Alps and the Massif Central: the Rhône and its extension, the Saône. As the Saône stretches northward, it ultimately skirts a low mass of hills called the Morvan, in the heart of Burgundy. Arising from, or passing near, this small *massif* are a number of other rivers—the Meuse, the Moselle, the Marne, the Seine, the Yonne, and the Loire among them. Thus, a short and not impossible portage over these hills allowed communication with rivers running into such diverse waters as the North Sea, the English Channel, and the Bay of Biscay. Consequently, Burgundy became the natural overland link between the Mediterranean world and the newly developing markets in northern Europe. The main road from Rome to Britain ran through it, as did the one to the Roman colonies on the Moselle and in the Low Countries. Its towns, such as Augustodunum—now corrupted to Autun—and Dibio, the "Divine"—now Dijon—became trading centers and entrepôts of considerable importance.

Exactly when the vine was first planted in Burgundy is anyone's guess, and there have been plenty. It is known that by 312 A.D. the vine had been there for some time. That year a panegyric was directed to the Emperor Constantine in which the vines of the Côte de Nuits and Côte de Beaune were singled out for their special excellence. Working back from this, one may assume that sometime around 200 A.D., eighteen centuries ago, good wine was being produced on the Côte d'Or, as the Côte de Beaune and Côte de Nuits are jointly called. There can be little doubt that the names of some of Burgundy's most splendid vineyards—Romanée Saint-Vivant, Romanée-Conti, and La Romanée—hearken back to this epoch.

Rome collapsed in 410, and what was left of the empire fell into a time of trouble as barbarian waves swept over it toward the end of the fifth century. The western section was overwhelmed by Germanic tribes. Some, such as the Goths and the Vandals, simply wandered through, looting what they could carry and burning the rest. Two of them, however, the Burgundians and the Franks, moved in and settled down to stay. Much of the next thousand years was devoted to determining which would master. And though the Franks were nearly always on top, the Burgundians were to have moments of splendor.

The mightiest king of the early Franks was Charlemagne, or Charles the Great, nominal Emperor of Rome and ruler over a territory that closely coincides with the present Common Market. Charlemagne must have been one of Charles de Gaulle's favorite great men; by strength of character, stratagem, and force of arms he imposed the will and influence of the Franks over a turbulent half continent. He unified Europe, drove out the foreigners, kept the Anglo-Saxons at a cool distance, and even made an opening to the East by arriving at an agreement with the powerful caliph of Baghdad, Harun al-Rashid.

Charlemagne was also a great enthusiast of wine. Though unable to write (he was not quite illiterate, as he could read), he was still a fervid encourager of letters, arts, and crafts, wine making among them. Apart from his great natural intelligence he was observant. He is said to have noticed from his palace at Ingelheim on the Rhine that the snow on the opposite, southward-facing slope melted sooner than elsewhere. He ordered that the slope be planted with vines, and thus the Schloss Johannisberg, one of the world's most magnificent vineyards, was begun.

In Burgundy, too, Charlemagne proved his interest in the vine by acquiring the vineyards on the prow of the hill overlooking Aloxe-Corton on the Côte de Beaune. He donated these to the Abbey of Saulieu, and to this day one of Burgundy's finest white wines comes from them. It is called Corton-Charlemagne, a fit memorial to a great emperor.

Charlemagne died in 814, leaving his empire to his son, Louis the Debonair. Within a short time there was the usual family squabbling over the inheritance. The three main contenders were the sons of Louis: Charles the Bald, Lothair, and Louis the German. After much battling, they divided the empire. Louis the German was given the eastern kingdom and Lothair received a center strip, part of which later became the province of Lorraine. Charles the Bald got the western third, including half the kingdom of the Burgundians. Henceforth his section was the basis for the Duchy of Burgundy, the rest of the kingdom becoming Franche-

Comté, Provence, and Savoy. Thus was born a duchy that was for six hundred years one of the most famous in Christendom. With inspired symmetry, it began with the victory of Charles the Bald in 843, and ended in the defeat of Charles the Bold in 1477. Between those dates the power of its dukes and its militant church orders was felt the breadth of the known world. Its riches were marveled at and its court set a style in ceremony that was aped by most of the kingdoms of Europe. Its rulers dubbed themselves the "Grand Dukes of the Occident," a title that few then disputed, and considered themselves on a par with kings.

The heyday of Burgundy was from the eleventh to the fifteenth centuries. By marriage or war its dukes extended their domains until they included much of present Holland, Belgium, northern France, and all of Luxembourg. Because of Burgundy's running feud with the French, it sided with the English in the Hundred Years' War. It was the Burgundians, it may be remembered, not the English, who finally managed to capture Joan of Arc, the first step on her way to martyrdom at the stake.

In 1467 Burgundy's last Duke, Charles the Bold, came to power. He was intelligent, noble, generous, impulsive, and brave. It was his fate to have as his mortal rival an exact opposite in temperament. Louis XI of France was called for good reason the "spider." He was small, mean, stingy, calculating, and utterly unscrupulous. And, of course, as so often is the case outside of storybooks, the worse man won. Louis encouraged Charles in his rashness. By a series of clever stratagems he enmeshed him in wasting wars with neighbors, Lorraine and the Swiss in particular. While Louis watched, Burgundy was bled white. Charles' star waned, and he began losing battles. He ultimately was killed outside of Nancy, the capital of Lorraine, in 1477. When the corpse of the last Grand Duke of the Occident was found, it had been stripped of clothing and armor and half devoured by wolves. The duchy collapsed into the arms of the waiting Louis.

From the gourmet's point of view, the history of the Duchy of Burgundy may seem somewhat like an underdone piece of meat, a little too bloody. But there is more to it than that. One result of its constant political struggles is that the best place in Europe to get a bottle of Burgundy—apart from Burgundy itself and a few superlative French restaurants—is Belgium. In England a bottle of "Burgundy" is likely to be some bizarre concoction of the local wine merchant, but it is more difficult to fool the Belgians, who demand the best. They, after all, belonged to Dukes of Burgundy for some centuries, and during that time they learned how a Burgundy should be.

Another result was the widespread recognition of the glories of the Burgundian cuisine, today hailed as one of the finest of France, and hence the world. The Dukes were splendid not only in their pomp at court; they also set a grand table—grand in both senses of the word. The cuisine was superlative, as no less a person than Charles VI, King of France, attested. It also must have been copious, as they thought nothing of having a small supper for three or four hundred in the ducal palace. Feeding this horde was, of course, rather complicated, and so a kitchen was built that must be one of the culinary wonders of the world. It still exists today in Dijon, and should one pass that way, it is certainly worth a visit. The whole room is, in effect, a huge chimney, and around the edges were a host of fires for roasting, grilling, broiling, boiling, baking, and turnspitting.

Among the innovations that came as by-products of the ducal hospitality was the menu. Up to then, food was prepared and presented "blind." The visiting trencherman smacked his lips, tasted, then mused over what it was that he had eaten. It took a woman to do something about this. A perennial visitor at Dijon was Queen Isabeau of Bavaria, wife of the aforementioned Charles VI. She decided to have written down a list of the dishes in order of service and to present this to the guests. The word for this granddaddy of the menu was *escriteau,* a term one notices coming back in France in those cute, pseudomedieval restaurants favored by the would-be fashionable.

The Dukes were interested in more than cuisine—they also took great care to protect their self-given title of "Seigneurs of the Finest Wine in Christendom." Probably their most outstanding contribution to this cause was persuading the Cistercian monks to become winegrowers. Burgundy's vineyards owe much of their glory to the knowledge, diligence, and good taste of its monks. Several of the orders owned extensive tracts of vineyards there, among them the Knights of Malta, Carthusians, Carmelites, and, most important, the Benedictines and Cistercians.

The Benedictines and Cistercians were based in Burgundy.

During much of the Middle Ages they were major forces within the Church. The magnificent mother abbey of the Benedictines was at Cluny, a village tucked in the rolling green hills behind Macon. Its main church was for centuries the largest in Europe and its abbot-superior was frequently on a par with the Pope, whom he served as guide and counselor.

But if power corrupts, the Benedictines proved no exception. Consequently, in 1098 Saint Robert of Molesmes founded a reformed Benedictine order in the marshland about eight miles east of Nuits-Saint-Georges, basing the rule of his abbey on that of the original Saint Benedict. The abbey was called Les Cîteaux— the "Cisterns"—after some nearby wells in the damp ground, and the new order took the name Cistercians.

The Cistercians are an austere order. One of their disciplines is hard physical labor, and their energy is legendary. At first they shunned vineyard tending, afraid that the corrupting powers of Bacchus would undermine their monastic virtue. However, after much soul-searching, they were persuaded in 1162 by Pope Alexander III and Duke Eudes II of Burgundy to have a try at the vine. The results of their work were extraordinary. Although their vineyards were dissolved at the time of the French Revolution, to this day remnants spangle the map of Burgundy, indeed of Europe. Among them are the Clos de Vougeot, Corton, sections of Savigny, Pommard, and Meursault, and, farther afield, that paragon of German vineyards, Steinberg.

Apart from the momentous act of persuading the Cistercians to cultivate the vine, the Dukes also promulgated decrees governing when the grapes could be picked, what kinds of grapes were permissible, and several other ordinances to uphold the quality of Burgundy's vintages. One of Burgundy's most famous Dukes was Philippe le Hardi, son of John the Good, King of France. Philippe has earned his niche in wine's pantheon by being the first to have laws passed encouraging the growth of the noble "Pinoz" vine. He also castigated ferociously the planting of the "*très mauvais et très desloyaux plant nommé Gamay*"—the "very wicked and disloyal plant named the Gamay."

In fairness to the present Gamay grown in Beaujolais and Maconnais, Philippe was probably not referring to it. Gamay is rather a large family of grapes, and his abuse was doubtless aimed at *le gros gamay,* a grape with little to commend it except that it produces a great deal of juice. Its more elegant cousin—the *Gamay noir à jus blanc,* called the Dôle in Switzerland and the Gamay du Beaujolais in California—produces in the right circumstances charming little wines of justifiable renown.

By the end of the Middle Ages, the wines of Burgundy had taken more or less their present form. Their style was based essentially on the type of grape used, the vinification, and the geographical and geological position of the vineyards.

BURGUNDIAN GRAPE TYPES

In Burgundy all great wines are made from unblended grape must. In this they are similar to the great wines of the Rheingau and Moselle and unlike those of Bordeaux and the Rhône, which are made of a mixture of juices from several grape varietals.

Red Wines

Pinot Noir. This is one of the finest red-wine grapes in the world. (In Champagne it is also used to produce a full-bodied white wine to blend with the lighter Pinot Blanc and Pinot Chardonnay.) In Burgundy it is used almost exclusively to make red wine, and to it the wine of Burgundy owes its full, elegant, grand, *racé* flavor. The Pinot Noir has been transplanted all over the world—in Germany as the Spätburgunder—and in Chile, Australia, and California. Though none manages to match the wines coming from its native habitat, the Pinot Noir flourishes creditably in all those places.

Gamay (Gamay noir à jus blanc). This is not as elegant a grape as the Pinot Noir, but it does produce juice in great quantity. And in some areas, such as Beaujolais, southern Maconnais, and California (where it is not called Gamay, but Gamay du Beaujolais), it produces delightful, fruity, robust little wines that are reasonably inexpensive. When it is good, it makes what is justifiably one of the world's favorite table wines—not grand, but as a good friend should be, easy to take in large quantities.

Passe-Tout-Grain is not often seen in the United States. It is essentially a wine made from the Gamay with an admixture of

Pinot Noir to add delicacy and finesse. It must state Passe-Tout-Grain on the label. A great many very good and rather inexpensive little Burgundy town wines are so made.

White Wines

Pinot Chardonnay and *Pinot Blanc.* These are two closely related grapes that produce all of the great white wines of Burgundy. They are without doubt two of the finest white-wine grapes in the world, and they have been widely transplanted with varying success in North and South America, and in Australia.

Aligoté produces an inexpensive, astringent little wine of no particular merit, though it does have its admirers in Burgundy, usually among those who grow it. It is the ordinary Burgundian carafe wine, and also serves as the basis for Kir, a drink named after the delightfully eccentric nonagenarian priest-mayor of Dijon. This drink is made of a mixture of cool Aligoté wine and a slug of cassis—sweetened red currant syrup—which improves it considerably.

Major Wine Areas of Burgundy

The major wine areas of Burgundy are six—one an island off to itself, the other five forming a long chain down the southeastern flank of the Morvan hills facing out over the river Saône.

Chablis. This is the region that is off alone. It is tucked in a small river valley on the northern side of the Morvan *massif.* Though it uses the noble Pinot Chardonnay to produce its fine white wines, the wine turns out quite differently from those made on the Côte d'Or. It is drier, harder, and more astringent, making it the perfect and time-honored companion for shellfish, particularly the oyster.

The *Côte d'Or,* the "Slope of Gold," is the heart of Burgundian wine making, and it is the northernmost region of a chain of vineyards that extends from just south of Dijon to just north of Lyon, a distance of nearly 120 miles. The Côte d'Or is divided into two sections. They are Côte de Nuits and Côte de Beaune.

Côte de Nuits. The northern half of the Côte d'Or is called the Côte de Nuits after the town of Nuits-Saint-Georges on its southern perimeter. The heart of it is a six-mile stretch of vine-yards on the flanks of a low-lying ridge of hills between the towns of Gevrey-Chambertin and Nuits-Saint-Georges. The best vine-yards usually lie along a narrow band a third of the way up the hillside. The *tête de cuvée* vineyards total a little over six hundred acres, the size of a single small California vineyard. Though some white wine is made on the Côte, and a little deservedly unknown rosé, the region is primarily famous for its splendid reds, perhaps the finest in the world, certainly the most expensive. Only the Médoc region of Bordeaux can rival the renown of the Côte de Nuits, and the question as to which is better is a classic destroyer of old friendships. Suffice it to say that on the Côte are such vineyards as Romanée-Conti, La Tâche, Richebourg, Musigny, and Chambertin—vineyards whose names must arouse the thirst of even the surliest claret lover. They are, like the grand dukes who once ruled over them, powerful, rich, filled with themselves, and, in the best sense of the word, ostentatious. They are splendid companions of game birds, venison, and beef.

Côte de Beaune. This is the southern section of the Côte d'Or and is named after the ancient wine town at its center. It produces some delightful reds, generally lighter and more delicate than those of the Côte de Nuits, thus ideal complements of roast domestic fowl or a *gigot*. However, the region is most famous for its remark-able dry white wines, certainly the finest of their type on earth. Mon-trachet, Meursault-Perrières, and Corton-Charlemagne are among the roster of splendid vineyards, and in a great year they produce a full-bodied, *bouqueté* dry white wine which adjectives cannot come close to describing.

Côte Chalonnaise. Ten miles south of Beaune there is a break in the hills as Route Nationale 6 slips down from the Morvan hills onto the flat valley of the Saône River. On the other side of the break the hills pick up again and for about twenty miles run due south behind the city of Chalon-sur-Saône. The eastward-facing slope of this is called the Côte Chalonnaise, and it is geologically an extension of the Côte d'Or. It produces some good red wine, especially in the townships of Givry and Mercurey, that is light and elegant in character, similar in many respects to the red wines of the neighboring southern section of the Côte de

Beaune. In the communes of Rully and Montagny an agreeable but not terribly distinguished white wine is made.

Maconnais. The next extension of the hillside running south is the Maconnais, most famous for its excellent white wine from the communes of Pouilly, Fuissé, Loché, Vinzelles, and Solutré. A quite agreeable little red also comes from the region. Made from the Gamay grape, it resembles in many ways the ordinary wine of Beaujolais.

Beaujolais has become in recent years one of the best-known names in winedom. Here the Gamay, the somewhat denigrated grape, seems to have found its perfect environment. The resultant red wine is fruity, refreshing, unpretentious, and it disappears with alarming alacrity. Wine snobs have a habit of pooh-poohing Beaujolais, but that hasn't stopped the world from taking it to its bosom. However, though Beaujolais is quite a large vineyard area, a great deal more wine carries its label than the region could hope to produce. If you want to get a legitimate bottle, look to the reputation of the importer or the shipper.

As a rule of thumb, Burgundy red wines should have been aged about five years before being served. Exceptions are those wines made from the Gamay grape, such as Beaujolais and some Maconnais wines. An obvious tendency among sellers is to try to have the public drink wines that are younger and younger. There is a world-wide shortage of good wine, so it behooves those who distribute it to sell what they have, dipping back into their aging inventories. Beaujolais, especially ordinary Beaujolais, is consumed while young and fresh, but a good one needs a little time, not so much as a Pinot Noir wine, but two or three years will not do it any harm.

A great white wine needs at least three years. To drink one at less than that is child murder.

Chablis

The fame of the tiny village of Chablis and its carefully delineated few acres of vines girdles the globe. If it is true that imitation is the sincerest form of flattery, Chablis is, acre for acre, the most flattered of wines. Never has so small an area had its name so copied and abused. Spanish "Chablis," Chilean "Chablis," Californian "Chablis," and Australian "Chablis" are some of the wines that have been so designated.

One reason for this name stealing is that Chablis is a classic companion for all kinds of shellfish—the oyster in particular. A *belon* or *marenne* could ask for no finer irrigation than a bottle of its compatriot wine—but then neither could a Whitstable, Chesapeake, or Blue Point. Clams, crabs and mussels, lobsters and crayfish all have their delicate flavor amplified and harmonized by goblets of this green-tinged wine. To quote an old piece of French doggerel:

> *Avec les huîtres,*
> *Que le Chablis est excellent!*
> *Je donnerais fortune et titres*
> *Pour m'enivrer de ce vin blanc*
> *Avec des huîtres!*

The reason for this affinity is elementary. The flavor of delicate fish and shellfish is brought out by a touch of acidity—hence the slice of lemon that so often accompanies them. Chablis is the northernmost region of Burgundy, and, as has been pointed out, the pale northern sun produces wines that are relatively light in sugar but high in acidity. Chablis thus has a pleasant, clean, slightly astringent taste that ideally complements delicately flavored fish and crustaceans.

The village of Chablis is about a hundred miles southeast of Paris. To the visitor it has much to offer. The nearby valley of the Yonne is justifiably regarded as one of the most charming in France and is a favorite weekend spot for discerning Parisians. But better than that, Chablis is surrounded by several extremely agreeable restaurants and hostelries of far more than local notoriety. Three deserve special mention. The intrepid gastronaut, in a day's motoring tour from Paris, can with luck and a strong constitution bracket his afternoon's visit to Chablis with at least two of them.

Forty miles east of Chablis is the pretty town of Chatillon-sur-Seine, on the headwaters of the stream that later rolls through Paris. It is famed for its charming hotel-restaurant, the Hôtel de la Côte-d'Or, which has a lovely garden, a splendid wine list, and a delicious menu with such *spécialités* as *terrine de caneton au foie gras truffé* and *coq au vin nuitonne*. The ambience is delightfully rustic, but the prices are considerably more metropolitan.

About thirty-five miles southeast of Chablis lies Montbard, birthplace of the great eighteenth-century naturalist Buffon. George Bernard Shaw relates that his uncle, the Anglo-Irish accent being what it is, always referred to Monsieur de Buffon as the "admirable Buffoon," which caused some confusion among

---

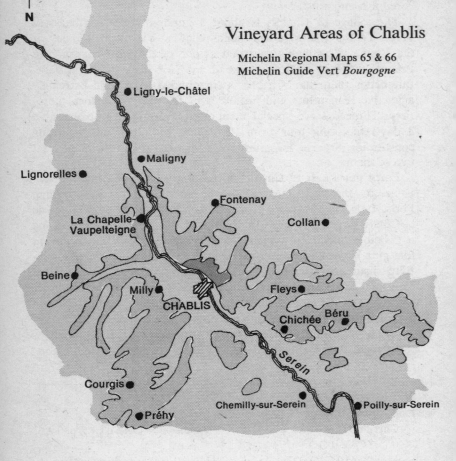

DAY 4
Itinerary p. 19

Vineyard Areas of Chablis

Michelin Regional Maps 65 & 66
Michelin Guide Vert *Bourgogne*

N

Ligny-le-Châtel

Maligny

Lignorelles

La Chapelle-
Vaupelteigne

Fontenay

Collan

Beine

Milly

CHABLIS

Fleys

Chichée   Béru

Serein

Courgis

Préhy

Chemilly-sur-Serein

Poilly-sur-Serein

CHABLIS GRAND CRU

CHABLIS PREMIER CRU & CHABLIS

PETIT CHABLIS

his more cosmopolitan friends. At any rate, Montbard is covered with mementos of the distinguished scientist. There is a *Parc Buffon*, a *Cabinet de Travail de Buffon*, a *Chapelle de Buffon*, and Buffon's mansion. But since this is such a gastronomic center, certainly the greatest honor to de Buffon is a dish named *truite farcie "caprice de Buffon"*—a stuffed trout with a banana accompaniment.

A short distance outside Montbard is the Abbaye de Fontenay, another attraction that is well worth a visit. This is a lovely abbey of the Cistercians, founded by Saint Bernard in 1168. However, the gastronome will visit Montbard with quite a different goal in mind. Here, in the Hôtel de la Gare, of all places, is a fine restaurant at which the specialties are pure Burgundian—*escargots de Bourgogne, saulpiquet montbardois* (ham with a highly spiced cream sauce), and, of course, *truite farcie "caprice de Buffon."* The décor is not especially noteworthy, but the food is superb, and the prices are, *mirabile dictu*, modest.

But certainly the most famous of the great restaurants that encircle Chablis is Monsieur Hure's sublime Hostellerie de la Poste at Avallon, twenty-two miles to the south of Chablis. It is staggeringly expensive but ravishing, with a lovely dining room, charming bedrooms, superlative food, and a wine list that will make the oenophile weep. The Poste is one of the great restaurants of France, and every moment in it is a delight; up to the last, that is, which would make even Croesus wince. Someone has remarked that perfection is never cheap, which saying aptly describes the Poste. It is a splendid place to suggest if you're

---

GRANDS CRUS	PREMIERS CRUS
Vaudésir	Montée de Tonnerre, Chapelot, Pied d'Aloup,
Preuses	Vaucoupin, Monts-de-Milieu, Vaulorent,
Les Clos	Fourchaume, Côtes de Fontenay, Vaupulent,
Les Grenouilles	Vaulorent, Beauroy, Troëme, Côte-de-Léchet,
Bougros	Les Lys, Séchet, Chatain, Vaillon, Beugnon,
Valmur	Mélinots, Butteaux, Les Forêts, Montmain,
Blanchots	Vosgros, Vaugiraud, Roncières

being taken out to dine, or if you have the good fortune to be on an expense account. Otherwise, you'd better drink up; you'll need something to soften the blow. You will encounter dishes such as *soufflé de brochet, pintadeau à la Riche,* or *timbale gourmande,* a delicious pastry shell filled with creamed *fruits de mer,* which goes down excellently with a *grand cru* Chablis of a good year. As those who like to exhort us to good works say, "We must not count the cost!"

Chablis lies on the frontier of Champagne. Separated from Burgundy's other vineyards by seventy-five miles of hilly country, it is a pocket of excellence lying between the Côte d'Or and the vineyards of Reims and Épernay. The character of its wine is thus quite unique. Lighter, drier, and harder than its counterparts of central Burgundy, it nevertheless has more body and bouquet than the still white wines of Champagne. In effect, its flavor reflects its geographical position, somewhere between the two.

Chablis takes its name from a charming little town nestled in the valley of a stream called the Serein. The town itself dates to Roman times, its name allegedly being a corruption of the word for a cable, as the Romans had a cable ferry crossing what must have been then a considerably wider river. The town is somnolent and small, with a population of a little over sixteen hundred. It is surrounded by good game country, and the local streams abound with fish. The *vignerons* of the town, when they aren't tending their vines, can usually be found out in the bush trying to get some of nature's other provender—a little *gibier* to fatten up the larder. Life in Chablis seems delightful. Tied to nature, it moves at a pleasant pace.

It has not always been so. The town and its vineyards have had their ups and downs. During the early Middle Ages, it was the refuge for the monks of Saint Martin of Tours fleeing the valley of the Loire from the depredations of the water-borne Norsemen. Charles le Chauve, the first king of modern France, gave them land in Chablis as a refuge. They then set up their abbey there and brought along relics of their founding saint. For a while Chablis was an important ecclesiastic center of western Christendom, and as such it prospered mightily.

A few centuries afterward, the Cistercians, the most energetic of medieval monks, arrived. After much bickering they managed to exact permission from the rival Order of Saint Martin to plant vines in Chablis. Though Chablis had been making wine since Roman times, the Cistercians brought new techniques and new grape types, and soon set a new standard that caused Chablis's fame to spread. With their usual astute eye, they singled out the best spots for vineyards and proceeded to plant them. These have produced noteworthy wines ever since.

All this sounds rather placid. But Chablis has tasted the misfortunes of war more than once. During the Hundred Years' War, Burgundy was an ally of the English against France. Chablis, as a border town, was overrun and occupied frequently by both sides. But the greatest misfortune to strike Chablis took place within our lifetime. In June, 1940, when France was collapsing under the hammer blows of Hitler's *Herrenvolk*, Mussolini decided to show that he, too, was tough. At the last minute he declared war on France, and as a gesture added his air force to the bombardment. One night in June an air fleet came over the Alps to do its worst. Why they picked on Chablis no one has ever found out. The town had no military significance whatsoever. There were no forts or factories, no major crossroads. They may have been aiming at Auxerre, Joigny, or Sens—all nearby, all on a river like Chablis, all with bridges that, if destroyed, would cut Route Nationale 6, France's vital north-south road. Or perhaps Mussolini's air force, with characteristic Italian intelligence about the folly of risking one's life, simply decided to dump its bombs while the dumping was good and scoot for home.

Whatever the reason, Chablis, to its surprise and dismay, found itself in a storm of fire. The center of the village was blasted, and, because an aqueduct that crosses the river on the bridge was destroyed when the bridge was hit, the fires could not be put out. They raged on for three days, and the old part of Chablis went up in smoke. When I made my first postwar visit to Chablis with my father in 1947, the effect of the hideous events of seven years earlier was all too apparent. Since then the damage has been repaired, but that day of destruction is still remembered grimly by the older inhabitants of the town.

Not all of Chablis's troubles have been caused by war, however. Chablis lives off the vine and is therefore especially vulnerable when the vine fares badly. The particular trouble in Chablis is caused by the Serein, the same river that gives the village its charm. The Serein, which means the "serene," seems misnamed; although it is placid in appearance it has the most damaging companions. Frost is the worst. This danger, which always exists in northern climes, is amplified and concentrated by the Serein. When a frost arrives, it sinks into the river bottom and hovers there for days, searing the delicate vines on the river's banks. During the 1950's there were five crippling frosts; five out of ten precious vintages were lost. Considering that it is lucky in these northern latitudes to have one good vintage in three, one can imagine the despair of the hard-working *vignerons* when, on top of that, half of all the vintages were destroyed. An especially bad year was 1953, when one of the best vintages of the decade was badly cut in size.

Few vinegrowers in the world would continue in the face of such odds: ten years of steady labor for only three copious, fine vintages—1952, 1955, and 1959. And, indeed, at the end of this miserable period there was talk of uprooting the beloved vines and replacing them with some steady source of income such as vegetables. We may be grateful that the weather later changed for the better and that this alarming plan was dismissed.

There have been a number of good, full vintages these past fifteen years and planting of Chablis's vines has increased with each success until now they are near the limit Appellation Contrôlée will allow.

As anyone who has tried them seriously knows, Chablis wines are unique in taste and bouquet. The characteristics of a true Chablis are an extraordinary dryness, a subtle and complex bouquet, an extremely light, limpid color tinged with green, and an ever so faint flinty taste. In 1759 the Canon Gaudon described Chablis in a letter to Madame d'Épinay: "My wine of Chablis this year is filled with life and bouquet; it soothes and enchants the palate, leaving behind the delicate fragrance of the subtlest of mushrooms." Such a description is difficult to improve upon.

The qualities of a Chablis result from a number of factors. Its dryness, crispness, and touch of astringency are due partly to the location of the vineyards. Chablis lies just south of the forty-eighth degree north latitude, a parallel that runs north of Seattle on our continent. White wines in particular need a certain amount of acidity to carry their flavor and bouquet and to allow them to age, and the pale northern sun of Chablis seems perfect for making it.

Another factor in a Chablis's flavor and bouquet is the grape varietal used. It is the Pinot Chardonnay, the great white-wine grape of Burgundy. In Chablis it is usually called Le Beaunois, doubtless because the Cistercians brought it up from the Côte d'Or, the center of which is Beaune. Its bunches are as small as those of its cousin, the Pinot Noir, but longer in form and less dense. The grape is a shy bearer, producing little juice for the area planted, but the quality of the resultant wine has given it a reputation of being one of the very best white-wine grapes. It is a noble vine.

Still a third element is the soil. The best Chablis is grown on Kimmeridgian, a chalky clay filled with pebbles and rich in limestone. This type of soil is also found in Champagne, and is one of the reasons for the wine's "clean taste reminiscent of hard spring water," as P. Morton Shand once put it.

The wines of Chablis are divided into four categories: Chablis Grand Cru, Chablis Premier Cru, Chablis, and Petit Chablis. All must come from a strictly delimited area more or less described by a three-mile radius around the village.

Chablis Grand Cru is the highest appellation. Such wines must have at least eleven percent natural alcohol. The vines must be cropped back so that only their best grapes remain: only 308 gallons—about 150 cases of wine—are allowed to be produced per acre. The wine must come from seven carefully described vineyards, all on the right bank of the Serein opposite the village of Chablis. There are only some five thousand cases of Chablis Grand Cru in a good year, an average of about 750 cases per vineyard. With such high standards and such limitations of supply, it can easily be understood why a Chablis Grand Cru can never be cheap. The seven Chablis Grand Cru vineyards are Vaudésir, Preuses, Les Clos, Grenouilles, Bougros, Valmur, and Blanchots.

Chablis Premier Cru wines are next in quality. Wines with this appellation must have a minimum of ten percent natural alcohol, produce no more than 356 gallons of wine per acre, and come from twenty-four specific vineyards near Chablis or the hamlets that encircle it. These vineyards are Pied d'Aloup, Vaupulent,

Roncières, Monts-de-Milieu, Montée de Tonnerre, Chapelot, Vau-lorent, Vaucoupin, Côte-de-Fontenay, Fourchaume, Les Forêts, Butteaux, Montmain, Vaillon, Séchet, Chatain, Beugnon, Mélinots, Côte-de-Léchet, Les Lys, Beauroy, Troëme, Vosgros, and Vogiros.

Following the wines of the Premier Cru are those called, simply, Chablis. These must reach ten percent natural alcohol and may come from a slightly broader region than a Chablis Premier Cru. Otherwise, they must fulfill the same qualifications. The word Chablis may be followed by the name of the vineyard, but it usually isn't.

Petit Chablis, the fourth category of Chablis, must reach nine and one-half percent natural alcohol and comes from twenty communes within a three-mile radius of Chablis. No more than 356 gallons of wine may be produced per acre.

In all the classifications it will be noted that the word "natural" is used to describe the necessary percentage of alcohol. To have the appellation, the grapes must contain enough sugar to ferment to the required degree. Once the appellation is acquired, the wines may be legitimately chaptalized (that is, sugar may be added) to bring the percentage of alcohol up a degree or two. In northern latitudes, this is often necessary.

Côte de Nuits

Northern Section

Where the greatest red wine in the world comes from is a source of endless debate. Every area that produces a better-than-average vintage puts forth its candidate, usually with considerable passion. Self-advocacy, however, is always a little suspect.

Among most knowledgeable oenophiles, the two preferred champions are the Médoc-Graves region of Bordeaux and the Côte de Nuits of Burgundy. Champion, of course, is a boxing term, and if we continue the metaphor, these two wines are the reigning heavyweights. Others are lighter and fleeter, but they lack the depth of flavor and bouquet; still others are burlier of body, but they fail to have that nuance and subtlety that spell elegance of style.

The Médoc-Graves region produces wines that, when young, are tart of taste and rather difficult to take. But as they age they develop a sinuous, subtle beauty that marks them as champions among champions. At their peak they are sophisticated, beautifully balanced, and depend almost more on their gracefulness and elegance than on their power. The wines of the Côte de Nuits are big, full in taste, virile, powerful, and robust. Yet they have a velvety grace and nuance of flavor and bouquet that set them apart as far more than ordinary "big" wines. They are, to say the least, extraordinary.

Which is the winner? The classic Bordeaux or the *grand vin de Bourgogne*? It would be virtually impossible to decide. One

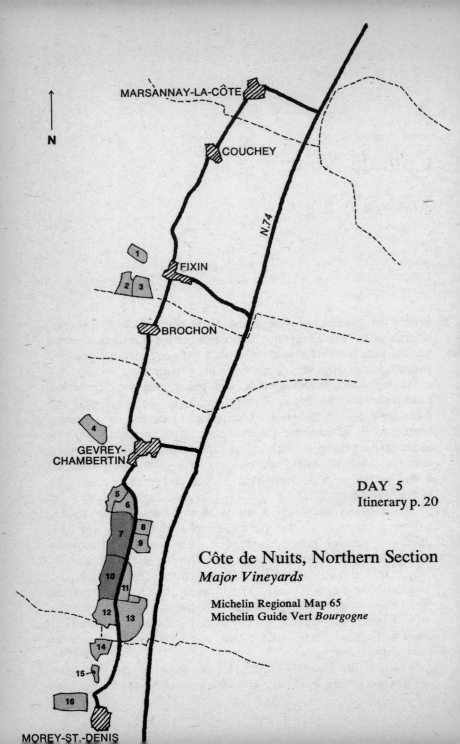

N

MARSANNAY-LA-CÔTE

COUCHEY

N.74

1

FIXIN

2 3

BROCHON

4

GEVREY-
CHAMBERTIN

5
6
8
7
9
10
11
12 13
14
15
16

MOREY-ST.-DENIS

DAY 5
Itinerary p. 20

Côte de Nuits, Northern Section
Major Vineyards

Michelin Regional Map 65
Michelin Guide Vert *Bourgogne*

can only agree with the jurist of the *ancien régime* who, when asked by a marquise at supper one evening which he preferred, answered, "Madame, in this sort of trial I get so much pleasure examining the evidence that I postpone giving my verdict from week to week."

The Côte de Nuits, a scant ten miles long, is the northern half of a southeastward-facing slope of long, low hills called the Côte d'Or. It is named after the town of Nuits-Saint-Georges near its southern end. The Côte is spangled with vineyards of world renown, and to say which is the best would require an audacity bordering on foolishness. However, by general consensus, and, even more indicatively, by the prices they command, there are in this plethora of stars three brilliant points of focus. These are centered around the vineyards of Chambertin to the north, Musigny in the middle, and Romanée-Conti to the south. Around each of these superlative vineyards are a host of other excellent ones which generally share the characteristics of the three regional leaders. This first chapter on the Côte de Nuits will discuss the general reasons for the quality of its wines and its vineyards as far south as the galaxy around Chambertin.

One reason for the uniqueness of the great vineyards of the Côte de Nuits is the grape type used. By law these wines are made exclusively of a single grape varietal, the Pinot. The great reds are made of the Pinot Noir; the few whites are made of the Pinot Chardonnay or Pinot Blanc. Few other areas on earth demand this. No other region has such stringent laws enforcing it.

GRANDS CRUS

10 Chambertin
7 Chambertin-Clos de Bèze

4 Clos Saint-Jacques
5 Ruchottes-Chambertin
6 Mazis-Chambertin
8 Chapelle-Chambertin
9 Griotte-Chambertin
11 Charmes-Chambertin

12 Latricières-Chambertin
13 Mazoyères-Chambertin
14 Clos de la Roche
15 Clos Saint-Denis

WELL-KNOWN PREMIERS CRUS

1 Les Hervelets
2 La Perrière
3 Clos du Chapitre
16 Clos des Lambrays

To be sure, most great German vineyards use the noble Riesling, but they are not obligated to do so entirely. In California, where, happily, the use of the best European grape varietals is spreading among the more reputable growers, the vintners are legally obligated to use only fifty-one percent of the grape type to carry its name on their label, though many voluntarily use more. The red wines of Bordeaux are almost inevitably of several grape varieties—the Cabernet Sauvignon and Cabernet Franc, the Merlot, Malbec, and Petit Verdot among them. A Rhône may be made from up to a dozen grape varietals, the blend depending on the taste the region or the vintner has developed as typical. And so it goes, except on the Côte d'Or. Here one grape is used in all great vineyards—the noble Pinot.

Exactly when the Pinot was first used in Burgundy is anyone's guess, and there have been several. Some think it is a development of vines brought by the Greeks or Romans. Others contend that it is a native of the region. Still a third group maintains that it resulted from monkish experiments to find the perfect Burgundy grape in the Middle Ages. We do know that it was mentioned firmly in one of the decrees of Philippe le Hardi in 1394, and it may be safely assumed by his favorable tone that it had been around for some time even then.

Whatever its history, the Pinot is a glorious grape, and, with the Cabernet Sauvignon, one of the greatest red-wine grapes in the world. With its variants, the Pinot Chardonnay and Pinot Blanc, it also makes some of the world's finest white wines. If any vines deserve the title of "noble," the Pinot is certainly one of them. Nobility of character is a rare quality, so it is only apt that this noble vine should be a shy bearer. Many vines produce

---

more juice, but they have less elegance and less breed. The Pinot's bunches are tight little packs of small grapes, each, in a good year, a miniature bomb of flavor. Wholesale nibbling in the vineyards, however, is much frowned upon. A kilo of Chambertin's grapes pressed makes about a bottle of wine. They are thus among the most precious fruit in the world. There is no welcome mat out for itinerant grape fanciers in Burgundy.

The quality that the Pinot Noir gives the great red wines of the Côte de Nuits is unmistakable. The wines are velvety, round, smooth, full, and usually not high in tannin, as a Bordeaux may be. Though the grape has been transplanted to many other climes and continents, in none does it reach the complexity and balance of taste that it gains from its native habitat. The reasons for this are many; one is, doubtless, the northern latitude, with its long summer days but weak sunlight. Since it is sunlight that produces sugar in plants, the Pinot grown here does not always contain enough sugar to ferment into the desired degree of alcohol. Chaptalization is thus a common practice in mediocre years. But there is also an advantage to such a climate, which balances this occasional defect. All wines need a certain measure of acidity to hold them together; this is the skeleton to which the wine's flesh holds. Without it a wine is soft, flabby, and short-lived. Too much sun means low acidity, and the Pinot grown in a more southern, sunny clime suffers from this lack.

Another factor in the character of the wines of the Côte de Nuits is the nature of the soil, a mixture of clay, silica, and quite a bit of limestone. And for fifteen hundred years the soil has been enriched by a compost made solely from a mulch of the leaves and cuttings of the vines themselves. History reveals that great civilizations do not spring up overnight, but usually evolve from a rich and slowly developed past. Analogously, the Pinot seems to thrive on the roots and verdure of its previous ages. "I sometimes think that never blows so red/The rose as where some buried Caesar bled," wrote Khayyám. And if the Pinot is the emperor of vines, so too its descendants flourish on their own lineal decay.

The topographical position of the vineyards also contributes to the glory of the Côte de Nuits wines. The Pinot seems to like steady warmth spread throughout the day rather than a tepid morning followed by hot middays and afternoons. The desired evenness of temperature is achieved by placing the vineyards on a slight tilt at the base of the Côte's hillside, facing southeast. This way the vines directly face the rising sun as it begins to dispel the chill night airs, but as the sun moves into its hot meridian and afternoon, its rays strike the slope at an oblique angle. The result is the evenest possible absorption of the sun's warmth and radiation over the daylight hours. This is one reason why nearly all of Burgundy's great vineyards face southeastward on the lower third of a hillside, just where it begins its steep ascendancy.

Grape, soil, latitude, and topographic position of the vineyard are all important in developing wine's qualities. Which is paramount is impossible to say. The chemical structure of wine is extremely complicated and continues to change until the wine is dead. It arrives at its shifting combinations by a series of variables, any one of which, if changed, would alter the later character of the wine. The permutations and combinations are endless, each triggering off countless sequences. Generalizing under such circumstances is difficult, but some observations may be useful.

Sunny years generally produce wines high in alcohol but low in acidity. They are inevitably hailed as the "year of the century" by some members of the wine trade (and by the less discerning public) because they can be sold easily and quickly. They mature with extraordinary rapidity. Like a rocket they dazzle with their spectacular ascent but they fall just as quickly. Their peak is evident, startling, and magnificent, but is not held. Examples were 1959, 1953, and 1947.

Cloudy years with little sunshine are likely to produce lean, hard wines high in acidity, which take a long time to mature and then are no great shakes. To be palatable they have to be chaptalized.

Rainy years produce similar wines, which are watery to boot, and have little to commend them. They also must be chaptalized.

Great years, such as 1961, 1964, 1966, 1969, and 1971, are an amalgam of sun, rain, and clouds. Consequently, they were a perfect balance of alcohol, tannin, sugar, and acidity.

There are, of course, exceptions to these generalities. Local weather conditions or maladroit vinification can reduce a great year to a mediocre one. Wise and imaginative vinification, on the other hand, can produce extraordinary wine even in a mediocre year. Because more is now known about the processes and control of vinification, good and interesting wine is being made from vintages that a generation ago would have been undrinkable. Often a relatively rainy or cloudy year will produce light, elegant wines that are not typical Burgundies, but are lovely nonetheless. There were several '63s in this category.

"The Côte d'Or is little more than a rather ugly and dried-up small mountain," Stendhal wrote, "but at every moment one runs across an immortal name." Stendhal was a little harsh in describing the landscape; it is a pleasant if not grandiose part of the world. However, the second part of his statement brooks no argument. Every village, indeed, nearly every vineyard, is a name that gives a shock of recognition. The towns themselves are usually not too prepossessing—a small church encircled by a cluster of granite houses. But lapping on their flanks like waves on an island is a green sea of vines.

The Côte de Nuits starts just south of Dijon, a city famed in earlier days as the capital of Burgundy and now known as a transportation hub as well as the world's center of the production of fine mustard. Eight thousand tons of mustard flow out of Dijon every year, enough to float a small freighter. The city is also known for its gingerbread and its cassis. In days gone by, the environs of Dijon produced wines of some notoriety. Crébillon, a hamlet on its outskirts, was in particular a viticultural center to be reckoned with. Now, however, it is known primarily as the place that gave its name to Claude de Crébillon, the great eighteenth-century master of erotica who wrote *Le Sofa*, surely one of the best goads ever devised to lure schoolboys into poring over their French lessons.

At present the only town on the Côte de Dijon of winey notoriety is Marsannay-la-Côte, five miles south of Dijon. Here a rosé made from the Pinot Noir is much admired by the local inhabitants. Here, also, is an extremely agreeable, rustic inn named Les Gourmets. It is run by Daniel Gauthier and his wife, chef, and chatelaine. They are assisted by the chef's brother, René, who serves as headwaiter. The latter, who once worked in California, has the face and gestures of one born to be a comic in the silent movies—fifty years too late, alas. There is a charming garden in which are displayed brightly polished brass cauldrons and a nineteenth-century fire engine. The menu includes such Burgundian specialties as *escargots* and *jambon persillé* as well as, when I was there, *terrine de volaille, andouillettes au vin blanc* (pork tripe sausages in white wine), and, during the season, game. The wine list has an excellent collection of Burgundies, as well it might, considering the vineyards that lie within a long stone's throw. Les Gourmets is thus the perfect place to taste the liquid and solid provender of the northern end of the Côte de Nuits. However, a telephone call to reserve a table is not a bad idea. The restaurant is near enough to Dijon, a city filled with admirers of good cuisine, to attract many plump burghers who want a breath of fresh air as well as inner satisfaction.

From the wine lover's point of view the Côte de Nuits begins seriously at Fixin, a tiny village two miles south of Marsannay. It contains one pleasant restaurant, Chez Jeannette, and five very good vineyards, among them Clos de la Perrière, a twelve-acre plot that produces a long-lived, robust wine which presages its great neighbors in Gevrey. Fixin is also the site of a monument sculpted by Rude, commissioned by an old soldier of the Napoleonic wars in honor of his emperor. It is called the *Awakening of Napoleon* but is no "rude awakening." It is lyrical and dreamy —indeed, camp at its highest, and for those who like that sort of thing it should not be missed.

A short distance south of Fixin is the town of Gevrey-Chambertin, a name known to wine lovers throughout the world. In it lie two equally great vineyards whose reputations rank among the very top red Burgundies, hence among the best red wines on earth. They are Chambertin and Clos de Bèze. The latter may legally call itself Chambertin if it so chooses, but Chambertin may not call itself Clos de Bèze.

Chambertin received vast publicity during the early years of the nineteenth century as Napoleon's chosen wine. In June, 1812, the *Grande Armée*, under the personal command of the emperor, struck into Russia and marched toward Moscow. The first three months brought nothing but victories; the last three a series of disappointments and catastrophes. In the end the *Grande Armée* was reduced to a shadow of its former grandeur, recoiling from a blazing Moscow across the freezing steppes, harassed every inch by Cossack, wolf, and merciless cold. Of the five hundred thousand men who entered Russia in early summer, only one in twenty lived to see his native land again. It was the greatest debacle of the century.

Napoleon, however, managed to fare quite well, for he always had the sense, or the cynicism, to look after himself. While his soldiers froze, he insisted that his linen be white; while Marshal Ney, *"brave des braves,"* held back the circling Cossacks with a handful of frozen men, Napoleon took solace that no matter what, no matter where, he would still be served his Chambertin to drive away the Russian cold. For despite his unprepossessing appearance and his general neglect of food, he was a lover of wine. And when his fiascoes had been forgotten, the wine he loved best was remembered. Chambertin was incorporated into Napoleon's legend and thereby became one of the most famous wines in the world.

As a result, though Clos de Bèze might conceivably want to call itself Chambertin, the opposite contingency is hardly likely to arise. Small matter. The two vineyards lie side by side, forming a continuum of sixty-eight acres of some of the finest vines on earth. Together they produce about six thousand cases in a good year.

The commune of Gevrey-Chambertin was probably planted with vines during Roman times, though the first clear mention of it is in 630 A.D. when the Burgundian Duke, Amalgaire, bequeathed a vineyard to the Abbey of Bèze, which became Clos de Bèze. In due course all the vineyards of Gevrey, excepting a pasture next to Clos de Bèze, fell under the sway of the Benedictine Order. Legend has it that some time during the twelfth century the owner of this field, a peasant named Bertin, decided that since the wine made by the monks in Clos de Bèze was so good he would do well to plant vines himself. He did, and five years later, when the resultant grapes were picked, the wine made from them was marvelous. The "field of Bertin"—*champ de Bertin*—was on its way to joining the immortals. The wine itself is certainly extraordinary. Virile, full, pungent of bouquet, velvety, and filled with finesse, it deserves its grand reputation. Perhaps the most delightful description of it is P. Morton Shand's quotation from a Burgundian *vigneron: "On croit avaler le bon Dieu en culottes de velours"*—"One seems to have swallowed the good Lord himself wearing velvet pants."

The classification of the wines of the commune of Gevrey-Chambertin is extremely complicated. There is very little rhyme or reason to it; it must be learned by heart or written down. At the head of the list, in a category all by themselves, are the vineyards of Chambertin (thirty-two acres) and Clos de Bèze (thirty-six acres). For these the maximum permissible yield per acre is 264 gallons, and the minimum natural alcoholic strength is eleven and a half percent.

Slightly lower in quality are the seven vineyards adjacent to Chambertin and Clos de Bèze, which are allowed to hyphenate their names with "Chambertin." They are Charmes-Chambertin (thirty-one acres), Mazoyères-Chambertin (forty-seven), Griotte-Chambertin (thirteen and a half), Latricières-Chambertin (seventeen and a half), Mazis-Chambertin (thirty-one), Ruchottes-Chambertin (seven and a half), and Chapelle-Chambertin (thirteen and a half). For these the maximum permissible yield per acre is 282 gallons, and the minimum natural alcoholic strength is eleven and a half percent.

Following these is a vineyard that is not allowed to hyphenate its name with Chambertin because it is on a separate knoll with different soil and exposure. But the price it deservedly commands is just under that of Chambertin itself. It is the Clos Saint-Jacques. Legally in the same Premier Cru category, but a long step beneath it, are twenty-four vineyards that may carry their own name if they wish but must precede it with the name of the commune, Gevrey-Chambertin, as must also the Clos Saint-Jacques. These wines are usually called simply Gevrey-Chambertin Premier Cru. All told they make up about a thousand acres. Their maximum permissible yield per acre is 308 gallons, and the minimum natural alcoholic strength is eleven percent.

Finally in Gevrey-Chambertin are those wines called simply Gevrey-Chambertin. They must reach only ten and a half percent alcohol. Their quality depends primarily on the reputation of the grower, or, if this is not known, of the importer. They are similar to regional wines in that they vary radically from vineyard to vineyard.

The wines of Gevrey-Chambertin are an admirable choice to

accompany full-flavored meats, in other words all types of beef and game.

The town of Gevrey-Chambertin has another blessing in addition to its wines, and that is a fine restaurant, La Rôtisserie du Chambertin. The setting is lovely, the building one of the prettiest houses in town with a beautifully decorated *cave* beneath. The food matches the elegance and originality of the site, as does, of course, the wine list. Monsieur Menneveau is the host.

The next town south of Gevrey-Chambertin is Morey-Saint-Denis, another place where the vineyards owe much to the work and devotion of the Cistercians. It lies between two famous neighbors, Gevrey-Chambertin and Chambolle-Musigny. The excellent wines of Morey-Saint-Denis have two sets of characteristics: the wines of its vineyards to the north, Clos de la Roche and Clos Saint-Denis, resemble in their fullness those of the adjacent Mazoyères-Chambertin. With these, the chain of vineyards of the Chambertin family ceases, and from here on, beginning with the next vineyards of Morey to the south, the wines take on a more delicate, feminine grace as they approach the great Musigny.

Côte de Nuits

Southern Section

The southward tour of the Côte de Nuits ended in the preceding chapter in the middle of the commune of Morey-Saint-Denis. The reason is that Morey is Janus-faced. Half of its vineyards, led by Clos de la Roche and Clos Saint-Denis, resemble their neighbors to the north, the virile wines of Gevrey-Chambertin. The other half, with such vineyards as Clos de Tart and a fraction of Bonnes Mares, begin to take on the *douceur* of their southerly neighbor —the town of Chambolle-Musigny.

This split acreage has cost Morey dear. The average wine bibber associates a great vineyard or wine type with its commune, a fact well demonstrated in Burgundy by the rather dubious practice of adding the name of a town's greatest vineyard to its own name.

But what does one commune do with two sets of vineyards, each with characteristics quite different from the other? The result, in advertising argot, is a "blurred image." The unsure oenophile, consequently, is likely to avoid the wines of Morey, sticking to its great neighbors that produce wines of a single type. So much the better for the rest of us. Morey's best vineyards are top-notch, just under the very finest in Burgundy. And because they are comparatively unknown, they will usually be very good values.

At the north Clos de la Roche produces splendid wine that in many ways resembles the great Chambertin. This is not too surprising, for Clos de la Roche is not only a continuation of the same slope of hill, but is also flat up against the Gevrey-Chambertin border. Three hundred yards away the vineyard of Chambertin ends. Between the two lie such excellent vineyards as Latricières-Chambertin and Mazoyères-Chambertin. Nothing seems to break the sea of beautifully tended vines except an occasional sign announcing the end of one vineyard and the beginning of another.

To the west of Clos de la Roche and slightly uphill from it is a vineyard called Monts-Luisants. The lowest part of it, the section adjacent to Clos de la Roche, is allowed to be considered part of the Clos. The upper part produces a rather full white wine.

South of Clos de la Roche is Clos Saint-Denis, after which the town is named. Its vines, which lap up against the walls of Morey itself, produce another manly wine of Chambertin-like temperament.

Below Clos Saint-Denis the wines of Morey begin to change in character. The first two vineyards are Clos de Tart and Clos des Lambrays, the former considered the finer of the two. Its odd name hearkens back to ownership in medieval times by the nuns of Notre-Dame-de-Tart near Dijon. The nuns, in fact, had a great deal to do with the wines of Morey. Clos des Lambrays was also once owned by a nunnish order, the Abbey of Lieu-Dieu. To this day many wine lovers find in these two wines a dulcet, almost feminine quality. As P. Léon Gauthier wrote, "Softer than the Musignys and Chambertins, their illustrious neighbors, the wines are distinguished by their finesse and bouquet"—feminine characteristics that come, perhaps, from their nun-influenced past. The southernmost vineyard in Morey is a sliver of the renowned Bonnes Mares, five of its thirty-six acres falling within the commune, the rest within that of Chambolle-Musigny.

The great vineyards of Morey-Saint-Denis are thus Bonnes

RESTAURANT

Vosne-Romanée (Côte-d'Or)   La Toute Petite Auberge   p. 21,
p. 99

HOTELS   p. 101

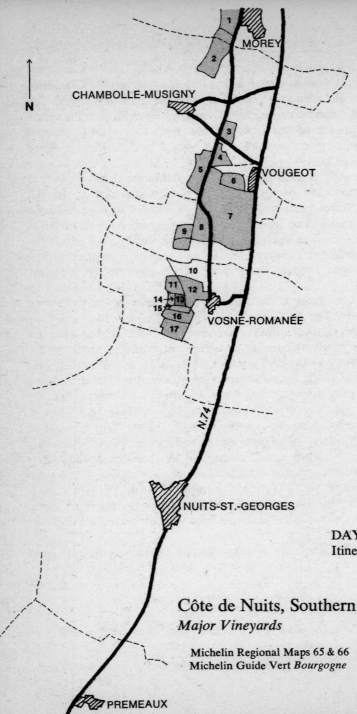

N

MOREY

CHAMBOLLE-MUSIGNY

VOUGEOT

VOSNE-ROMANÉE

N.74

NUITS-ST.-GEORGES

DAY 6
Itinerary p. 20

Côte de Nuits, Southern Section
Major Vineyards

Michelin Regional Maps 65 & 66
Michelin Guide Vert *Bourgogne*

PREMEAUX

Mares (five acres out of thirty-seven), Clos de Tart (seventeen and a half), Clos de la Roche (thirty-eight), and Clos Saint-Denis (sixteen and a quarter). All of these wines are red, and to be allowed to carry their names under Appellation Contrôlée, they must have at least eleven and a half percent natural alcohol, and no more than 264 gallons of wine may be produced per acre. In a category slightly beneath these is Clos des Lambrays (fourteen acres). Its wines must reach eleven percent natural alcohol, and no more than 282 gallons may be produced per acre. As with all Burgundian wines beneath the rank of *grand cru*, the vineyard name must be preceded by the name of the town, Morey-Saint-Denis.

The village of Chambolle-Musigny has its roots deep in antiq-

---

PREMIER DES GRANDS CRUS

  13   La Romanée-Conti

GRANDS CRUS

   1   Clos de Tart
   2   Bonnes Mares
   5   Musigny
   6   Vignes Blanches de Clos de Vougeot
   7   Clos de Vougeot
   8   Grands Échézeaux
   9   Échézeaux
  11   Richebourg
  12   Romanée-Saint-Vivant
  14   La Romanée
  16   La Tâche

WELL-KNOWN PREMIERS CRUS

   3   Chambolle-Musigny Les Charmes
   4   Chambolle-Musigny Les Amoureuses
  10   Vosne-Romanée Les Suchots
  15   Vosne-Romanée La Grande Rue
  17   Vosne-Romanée Les Malconsorts

uity. A tiny stream comes down from the hillside and cuts across
the commune. When the spring rains came, this rivulet used to
turn into a roaring little river, inundating the land on its flanks.
Consequently, the Romans called the area *Campus Ebulliens,* the
Boiling Field, and this became in French *Champ Bouillant,* later
corrupted to Chambolle. The stream has since been tamed, but
the name lives on.

The first vineyard across the Morey-Chambolle town line is
the thirty-two acres of Bonnes Mares within the limits of Chambolle. Where the name Bonnes Mares came from is a subject of
some conjecture. *Mare* in French means a stagnant pool, and in
the days before grapes were grown, there may have been *bonnes
mares* here for cattle to drink from. Another meaning is suggested
by the medieval French verb *marer,* which encompasses the care
and labors associated with vine tending. In this case the words
would mean something like "the good labors." Whatever the
origin of the name, the vineyard is excellent. Though perhaps not
as subtle or delicate as the great Musigny, its wines are more so
than the other wines of Morey. As one moves southward toward
the Vouge, the stream that separates Musigny from Clos de Vougeot, the wines become progressively more elegant and delicate.
Bonnes Mares still has a touch of the virility of the northern
Chambertins, but one can taste that it is two-thirds of the way
toward Musigny. All in all, it is a splendid wine, one of the
greats of Burgundy. Not being too well known, it is usually a
good value.

A little way south of Bonnes Mares is the pretty village of
Chambolle, stuck in a cleft in the hillside. Unlike most towns on
the Côte d'Or, it has inclined streets along the hill's flanks. The
Route des Grands Crus, which up to this point follows quite a
straight line through the vineyards all the way from Gevrey-
Chambertin, is lost for a moment in a maze of alleyways. But if
one takes the lane east from Chambolle toward Route Nationale
74 at Gilly, one comes to a crossroad after about five hundred
yards. Directly in front lie two superb vineyards: to the left,
Les Charmes, and to the right, Les Amoureuses, "the ladies in
love," one of the most charming names and wines in Burgundy.
It is no misnomer. For the wine is exactly that—feminine, soft,
and lyrical. If it didn't lie right beside Musigny, it certainly would

be considered one of the very top in Burgundy. But fate has put it next to its archetype, and it sits in its shade. For, turning right at the above-mentioned crossroad and proceeding about two hundred yards, one arrives at the vineyards of Musigny itself.

Vineyards, plural, is just the term, for Musigny consists of four small vineyards stretched out like a diadem of pearls along the brow of the hillside. They are Les Musigny, followed by Les Petits-Musigny, then the two sections of La Combe d'Orveau. All produce wines of extraordinary fineness and delicacy. They are not great, burly Burgundies but elegant and subtle wines, and, as such, are about the only red wines of the Côte de Nuits that accompany such delicately flavored red meats as lamb. Musigny is, as Gaston Roupnel once wrote, "the wine of silk and lace"— utterly feminine and charming.

With Musigny, the Route des Grands Crus enters its golden mile. In a short half-hour's stroll one passes a parade of superb vineyards. Across the lane are the rolling vines of Clos de Vougeot. Crossing the town line of Flagey, one runs into Grands Échézeaux, followed closely by Richebourg, Romanée Saint-Vivant, Romanée-Conti, La Romanée, and La Tâche. All are immaculately tended. They are probably the most valuable plots of agricultural land in the world.

The *grands crus* of Chambolle-Musigny are Les Musigny (twenty-five acres) and Bonnes Mares (thirty-two out of thirty-seven). Both of these are red. They must reach eleven and a half percent natural alcohol, and no more than 264 gallons may be produced per acre. Musigny Blanc is the name given to a small quantity of white wine made in the vineyards of Musigny. This must fulfill the same stipulations as the red wine, except that it must reach twelve percent natural alcohol.

The two best-known *premier cru* vineyards are Les Charmes (two acres) and Les Amoureuses (thirteen). For both wines the name of the town, Chambolle-Musigny, must precede the name of the vineyard. No more than 308 gallons of wine may be produced per acre, and it must reach eleven percent natural alcohol. There are seventeen other *premier cru* vineyards, usually only identified by the words Chambolle-Musigny Premier Cru. They must follow the same rules.

In the last category are wines called, simply, Chambolle-

Musigny. These are wines from the town that have reached a natural alcohol strength of ten and a half percent and come from certain delineated vineyards that are allowed to produce no more than 308 gallons of wine per acre.

Immediately downhill from the vineyards of Musigny, in the commune of Vougeot, lies the hulking form of a medieval château. Its solid bulk traces what is certainly one of the most famous outlines in winedom. What the Eiffel Tower is to steel construction and the Coliseum is to amphitheatres, this building is to wine. Its history is colorful, its present is well publicized, and the vineyard that surrounds it is not only the largest of the great Burgundian vineyards but among the best. It is, of course, Clos de Vougeot.

The history of the Clos is intimately intertwined with the Cistercian brotherhood. Shortly after the monks were convinced, in 1162, to commit their formidable energies to wine making, they began amassing the land that was to be the center of their efforts. Through bequests, purchases, and arrangements with rival orders, they gradually garnered these magnificent 125 acres. In 1336 they signalized their work by finishing a wall around the Clos, which still traces its boundaries.

The Cistercians graded the wines of the Clos in three categories. The top wines, fittingly enough, came from the highest part of the vineyard next to Musigny and Grands Échézeaux. They were not for sale, but were reserved for gifts to the high and mighty in the church. In 1359, Jean de Bussières, Abbot of the Cistercians, sent thirty kegs of this wine—the equivalent of a little over nine thousand bottles—to Pope Gregory XI. Four years later, just enough time for the wine to have settled down, he was awarded a cardinal's biretta, a modest return for so magnificent a present.

During the French Revolution, the properties of the Church were sequestered by the state to be sold later privately as *biens nationaux*. One of these was Clos de Vougeot. The last Cistercian *chef de cave* was a lay brother with the apt name of Dom Goblet, and when the bailiffs of the new republic came to evict him, he burst into tears. It is indicative of the French order of priorities— an order with which no true gourmet can disagree—that though the Terror was going full tilt, Dom Goblet was not only allowed to keep his head, but to go freely on his way. Moreover, to console him for his enormous loss, he was permitted to take a lifetime's supply of his beloved wine with him.

A short time later, a certain Colonel Bisson, marching his regiment to join the Army of the Rhine, where Rouget de Lisle had just written the "Marseillaise," found himself on the Route Nationale alongside Clos de Vougeot. It was the moment of greatest danger to the infant republic, for the crowned heads of Europe were throwing their armies at its frontiers to kill it before its revolutionary ideas could spread. The result of this was a burst of patriotism which, being French, took a winy turn. Colonel Bisson halted his regiment, commanded it to "left face," and ordered it to dip the colors to one of the great glories of France, Clos de Vougeot. This *beau geste* was never forgotten. Ever since, every French army detachment marching down the Route Nationale has stopped and saluted the great vineyard too.

For nearly one hundred years after the Revolution, the Clos remained in the possession of a succession of single owners. In 1889, unfortunately, it fell into the hands of a real-estate speculator, who split it up and sold it in bits to the highest bidders. It was bought by some for prestige, by others as an elegant plaything, and by still others to make fine wine. Seven hundred years of putting together and holding together one of the finest vineyards in Burgundy was unraveled. At present, the 125 acres of the Clos are owned by more than sixty proprietors, some making wine, some not, some bottling it under their own names, others selling to *négociants*. Standards, consequently, vary considerably, though a well-made bottle of Clos de Vougeot is still a memorable treat. Probably the most dependable guarantee of quality is the good reputation of the grower, shipper, or importer.

The château of the Clos was built by the Cistercians as a pressing shed and storage place in the fifteenth century. Its fame today rests on far more than a colorful past, however. It is at present owned by that bibulous fraternity of Burgundy enthusiasts, the Chevaliers du Tastevin, who periodically throw splendid soirées in its massive hall. About five hundred people are wined and dined at a clip, the medieval rafters ringing with the boisterous songs of the Cadets de Bourgogne. The glories of the wines of Burgundy are extolled, and drunk, hugely. The food served is excellent, and by some miracle of organization it is presented on plates that are piping hot. The whole show may be, as some cynics claim, nothing more than a vast publicity stunt, but even so, it is a splendid one, and not to be missed if one has the opportunity to be there.

Although the Clos proper produces only red wine, there is a small vineyard across the road from the château that makes an excellent white. Called Clos Blanc de Vougeot, it is one of the few whites of the Côte de Nuits that can match those of the Côte de Beaune. It is quite expensive, and justifiably so. There are a few other vineyards in the commune of Vougeot, but none to match the fine wines of the Clos.

In the commune of Vougeot the *grand cru* wine is Clos de Vougeot (125 acres). The maximum production permitted is 264 gallons per acre and the minimum natural alcoholic strength is eleven and a half percent.

The *premiers crus* of Vougeot total thirty acres. They are Clos Blanc de Vougeot, Les Petits-Vougeots, Clos de la Perrière, and part of Les Cras. To be classified as first growths, the reds must reach a natural alcoholic strength of eleven percent and the whites eleven and a half percent, and no more than 308 gallons of wine may be produced per acre.

The commune of Flagey-Échézeaux is an oddly shaped gerrymander. The town and the bulk of the land under its jurisdiction lie off on the flats to the east of the Côte de Nuits, separated from it by Route Nationale 74. However, there is a thin, key-shaped sliver of land that crosses the road, runs up the edge of the Clos de Vougeot, and then, reaching the back of it, broadens into an island. This island contains two of the finest vineyards in Burgundy—Échézeaux and Grands Échézeaux. There is ample cause for their greatness. On the north they are bounded by Musigny, and on the east by Clos de Vougeot. To the south, two hundred yards farther along the same flank of hills, lies the complex of Richebourg, Romanée Saint-Vivant, La Romanée, La Tâche, and Romanée-Conti.

Of the two vineyards, Grands Échézeaux is in the key position, and its body, bouquet, and flavor reflect this. The vineyard lies against the wall that marks the boundary of the best part of Clos de Vougeot. The wines of the Clos tend to get better as they ascend the hillside. Taking this as a principle, the wines of Grands

Échézeaux would be, if they were part of the Clos, its *crème de la crème,* for they are an extension of its highest part. Échézeaux itself is a superb wine, but it lacks some of the fullness and breed of Grands Échézeaux. It is a much bigger vineyard—vineyards, really—as it is made up of several that describe a large semicircle around Grands Échézeaux. For reasons that may have to do with pronunciation, these two wines are not well known in Anglo-Saxon countries. Consequently, they are likely to be good values.

The *grands crus* of Flagey-Échézeaux are Grands Échézeaux (twenty-two and a half acres) and Échézeaux (seventy-nine). Both wines are red, and must reach eleven and a half percent natural alcohol. No more than 264 gallons may be produced per acre.

Other good, lesser growths of the commune may appear under the name of the neighboring town, Vosne-Romanée.

A little over a mile north of Nuits-Saint-Georges lies the cluster of granite houses that comprise Vosne-Romanée. It is a pretty village, but not overpoweringly so, and certainly the fact that it contains only a few more than 650 inhabitants has earned it no great niche among metropolises. Yet its name is known to the cultured or the sybaritic the world over. The reason for this renown is a flourish of vineyards that start directly on the back steps of the town and climb the gentle slope behind it. They are five in number—four of them being princes of the blood, and the fifth, by general agreement, the sovereign of the red wines of Burgundy. The princes are Romanée Saint-Vivant, La Romanée, Richebourg, and La Tâche. The sovereign is Romanée-Conti.

The word Romanée figures large in the naming of the great vineyards of Vosne, and this doubtless hearkens back to the days of the Roman occupation. In 312 A.D., the rhetor of Autun directed a panegyric to the Emperor Constantine in which he praised the *pagus arebrignus* as "this famous canton, distinguished for its culture of the vine." The *pagus arebrignus* was the country around what is now Nuits-Saint-Georges, and so there can be little doubt that the Romans discovered and developed this most elegant slope of all.

In the Middle Ages, the town came under the sway of a rival order to the Cistercians, the Priory of Saint-Vivant, and during this time the four and a half acres of what later was to be called

Romanée-Conti was known as *Le Cloux*. In Middle French this meant "the best." The vineyard received its present name in the eighteenth century from Louis François de Bourbon, Prince de Conti. The prince was an excellent general and an astute diplomat, and for a while he was considered a possible candidate for the crown of Poland. Failing in this, he became secretary to his cousin, Louis XV, the closest thing that France then had to a prime minister. His nemesis, however, proved to be Madame de Pompadour. That marquise, once she had become firmly ensconced as the king's mistress, took on regal airs. Copying her rival, the queen, she had all the chairs removed from her waiting rooms so that everyone had to stand in her presence. The prince heard of this, and one day went to visit her. Finding no place to sit, he plumped himself down on her bed with the remark that it looked as if it had a rather comfortable mattress. The marquise was outraged, and a feud began that was to lose the prince his job, and France one of its wisest counselors.

The squabble sputtered for a decade across the court at Versailles, reaching its most acid point when both Pompadour and the Prince de Conti heard in 1760 that the finest vineyard in Burgundy was up for sale. Both wanted it, and it became a matter of personal honor for each to win. Pompadour tried to bend the king's ear, but the prince, after all, was of royal blood and had been a hero and statesman of France besides. He got the vineyard for eighty thousand *livres* and one hundred *louis de chaine*. But with that his official days were numbered. He was removed from royal favor because of the influence of Pompadour and became the head of the elegant opposition to the crown's policies. He died in 1776, but not before his family had become the patrons of such fashionable critics of the regime as Jean Jacques Rousseau.

During the Revolution, the property was sequestered and sold as a *bien national*. It changed hands a few times in the nineteenth century, before being purchased in 1869 by Monsieur Duvault-Blochet, great-grandfather of the present half-owner, Monsieur de Villaine.

Recently, Monsieur de Villaine formed a partnership with Monsieur Henri Le Roy to acquire and develop other great Burgundian vineyards. It is called the Société Civile du Domaine de la Romanée-Conti, a rather unwieldy mouthful, and has come to control the greatest collection of vineyards in its section of the Côte de Nuits. Indeed, the vineyards are thought by many to be the finest agglomeration in all of Burgundy—sixty acres, all of which are *grands crus*. They include Romanée-Conti in its entirety, all of La Tâche, part of Richebourg, a part of Grands Échézeaux, and sections of Échézeaux and Montrachet. Since 1966 the Société Civile has also been the *régisseur* of half of Romanée Saint-Vivant.

The *chef de cave* of the Domaine in charge of tending the vines, overseeing the wine making, and then bringing the wine up is André Noblet, a soft-spoken giant of a man of quiet charm and ineffable modesty. He is a kind of viniferous genius, and there is a marked difference between sections of the vineyards not under his control in entirety and those beside them. The vines look different and the resultant wines are even more markedly so. A few years ago he received the coveted title of Chevalier du Mérite Agricole from the French Minister of Agriculture. Here is part of the citation that went along with it: "Rarely has the distinction been given to anyone more worthy of it than Mr. Noblet. He has raised the culture of the vine, the vinification of the wine, and the subsequent care of it to the level of a religious service. He works constantly among his vines, stays up for nights on end watching over the must as it turns into wine after the picking, and speaks of wine like a poet; all this with the least conceit in the world, like every true Burgundian *vigneron*."

Of course, Monsieur Noblet has some of the finest vineyards in the world to work with, and the results are sublime. The Romanée-Conti itself is quite beyond description. Magisterial, full, laden with bouquet, velvety—all words fail to come close to describing it. It is the Burgundy par excellence. The sad part is that its vineyard is only a little over four acres in size, producing no more than five hundred cases of wine per year. Its cost is, consequently, astronomical, if the wine can be found at all. Like all really great wines, it takes longer to bloom than its lesser neighbors.

Half a step from Romanée-Conti are La Tâche and Richebourg. La Tâche is thought by many with a not too profound knowledge of French to mean a "spot" or "stain." The late Christopher Morley punned on this idea in his book, *The Romany Stain*. He was in error. A *tache* is a spot; a *tâche,* with a circumflex accent, is a task. This idea of labor is a concept broadly used in Burgundy in naming vineyards. Les Quatre Journaux, that section of Romanée Saint-Vivant owned by Louis Latour, means "the four days' work." Bonnes Mares, as has been mentioned, probably means "the good labors." The old French word from which La Tâche derives, *la tasque,* is actually closer to modern English than it is to French. But another lugubrious word stems from the old French in both languages. In the days of feudalism, before a money economy existed, the lord of the manor would exact work from his serfs to pay for the upkeep of his ménage. This was formally known as *la tasque,* and the verb was *tasquer.* From these our word "tax" derives.

In spite of this unhappy connotation, La Tâche is a superb wine. Its vineyard is about fifteen acres, producing about 2,200 cases of wine a year—a mere drop in the winy ocean, but at least a bigger one than Romanée-Conti. And, there are two thousand cases of equally splendid Richebourg, so the questing oenophile will probably run across at least one sample of this sublime trinity.

Two other excellent *grands crus* are La Romanée, owned by the Abbé Liger-Belair, member of a well-known Burgundian wine family, and Romanée Saint-Vivant, which is split up among several proprietors. La Romanée is a scant two acres, but Romanée Saint-Vivant balances this with a lusty twenty-three.

The wines of Vosne-Romanée can boast about sixty-five acres of *grand cru* vineyards. When combined with the neighboring section of Flagey-Échézeaux, as they usually are, the *grands crus* come up to 166 acres of top-notch vineyards, the largest, as well as probably the best, ensemble of red wines in Burgundy. In the commune of Vosne-Romanée are the following *grands crus*: Romanée-Conti (four and a third acres), La Tâche (fifteen), Richebourg (twenty), Romanée Saint-Vivant (twenty-three) and La Romanée (two). All must reach eleven and a half percent natural alcohol, and no more than 264 gallons of wine may be produced per acre. In addition to these are several superb *premiers crus*—always prefaced with the town name. Particularly well known are Les Malconsorts, Les Beaux-Monts, Les Suchots, La Grande Rue, Les Gaudichots, and Les Chaumes, wines that in any other locale would be *grands crus* in their own right.

Incidentally, on Route Nationale 74 outside of Vosne-Romanée is a very pleasant little rustic restaurant, La Toute Petite Auberge. It can't be missed, as it is painted bright red. The interior is just as cheery as the exterior. The food is good and remarkably inexpensive. The wine list is, of course, excellent; here is one of the few places that a *vin de pays* is likely to be supernal.

Nuits-Saint-Georges is a rather pretty little town of four thousand people on the southern end of the Côte de Nuits. Prémeaux is a hamlet just south of it whose vineyards are legally considered part of Nuits. In spite of the fact that the town of Nuits has given its name to the entire Côte, there is not a single *grand cru* vineyard in it. The town is better known as a center of the wine trade because a number of distinguished shippers have headquarters there. Almost all the wine of the twin communes is red, though a tiny amount of white is produced. The best-known *premier cru* vineyards are Les Vaucrains (fifteen acres), Les Saint-Georges (nineteen), and Les Cailles (nine). All these must reach a natural alcoholic strength of eleven percent, and no more than 308 gallons of wine may be produced per acre.

Côte de Beaune

Northern Section

A little over five hundred years ago, François Villon wrote, "*Je demande du Vin de Beaulne,/Qui soit bon, et non aultrement.*" Villon was the foremost poet of his age, and he lived as lustily as he wrote. His love of beauty, especially in feminine or bottled form, got him into a host of scrapes. Jail was his constant abode, and the murderous *bagarres* he fought resulted in two appointments with the hangman's noose. Luckily for poetry, he was pardoned both times. Rascal or not, Villon certainly had good taste, for the wines of the Côte de Beaune are among the best of their type. The reds, though lacking the grandeur and fullness of those from the neighboring Côte de Nuits, have a delicacy that makes them a nice match for dishes of subtle flavor. The whites are by common consent the finest dry white wines in the world.

The Côte de Nuits ends at Corgoloin, just south of Nuits-Saint-Georges. The southern half of the Côte d'Or, the "Slope of Gold" on which the great majority of Burgundy's famous vineyards grow, is the Côte de Beaune. For a short distance beyond Corgoloin, the hillside is barren of vines, giving itself over to farms and stone quarries. But at Ladoix-Serrigny the vines begin again in rank upon rank of ordered greenery. With them, the roster of famous names recommences—Aloxe-Corton, Pommard, Volnay, Meursault, and Puligny-Montrachet—a fifteen-mile swath of villages and vineyards that produce dozens of charming wines and nearly a score of great ones.

The Côte de Beaune owes its name to the town, it embraces. Beaune was a thriving community in Roman times, when it was known as Belna. There are even some local boosters who maintain that Beaune sits on the site of the pre-Roman Gallic capital of Bibracte. This should be accepted with discreet skepticism, however, as a more plausible Bibracte has been unearthed elsewhere.

During the early Middle Ages, Beaune was an important city in Burgundy. It was a rich town, and a ring of battlements was built around it to protect it from marauding enemies. These buildings still stand. Their *donjons* and fortresses no longer resound to the clash of pike upon broadsword, however. They are now used as wine cellars for some of the city's distinguished shippers. At the center of the city is another interesting edifice, a rather pretty fifteenth-century town house of the Dukes of Burgundy. It now serves as the site of the Musée de Vin, the wine museum. In it are life-size models of medieval vineyard workers using the tools of their times, a collection of winepresses and *cuves* spanning the centuries, and several other exhibitions covering a broad gamut of viticultural geology, geography, history, and lore.

A short way from the Musée de Vin is one of the most astonishing buildings in France. Called the Hôtel Dieu, the House of God, or Hospices de Beaune, it is a huge and extraordinary charity hospital over five hundred years old. It is Burgundo-Flemish architecture at its most extravagant—ornate fretwork, gabled courtyard, and a dazzling polychrome tile roof that makes anything this side of the psychedelic look square. Surprisingly, though both the exterior and interior seem straight out of the Middle Ages, the hospital still serves its original function. Tucked out of sight are X-ray machines, operating rooms, and other appurtenances of twentieth-century medicine.

Also in the Hôtel Dieu is an art collection of considerable renown. The pièce de résistance is a polyptych of the Last Judgment by the fifteenth-century master Rogier van der Weyden. He,

---

RESTAURANT-HOTELS
Beaune (Côte-d'Or)

*Hôtel de la Poste   p. 20, p. 104
*Hôtel du Marché   p. 21, p. 104

N

1

2 3

LADOIX

8

4 5

7

ALOXE-
CORTON

SAVIGNY

8

9

10
11

12

13

14

17 16 15

18

19

20

21

N.74

BEAUNE

N.73

23

24

22

POMMARD

25

27 26

28

29

VOLNAY

30
31
32

33

34

35

DAY 6
Itinerary p. 20

Côte de Beaune,
Northern Section
Major Vineyards

Michelin Regional Map 69
Michelin Guide Vert *Bourgogne*

like his confreres the Brueghels and Hieronymus Bosch, had a
particularly well-developed sense of the hideous. At the age of six,
when I was first taken to see the polyptych's vivid portrayal of
hell, my mother managed to terrify me into two weeks of good

GRANDS CRUS—RED

1 Corton Renardes
2 Corton Clos du Roi
3 Corton Bressandes
4 Corton: Grancey, Perrières, Les Maréchaudes, Chaumes,
   Languettes, La Vigne-au-Saint, Les Meix, Pougets, Grèves,
   Paulands

GRAND CRU—WHITE

6 Corton-Charlemagne

PREMIER CRU—CORTON

5 Les Chaillots

PREMIERS CRUS—PERNAND

7 Vergelesses
   Ile-de-Vergelesses

SOME PREMIERS CRUS—BEAUNE

8–9 Les Marconnets
10   En l'Orme
11   Les Perrières
12   Fèves
13   Bressandes
14   Grèves
15   Les Theurons
16   Les Cras
17   Les Coucherais
18   Champs-Pimont
19   Aigrots
20   Vignes Franches
21   Clos des Mouches

SOME PREMIERS CRUS—POMMARD

22 Petits Épenots
23 Charmots
24 Les Épenots
25 Rugiens
26 Frémiers
27 Jarollières

SOME PREMIERS CRUS—VOLNAY

28 Fremiets
29 Les Angles
30 Les Mitans
31 En l'Ormeau
32 Carelle
33 Champans
34 Caillerets

35 Les Santenots
    (in Meursault)

behavior by telling me that was where little boys went who acted as I did. Nothing has been as successful since.

The Hôtel Dieu was constructed in 1443 as a refuge for the poor by the Chancellor of Burgundy, Nicolas Rolin. During his time in power he was known as one of the most assiduous and efficient tax collectors that Burgundy had ever had. This led Louis XI—no friend of Rolin's—to remark that it was only right for him to have constructed a house for the poor, as he had made so many of them. The hospital is still functioning, in part because it has its niche in the wine world. Over the centuries, various Burgundian landowners have bequeathed vineyards to the Hospices to pay for its upkeep. These now total over a hundred acres of vines. Every autumn the wines from these vineyards are sold at a colorful wine auction. Though the wines are not necessarily the best in Burgundy, the sale is followed avidly by the wine trade, as the prices the wines command set a rule-of-thumb standard for the value of that year's vintage.

Beaune has yet more to offer than wine and history. It is also a star of considerable magnitude in the gastronomic firmament. One of its two outstanding restaurants is the Hôtel de la Poste. It is run and owned by a charming young couple, Monsieur and Madame Marc Chevillot, who are well known from their visits to this side of the Atlantic. Consequently their restaurant serves as a home away from home for many Americans exploring Burgundy. Its specialties are the classic Burgundian dishes as well as *écrevisses à la crème Victor Chevillot*. Another splendid dish is *sole à la bourguignonne*, a sole poached in a court bouillon of onions, carrots, parsley, garlic, shallot, bay leaf, thyme, and red Burgundy. It is sublime. The wine list of the Poste is, of course, magnificent.

Another excellent and very pretty hotel-restaurant is the Restaurant du Marché. Though smaller than the Poste, it also has a menu guaranteed to delight the visiting gastronome. The *quenelles de brochet en brioche* are especially memorable, as is the *jambon à la crème*. The wine list will bring a glimmer of thirst to the most sated of oenophiles, and, as at the Poste, there are rooms to be had. Monsieur Croix is the host.

The vineyards of the Côte de Beaune are divided into three regions, two of equal size, one smaller. Each produces wines with a character particular to itself. The northernmost and smallest of this trinity is a peninsula of vines facing southward on the prow of a hill pointing toward Beaune. It is famous for its magnificent red, Corton, and equally renowned for its superb white, Corton-Charlemagne. The center region encompasses Beaune itself, as well as Pommard and Volnay. Though some white wines are produced here, the region is primarily known for its soft and elegant reds. The most southerly of the three areas starts at Meursault and runs down through Puligny-Montrachet and Chassagne-Montrachet. This area produces a few good reds but it is best known for its peerless whites.

Peninsula of Corton is an arbitrary term used, so far as I know, by me alone. However, I think it is descriptive. The mountain of Corton sticks like a foreland into a sea of vines of the Côte de Beaune. Visually and geographically there is a clear difference between the two. The taste of their wines reflects it. This should not be surprising, for though the Côte de Beaune by ordinary definition starts a little north of the abutment of Corton, this prow is in reality the southernmost face of the chain of hills that makes up the Côte de Nuits. The wines mirror their geographical position. A red Corton is heavier and fuller than other reds of the Côte de Beaune. It resembles in fact what it is, an unrecognized brother of the great wines of the Côte de Nuits.

The top of the Corton promontory is fringed with a line of trees. Around the edges of the hill are three communes: to the east, Ladoix-Serrigny; to the west, Pernand-Vergelesses; and to the south the most famous of all, the little village of Aloxe-Corton, nestled halfway up the hillside.

The tiny town of Ladoix-Serrigny is not on the hill's flank, but down below on Route Nationale 74. Its vineyards, though, make up a good-sized chunk of those on the Mont de Corton, clambering as they do up its eastern side. However, one does not frequently run across the name of Ladoix, as its best vineyards are legally included among those of Aloxe-Corton and its lesser ones are often used in making up the wines called Côte de Beaune-Villages.

The village of Pernand-Vergelesses also shares some of the Corton and Corton-Charlemagne vineyards with Aloxe-Corton, but these great wines come out under their own proud appellations alone, without the town's name as a prefix. Pernand, however, is not quite as anonymous as Ladoix. In it is a very good *premier cru,* the Ile-des-Vergelesses, which has helped to spread the name of Pernand well beyond the confines of the Côte de Beaune. The great bulk of the wine is red, and it resembles on a somewhat diminished scale its better known neighbor, Corton. It is likely to be a good value.

X in French is occasionally pronounced double s; an example is Aloxe, pronounced Ah-loss. However one says it, Aloxe-Corton is one of the famous villages of Burgundy. In it are the vineyards that make up the heart of two of the most famous names in wine's *Almanach de Gotha*—Corton and Corton-Charlemagne. As if this weren't enough, Aloxe is blessed with a host of subsidiary vineyards of far above average quality.

The name of the Emperor Charlemagne is featured prominently in two of Corton's outstanding vineyards. This is not the work of some bygone huckster trying to make his vineyards known by appropriating a famous name. A good deal of the slope was indeed owned by the great king, who gave the vineyards to the Abbey of Saulieu in 775. This would seem like a rather silly thing for such a wine-loving monarch to do, unless one knew the customs of the times. Monks made a habit of giving the finest specimens of their work to the great in church and state. And since no one knew more about nor took more pains in making fine wines than the monastic orders, there can be little doubt that Charlemagne's magnificent gift was recompensed by the monks with the best wine they could produce. In effect, the emperor had provided himself, and probably his heirs, with a winy annuity of the most splendid sort. It was not stupidity that had made Charlemagne ruler of three-quarters of Europe.

Another well-known admirer of Corton was François Marie Arouet, better known to the world by his nom de plume, Voltaire. Because of his contentiousness and acid-tipped pen, he found it prudent to set up house in the town of Ferney on the Swiss border. Here he was within a stone's throw of several frontiers in case he had to scamper from some outraged arm of the law. Voltaire loved to entertain, and his salon outside of Geneva became known as a gathering point for the literate and the witty. Being a man of the world, he looked after his guests properly, but he took special care when it came to his house's most honored resident—himself. In a letter to the owner of Château Corton-Grancey he wrote, "While I give my friends a good little wine of Beaujolais, in secret I pour for myself your wine of Corton"—a trick many a wine lover has been tempted to emulate.

Voltaire had taste. Corton is certainly a magnificent red wine, the only wine on the Côte de Beaune that is judged in the same class as the Chambertins and Romanées of the Côte de Nuits. Like all great wine it needs time for its majesty to unfold—six or seven years at least—and it will go on for quite a while from there. It is, unlike the wines of Beaune, Pommard, and Volnay, full, pungent, and heavy with the flavor of the grape.

The legal Appellation Contrôlée of Corton is one of the most complicated in Burgundy. Wines with the word Corton in their names do not necessarily come from the vineyard of Corton alone. In fact, only part of this vineyard measures up to the standard set for the wine called Corton and only this part is allowed to call itself Corton *tout court*. The wine Corton is essentially the *crème de la crème* of a number of great vineyards around the prow of the Corton peninsula. Thus the wine comes out under a number of names. There is a Corton-Clos du Roi, for example, which comes from a vineyard once belonging to the king. Sometimes the grower doesn't bother identifying the rows of vines from which his Corton came; he just calls the wine Corton and leaves it at that. The esteemed grower Louis Latour doesn't even go this far—he bottles much of his Corton under the name of his estate, Château Corton-Grancey, and underneath, in small letters, puts Appellation Corton Contrôlée. This last phrase is the key. All legitimate Cortons will have it somewhere on the label. It is the legal guarantee, and if one sees it one may smack one's lips in pleasurable anticipation.

As famous as the red Corton is its sister, the white Corton-Charlemagne, which is considered, along with the *grands crus* around Montrachet and Meursault-Perrières, the finest dry white in Burgundy, and hence anywhere. It is magnificent and full, and has a trace of steeliness that differentiates it from its more luscious rivals to the south. It also needs time to mature. Five years will certainly do it no harm.

Corton-Charlemagne is as complicated an appellation as Corton. It, too, is the *crème de la crème* of several vineyards on the Corton promontory. In fact, many vineyards produce both wines, the difference of course being that the Corton section is covered with the Pinot Noir while the Corton-Charlemagne vines are planted in more Pinot Chardonnay. In general, most Corton-Charlemagne is made from vineyards on the westward-facing slope of the hill, whereas the red comes from those on the southeastward-facing side. This possibly may be explained by the fact that a red wine needs quite a lot of sun to bring it out, whereas a white should not have too much or it will be low in acidity.

Aloxe-Corton is also blessed with a number of other very good vineyards producing much red wine and a little white. They are Les Fournières, Les Vercots, Les Guérets, and part of Les Chaillots, Les Valozières, Les Meix, Les Maréchaudes, and La Pauland. In the commune of Ladoix-Serrigny, but allowed to be called Aloxe-Corton Premier Cru, are La Maréchaude, La Toppe-au-Vert, La Coutière, Les Grandes-Lolières, Les Petites-Lolières, and Les Basses-Mourottes.

The center of the Côte de Beaune extends from Beaune down through Pommard and Volnay, then up a little on the hillside, to Auxey-Duresses on the road to Paris. The great preponderance of wine produced is red, well over ninety percent, but there is a little very good white, too. In general the reds of this section of the Côte are softer and lighter than those of Corton or the Côte de Nuits, and they take less time to mature. They thus serve as ideal companions for such delicately flavored meats as roast chicken, turkey, and lamb.

A little stream called the Rhoin separates the mountain of Corton from the rest of the Côte de Beaune. On it is the village of Savigny-Lès-Beaune, about three miles northwest of Beaune. Though the commune has no *grand cru* vineyards, it does produce a number of *premiers crus*, five of which are a prolongation of the Corton slope—Les Vergelesses, La Bataillière, Les Lavières, Aux Gravains, and part of Les Fourneaux—and three on the south side of the stream that are extensions of the hillside behind Beaune—Les Marconnets, La Dominode, and Les Jarrons. The area of the vineyards is 945 acres, of which ninety-six percent produce a soft, early maturing, fruity red wine that is archetypal of a pleasant Côte de Beaune. Though the town produces no great wines, it does have some very good ones, and because the commune is relatively unknown they are likely to be good values.

Chorey-Lès-Beaune is a small village due north of Beaune and east of Savigny that produces red and white wines under its own name. They are pleasant, but not outstanding.

Beaune itself, a city of about sixteen thousand, serves as the headquarters of many of the Côte d'Or's most famous shippers. If any town could claim to be the capital of the Burgundian wine land, Beaune would be it. Apart from its commercial importance, Beaune contains a number of excellent vineyards, nearly all of which—ninety-seven percent—produce red wines. Its best vineyards include Bressandes, Les Fèves, Les Marconnets, Les Grèves, and Theurons. These are followed closely by Clos des Mouches, Champs-Pimont, En l'Orme, En Genêt, Les Perrières, A l'Écu, Les Cent Vignes, Les Toussaints, Sur les Grèves, Aux Cras, Le Clos-de-la-Mousse, Les Chouacheux, Les Boucherottes, Les Vignes-Franches, Les Aigrots, Pertuisots, Tielandry, Les Sizies, Les Avaux, Les Réversées, Le Bas-des-Theurons, Les Seurey, La Mignotte, and parts of Clos du Roi, Les Coucherais, Montée Rouge, Les Montremenots, Les Blanches-Fleurs, and Les Épenottes. Clos des Mouches, which is on the southern border of Beaune touching Pommard, produces, in addition to its red, a white that is esteemed as being probably the best of this section of the Côte.

Pommard is certainly one of the most famous names on the Côte de Beaune. Pommard's reputation is said to stem from its once having been a Protestant center. When Louis XIV revoked the Edict of Nantes, forcing the Huguenots to flee France, they carried the name of their beloved Pommard with them. The wine of Pommard is now not only one of the best known, but also one of the most widely drunk of all red Burgundies. Although Pommard produces a great deal of wine, more than any other commune on the Côte d'Or, a good deal more of what is imaginatively labeled Pommard is consumed throughout the world than the town could hope to produce. Most of the Pommards consumed in America are bottled in Burgundy under Appellation Contrôlée supervision, so this is likely to be less of a problem than in Great Britain where wine is often imported in bulk and bottled in the basement of whoever brought it in. Of course English wine merchants of hallowed repute do bottle legitimate Pommards, but there are, alas, others who know that no English law stops them from putting whatever label they want on the bottle. As Pommard is one of the most widely known Burgundies, the "Pommard" label is one of their favorites. Further, as in any commune or region that produces a large quantity of wine, the quality will vary radically. A Pommard that is not followed by the name of the vineyard can be a good wine if the reputation of the importer is known to be good, but otherwise beware. Pommard does contain a number of first-class vineyards that are some of the best on the Côte de Beaune, producing wines that are soft, elegant, and well-balanced. The finest of these are Les Épenots and Les Rugiens. Following them are Clos de la Commaraine, Clos Blanc, Les Arvelets, Charmots, Les Argillières, Les Pézerolles, Les Boucherottes, Les Sausilles, Les Croix-Noires, Les Chaponières, Les Fremiers, Les Bertins, Les Garellières, Les Poutures, Le Clos-Micot, La Refene, Clos de Verger, Derrière-Saint-Jean, and parts of Les Petits-Épenots, La Platière, Les Chanlins Bas, Les Combes-Dessus, and La Chanière.

After Corton, Volnay has the greatest reputation for red wines on the Côte de Beaune. It also produces a few very good whites. However, by mutual agreement with the neighboring town of Meursault, the white wine of Volnay is classified under Meursault and the red wine of Meursault is classified as a Volnay. An example is the very good vineyard of Santenots. Though actually in Meursault, it produces red wine, and so is called Volnay Santenots.

The wines of Volnay are elegant, delicate, subtle, *racé*, filled with bouquet, soft, and with a sort of velour that sets them above any other reds of the center part of the Côte. The finest ones are Les Caillerets, Les Caillerets-Dessus, Champans, Chevret—followed by Fremiets, Bousse d'Or, La Barre, Les Angles, En l'Ormeau, Taille-Pieds, Verseuil, Carelle-sous-la-Chapelle, En Ronceret, Clos des Ducs, Les Pitures-Dessus, Les Santenots (actually in Meursault), Les Petures (in Meursault), and parts of Clos des Chênes, Carelles-Dessous, Robardelle, Les Lurets, Les Aussy, Les Brouillards, Chanlin, and Villages-de-Volnay.

The next town along Route Nationale 73 south of Volnay is

Monthélie, a hamlet that produces a number of very good wines. Because until recently Monthélie was sold as a Pommard or Volnay, it is not particularly well known. This is good luck for the oenophile, for the fine wines of Monthélie owe apologies to no one, and they will usually be very good values. The best ones are Sur la Velle, Les Vignes Rondes, Le Meix Bataille, Les Riottes, La Taupine, Le Clos Gauthey, Le Château Gaillard, Les Champs Fulliots, and part of Les Duresses.

Route Nationale 73 follows a small indentation in the hills as it cuts off the main chain of the Côte d'Or. Then it begins to wind as it climbs the Côte's escarpment, looking down as it does so on the magnificent medieval château of La Rochepot. (In the village of La Rochepot is a very pleasant rustic restaurant, Le Relais du Château.) One of the last towns in this dent is Auxey-Duresses, which produces a number of rather good red wines. In this day of vaulting prices the better wines of Auxey are very good value indeed. The wine snob, the millionaire, and the person of limited memory follow the great names, which are splendid but astronomically expensive. Those few vineyards that pleased our grandfathers in the days before the population explosion and the spread of wealth are now pressured as never before with buyers, and their prices naturally have gone up. Not so the lesser names of the Côte de Beaune, and because of the increase in wine technology in the past fifty years these often produce wines that are the peers of the good growths made famous in times gone by. Because their reputation is less historic, they are likely to be a good deal cheaper. Auxey, Pernand, Savigny, and Monthélie all produce wines that fit into this category. The best wines of Auxey are Les Duresses, Le Bas-des-Duresses, La Chapelle, Les Grands-Champs, part of Clos du Val, Les Écusseaux, and Les Bretterins.

Behind Auxey, on the other side of Route Nationale 73, is the hamlet of Saint-Romain. A village comparatively unknown outside of Burgundy, it produces good wine that usually is not seen under its own name as it is used in the blending of Côte de Beaune-Villages. (A wine labeled Côte de Beaune-Villages is a red wine or a blend of red wines from any of the townships on the Côte de Beaune.) Since it is a regional wine, its quality depends entirely on the skill and honesty of the shipper; if he is trustworthy the wine is likely to be one of the best buys in Burgundy. During any vintage year, these townships will produce several good wines, so the astute, capable, and honest blender can make a very good wine out of them. All are made from the Pinot Noir grape, and their price will probably be a third of what you would pay for a bottle from any great single vineyard.

Côte de Beaune

Southern Section

The Côte de Beaune has a rustic and serene air. It seems a typical rural French scene—picturesque, perhaps even a trifle banal. But far from banal is the fact that each village hides a treasure, and, as with most treasures, it is buried beneath the ground. In unprepossessing cellars lie row upon row of oak casks filled with golden and ruby wines. Though there may be a question as to where the greatest red Burgundy comes from, there is none whatsoever about which region produces the finest white. It is the Côte de Beaune. Even more limiting than this, apart from the magisterial Corton-Charlemagne, all the greatest whites of central Burgundy come from a three-mile stretch of vineyards below the center section of the Côte, sometimes called the Côte de Meursault, which runs through the communes of Meursault, Puligny-Montrachet, and Chassagne-Montrachet. They are considered by most connoisseurs the *ne plus ultra* of the world's dry white wines. Several factors combine to produce them. One certainly is the soil. White-wine vines seem to thrive in earth that is high in limestone, or its near relation, chalk. Champagne, Chablis, even distant Jerez in Spain

RESTAURANT-HOTEL
   Chagny (Saône-et-Loire)   *Hôtel Lameloise   p. 21, p. 122

RESTAURANT
   La Rochepot (Côte-d'Or)   Le Relais du Château   p. 21

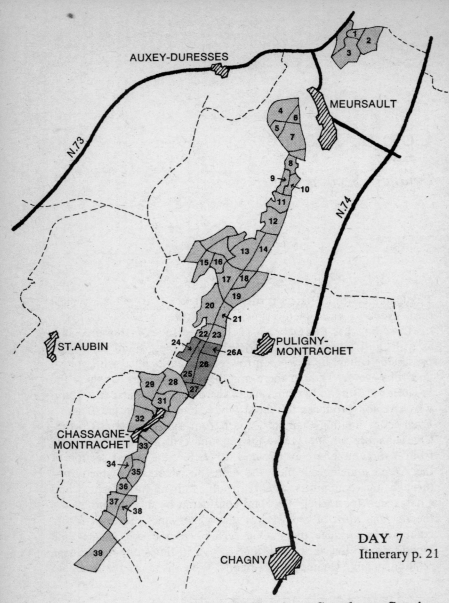

AUXEY-DURESSES

MEURSAULT

N.73

N.74

ST.AUBIN

PULIGNY-
MONTRACHET

CHASSAGNE-
MONTRACHET

CHAGNY

DAY 7
Itinerary p. 21

Côte de Beaune, Southern Section
Major Vineyards

Michelin Regional Map 69
Michelin Guide Vert *Bourgogne*

are famous for their chalky soil which seems to lend a fresh, clean taste to wine. Montrachet, the finest vineyard on the Côte de Meursault, is thirty-one percent limestone, a very high proportion.

Another factor is the grape type. All the finest white wine of Burgundy is made from either the Pinot Chardonnay or the Pinot

---

PREMIER DES GRANDS CRUS

25   Montrachet

GRANDS CRUS

24   Chevalier-Montrachet
26   Bâtard-Montrachet
26A Bienvenue-Bâtard-Montrachet
27   Criots-Bâtard-Montrachet

WELL-KNOWN PREMIERS CRUS—MEURSAULT

 8   Goutte d'Or
12   Genevrières
13   Perrières
14   Charmes

WELL-KNOWN PREMIERS CRUS—PULIGNY-MONTRACHET

15   Blagny
17   Champ Canet
18   Combettes
19   Referts
20   Folatières
21   Clavoillon
22   Cailleret
23   Pucelles

WELL-KNOWN PREMIERS CRUS—CHASSAGNE-MONTRACHET

33   Champs Gains
35   Boudriotte
38   Abbaye de Morgeot

Blanc—usually the first. These grapes, along with the Riesling, the Sémillon, and the Sauvignon, are the aristocrats of the world's white-wine grapes. The two Pinots produce what is generally considered the finest dry white wine extant, and they thrive best in Burgundy, their native environment. In northern Burgundy, where the rays of the pale sun are muted by the high latitude, the Pinots produce lean, somewhat astringent wines, the archetype of which is Chablis. Farther south, in the Côte de Meursault, the wines become fuller and have more body and flower. However, the sun is not so strong as to cut down the acidity necessary to hold the flesh of the wine. In more southerly climes than Burgundy, the Pinot, unless it is treated artificially, is likely to lack this acidity, and the resultant wines will be fat and flabby. The Côte de Meursault, however, is far enough north to provide the requisite acidity, yet far enough south to produce full flavor and body. The wines are thus ideally balanced.

Meursault, with seventeen hundred inhabitants, is the second largest town on the Côte de Beaune. Architecturally it is not especially noteworthy, though it does have a rather pretty fourteenth-century church, the spire of which is Meursault's most famous landmark. It is a normal Burgundian town—granite houses, leafy squares, and the smell of baking bread and wine drifting down on

---

OTHER MAJOR VINEYARDS

Meursault:

1	Santenots
2	Santenots
3	Pétures
4	Chevalières
5	Tesson
6	Charrons
7	Grands Charrons
9	Bouchères
10	Poruzots
11	Poruzots

Puligny-Montrachet:

16	Chalumeaux

Chassagne-Montrachet:

28	Chenevottes
29	Vergers
31	Macherelles
32	Clos-Saint-Jean
34	Caillerets
36	Petits Clos
37	Grand Clos
39	Gravières

the wind. Meursault's name, according to one legend, stems from an historical oddity. When Rome ruled Gaul, two kinds of roads were thrown across the countryside. One type consisted of the main roads, which were used by heavy traffic. These followed the easiest land contours, valleys where possible, and were traveled by chariots, carts, and the like. The other roads were little more than footpaths—narrow, straight lines that went directly over hill and dale from one point to another. These were military roads for the Roman infantry. In case of a rebellion in some corner of the land, the legions—leaving their heavy equipment, or "impedimenta" as it was called, to follow—took off, carrying no more than they needed to live on, and rushed by forced march to the point of disturbance. The rapidity of the Roman infantry was legendary, and because of it Gaul stayed safely Roman for over four hundred years. One of these roads in Burgundy crossed a brook flowing down from the Côte de Beaune. The ford across it was tiny, and the legions dubbed it rather derisively "the mouse's jump"—in Latin, *muris saltus*. A village sprang up near the ford, and time and the Gallic accent corrupted *muris saltus* to Meursault.

In 1162 the Cistercians arrived in Burgundy's vineyards and with them the standard of viticulture vaulted. Meursault's reputation spread and it has continued to do so ever since. Today the historical aspects of Meursault are usually ignored, the town's fame resting purely on its superb wines. Meursault produces not only excellent wine, but a great deal of it. It is the second largest wine-producing commune on the Côte de Beaune (after Pommard) with an average vintage of about 150,000 gallons. Ninety-seven percent of this is white wine. The small amount of red wine, by law, goes under the name of Volnay.

Meursault's two greatest wines—and they are splendid—come from the twin vineyards of Meursault-Perrières and Meursault-Charmes, both flat up against the border of the commune of Puligny-Montrachet. These two are closely followed by Meursault-Genevrières, then Meursault-Blagny, Goutte d'Or, Bouchères, Les Santenots Blancs, Les Caillerets, Les Petures, Les Cras, La Jennelotte, La Pièce-sous-le-Bois, and part of Le Porusot and Sous-le-dos-d'Ane.

High on the slope of the border between the towns of Meursault and Puligny-Montrachet lies Blagny, a hamlet surrounded by vines. It is famed for producing one of the best whites in the area. Not so well known is the fact that under its own name it produces a fine, subtle, delicate and elegant red which many find reminiscent of a good Volnay. Because it is small its reputation is known only to the cognoscenti, and because its fame is limited it is likely to be a very good value.

Within the confines of the pretty little townships of Puligny-Montrachet and its neighbor, Chassagne-Montrachet, lies the greatest galaxy of white-wine vineyards. Puligny and Chassagne not only have the ace of trumps in the form of Montrachet itself, but they have between them no fewer than five *grands crus* of white wines, more than all the rest of the Côte de Beaune. The vineyard of Montrachet is the *grand seigneur*. Like Château d'Yquem in Sauternes and Romanée-Conti on the Côte de Nuits, it is considered *hors de classification*—above and beyond classification. Alexandre Dumas stated that Montrachet should be imbibed only when one is bareheaded and kneeling. This is scant exaggeration. The wine is viscous, majestic, full, grand of taste, laden with nuance and bouquet. To drink it is an experience akin to first hearing the "Eroica."

Like too many Burgundian vineyards, Montrachet is lamentably small. There are eighteen and a half acres which produce an average of less than twelve hundred cases a year. Happily, Montrachet is flanked by four other superb vineyards only faintly beneath it in reputation. Bordering it to the west is the seventeen-acre Chevalier-Montrachet, and just to the east is Bâtard-Montrachet with its two adjacent subdivisions, Criots-Bâtard-Montrachet and Bienvenue-Bâtard-Montrachet.

The Chevalier vineyard produces another eleven hundred cases of wine, and the three Bâtards just under four thousand. Thus the total is something over six thousand cases in an average year, a mere drop in the winy deep, it is true, but enough to allow one to run across a bottle once in a while.

The name Montrachet is the cause of another etymological discussion. One school maintains that it comes from the medieval Burgundian pronunciation for a stripped or shaved hill—*mont rasé*. The English equivalent for this would be "Old Baldy" or "Baldtop." Almost as convincing is the notion that the name may come from the Latin—*mons racemus* or *mons recemorum. Racemus* in classic Latin meant a bunch of grapes, but it came to mean grapes in general, and later on even wine. Both the English and French languages have two words that stem from it, the same in both languages: raceme and raisin. In this case, the vineyard would have been called "Winevine Hill," or something of the sort. Either way—"Baldtop" or "Winevine Hill"—the name is descriptive, for Montrachet is on a hillock stripped of everything but its superb vines. And reflecting its derivation, Montrachet is still pronounced as though it were two words, with the middle "T" silent.

The root of the names of the neighboring vineyards is also lost in the mists of antiquity. However, there is a saucy tale told about them that inevitably gains in color and detail as the evening's glasses are emptied. It seems that once there was a noble *sieur* who owned the hillock of Montrachet and the best vineyards around it. He had a number of children, and as a generous parent, decided to give them the medieval equivalent of an outside income. He split his estates with them. For himself he kept the best, Montrachet. To his oldest son, who was a knight, or *chevalier,* he gave the next best, and this was named Chevalier-Montrachet. To his second son, the result of an illicit escapade, he bestowed the third vineyard, and this was descriptively dubbed Bâtard-Montrachet. His unmarried daughters got the fourth—Les Pucelles—the virgins.

Curiously, the character of the wines seems to mirror their names. Montrachet is the most impressive. It is full and regal. Chevalier is its obvious heir; it has the same fineness and nobility of taste but is somewhat lighter, more delicate, perhaps subtler. Bâtard has a marked resemblance to its father and half-brother. However, its hybrid vigor shows. It is a bit lustier, more apparent. Les Pucelles is a lovely, delicate wine, more retiring and timid.

The vineyards of Montrachet and Bâtard-Montrachet are divided between Puligny and Chassagne. All of Chevalier-Montrachet and Bienvenue-Bâtard-Montrachet are in Puligny alone. Slightly lower in quality are the wines of Le Cailleret and Les Combettes. Though these are classified as *premiers crus,* in any other village they probably would be *grands crus.* Other excellent *premiers crus* are Les Pucelles, Clavoillons, Champ-Canet, Les

Chalumeaux, Les Referts, Sous-le-Puits, La Garenne, Hameau de Blagny, and part of Les Folatières. Although ninety percent of Puligny's wine is white, it does produce a little red, the best of which is bottled under the name of Blagny, the hamlet mentioned before, which has vines in both Meursault and Puligny.

The town of Chassagne-Montrachet owes much of its reputation to its partial ownership of Montrachet and Bâtard-Montrachet and its possession of the entire Criots-Bâtard-Montrachet. One might therefore imagine that Chassagne is primarily a white-wine producing commune but this is not so. Of the fifty thousand cases of wine Chassagne produces during an average year, over thirty thousand are red. Much of this, though not the peer of the magnificent whites, is good, sound wine if properly matured, and an excellent value.

Most of the best vineyards in Chassagne produce both red and white wine, the reds, of course, made from the Pinot Noir, and the whites primarily from the Pinot Chardonnay.

The best red wines come from Clos Saint Jean, Morgeot, L'Abbaye de Morgeot, and La Boudriotte, followed by La Maltroie, Les Chenevottes, Les Champs-Gain, Grandes Ruchottes, La Romanée, Les Brussonnes, Les Vergers, Les Macherelles, and Le Cailleret. As these wines are *premiers crus*, their names must be preceded by the town name—Chassagne-Montrachet. The *premiers crus* whites of Chassagne are Morgeot, L'Abbaye de Morgeot, La Boudriotte, La Maltroie, Clos Saint Jean, Les Chenevottes, Les Champs-Gain, Grandes Ruchottes, La Romanée, Les Brussonnes, Les Vergers, Les Macherelles, and En Caillerets.

Up on the hillside above Chassagne lies the little village of Saint Aubin. Within its boundaries is the hamlet of Gamay, after which the Gamay grape is probably named. Although Saint Aubin has a number of vineyards that are *premiers crus,* these are rarely seen on the world's markets, so there is little point in listing them. They may be identified by the usual Burgundian practice of putting the town name, Saint Aubin, first, and following it by the vineyard name. Any Burgundian wine so labeled must be a *premier cru.* Much of the red wine of Saint Aubin is also used in the making of Côte de Beaune-Villages. Total production averages about twelve thousand cases a year, and of this two-thirds is red, one-third white.

Santenay is the last town of any importance on the southern end of the Côte de Beaune. It produces a minuscule amount of good white wine, but is primarily known for its reds. The whole town yields about fifty thousand cases of wine during an average year. The reds have the tendency at first to be a little hard and tannic, but with age they take on a pleasant delicacy and bouquet that make them good companions for such subtly flavored meat as lamb. The most famous *premiers crus* are Les Gravières, Clos Tavannes, and La Comme, followed by Beauregard, Le Passe-Temps, Beaurepaire, and La Maladière.

The three southernmost communes on the Côte—Cheilly-les-Maranges, Dezize-les-Maranges, and Sampigny-les-Maranges—share the not too distinguished vineyard of Les Maranges, hence their hyphenation. The three towns together produce about fifteen thousand cases of red and white wine during an average year. Little of it is exported, so the chances of running across it in the United States are slim. If one does, and if the wine comes from a reputable grower, shipper, or importer and is of a good year, it will probably be a good value. Much of the red wine is used in Côte de Beaune-Villages.

With these three little towns, the Côte de Beaune ends, but two more appellations remain to be explained. They are Côte de Beaune and Côte de Beaune-Villages.

A wine labeled simply "Côte de Beaune" has the higher appellation of the two. It must come from within the town limits of Beaune, plus a little over twenty-two adjacent acres that are considered worthy of the name. Côte de Beaune may also be used as a suffix after the names of Dezize, Cheilly, Sampigny, Chassagne, Puligny, Meursault, Auxey, and Chorey. This is a higher appellation than just the name of the village alone. All these wines are likely to be good, sound bottles.

The Côte de Beaune-Villages mentioned previously is a red wine made from any two or more wines from a township or townships of the Côte de Beaune other than Beaune. Provided the vintner is honorable and knows what he is doing, these can be very good bottles of wine at a modest price. In this day, when the prices of wines from small Burgundian vineyards have joined the astronauts in their race to the stars, it is a pleasure to run across sound wines of good value. A good Côte de Beaune or

Côte de Beaune-Villages is about the best bargain in terms of quality for price on the market today.

For the touring trencherman who wants to partake of both Burgundy's glorious liquid provender and its cuisine, the southern end of the Côte de Beaune has a splendid retreat. About two miles south of Puligny-Montrachet is the largish town of Chagny. It is just off Route Nationale 6, the Paris-Lyon road. In it is the Hôtel Lameloise, an old Burgundian town house that has been charmingly converted into a most agreeable restaurant by its owners, Monsieur and Madame Lameloise. The menu matches the ambience, with specialties of *terrine Lameloise aux foies de volailles, truite à l'Aligoté beurre échalote*, and *coquelet en pâte sauce Janick*. The wine list offers an excellent cross section of Burgundy's finest vintages with special emphasis on the southern end of the Côte de Beaune, the Côte de Meursault, and the Côte Chalonnaise.

Chalonnais & Maconnais

DAY 8
Itinerary p. 22

Michelin Regional Maps 69 & 73
Michelin Guide Vert *Bourgogne*

See Burgundy wine map p. 54

The Burgundy lover, confronted with the astronomical prices of the splendid but tiny vineyards of the Côte d'Or, is in a dilemma. As he flatters his palate, his wallet shrinks. Yet what can he do? To a true Burgundophile no other vintage will slake his thirst. He must either give up wine or resign himself to a denuded billfold.

His quandary isn't as hopeless as he may think, for just south of the Côte d'Or are Chalonnais and Maconnais, two regions that produce extremely agreeable wines. Though they may not match the grandeur of the top wines of this Côte, several are on a par with its very good ones. And because the fame of the two regions is not so widely touted, their wines don't plunder the privy purse.

The Côte Chalonnaise is a long, low line of hills that extends southward from the Côte de Beaune for about twenty miles. The break between the two Côtes comes at Chagny, eight miles north of Chalon-sur-Saône, after which this Côte is named. Chalon is an industrial town of about forty-five thousand on the banks of the quietly flowing Saône. One is likely to miss it entirely, as a bypass on Route Nationale 6 makes a broad sweep around it, as does the Autoroute. However, the gastronome and the archeologically inclined may well find a visit interesting. Chalon contains a pleasant hotel with a fine restaurant, the Hôtel Royal. Specialties include *truite en papillote* and *grenouilles sautées bressane,* just the things to go with a good white Rully from the hills behind the town.

A couple of hundred yards from the hotel is the Musée Denon, which is filled with a host of ancient artifacts including many items from pre-Roman Gaul. Those who assume that Rome and its legions civilized Gaul will be surprised to see that design and metallurgy were quite advanced in the centuries before Caesar. The museum also houses a room dedicated to one of Chalon's most famous sons—a man with the curious name of Nicéphore Niepce. In the very beginning of the nineteenth century he started to experiment in darkened rooms, examining the effects of light on such odd substances as bitumen and egg whites. After about fifteen years of puttering he came forth with a set of theories and inventions that were to be the basis of photography. It thus seems fitting that Chalon should be the site of one of the largest Kodak plants in Europe.

But the oenophile is interested in the Chalonnais because of

RESTAURANT-HOTELS

Chalon (Saône-et-Loire)
    *Hôtel Royal (8, rue Port-Villiers; tel. 48.15.86)   p. 124

Cluny (Saône-et-Loire)
    *Hôtel Moderne-Chanuet   p. 22, p. 130
    Hôtel de Bourgogne   p. 22

Tournus (Saône-et-Loire)
    *Le Greuze (4, rue Albert-Thibaudet; tel. 1.66)   p. 128
    Le Sauvage (pl. Champ-de-Mars; tel. 28)   p. 129

RESTAURANTS

Thoissey (Ain)
    **Hôtel Chapon Fin   p. 22, p. 132

Fleurville (Saône-et-Loire)
    *Restaurant Chanel (tel. 3)   p. 129

Macon (Saône-et-Loire)
    *Auberge Bressane (14, rue 28-Juin-1944; tel. 7.12)   p. 132

its wines, not its history. And for good reason. The wines of the Chalonnais are not only a geographic extension of the wines of the Côte d'Or, but the grape types used are the same too. The classified red wines are made from the Pinot Noir and the whites from the Pinot Blanc and Pinot Chardonnay. The soil, argill-calciferous for the Pinot Noir and calciferous for the Pinot Blanc and Chardonnay, is ideal for these varietals. Farther south, in Maconnais and Beaujolais, the red wines are made from the Gamay, a grape that thrives best in granitic rather than calciferous soil.

The northernmost town of winey importance is Rully, a village two miles south of Chagny and four from the great Montrachet. Although the town does produce (unfortunately) some sparkling Burgundy, it is known primarily for its excellent whites, which have, quite naturally, a marked resemblance to the wines from the nearby vineyards on the Côte de Beaune. They are dry and fresh, typical in fact of good white Burgundies. Of a total average production of ten thousand cases a year, over seventy-five percent of Rully's wines are white. Its first-growth whites must reach a minimum natural alcoholic level of eleven and a half percent; its first-growth reds, eleven percent. Town wines must reach eleven percent for the whites and ten and a half for the reds. Only 356 gallons may be produced per acre. The *premiers crus* of Rully are Margotey, Grésigny, Vauvry, Mont-Palais, La Bressande, Champ-Cloux, La Renarde, Pillot, Cloux, Raclot, Raboursey, Marissou, La Fosse, Chapitre, Préau, and Moulesne.

Two miles southwest of Rully lies the town of Mercurey, so named because in Roman times a temple to Mercury—god of commerce, conductor of souls to the nether regions, messenger from Olympus, and protector of travelers—crowned a hill above it. Nowadays, however, the town seems to have switched its allegiance to Bacchus, as it is surrounded by a green sea of vines. Wines bearing the Mercurey classification may come from the best vineyards of three communes—Bourgneuf-Val-d'Or, Saint-Martin-sous-Montaigu, and Mercurey itself. Ninety-five percent of the wine produced is red, and it has the reputation of being the finest of the Côte Chalonnaise, equal to the good town wines of the Côte de Beaune. It is, however, a little lighter in taste and color, though the latter is largely a result of vinification. Its subtlety of flavor makes it a splendid companion for more delicately flavored dishes such as lamb and roast fowl.

The Mercurey region produces not only the finest, but the largest amount of quality red wines of the Chalonnais. About ninety thousand cases are produced a year, ninety-five percent of which is red. Minimum alcoholic strength for first-growth whites is eleven and a half percent, and eleven for first-growth reds; for others, eleven for whites and ten and a half for reds. Each acre is permitted to produce a maximum of 308 gallons of wine. First growths are Clos-du-Roi, Clos-Voyen or Les Voyens, Clos-Marcilly, Clos-des-Fourneaux, and Clos-des-Montaigus.

Givry is the only town in the Chalonnais producing a red wine that comes close to vying with those of Mercurey. It lies about three miles south of Mercurey on the road that goes down to the massive remains of the medieval monastery of Cluny. Though there are no classified first growths in Givry, the red wines strike a high level of quality. About twelve thousand cases of wine, nearly all of it red, are produced a year—small by Mercurey's standard. To carry the Givry appellation, the red wines must reach ten and a half percent natural alcohol and the whites, eleven. A Givry is likely to be even lighter in flavor than a Mercurey, making it a good warm-weather wine. Maximum production permitted is 356 gallons per acre. Givry, incidentally, has a large eighteenth-century *arc-de-triomphe* structure near its entrance. As the town has a population of only about two thousand, the edifice seems rather charmingly pretentious. It serves as the symbol of the commune and houses the town hall.

The fourth and last area of any significance on the Côte Chalonnaise is Montagny, about six miles south of Givry. The wines of Montagny are all white. They are pleasant and fresh, and about twenty thousand cases are produced a year. Maximum production permitted is 356 gallons per acre. The *premiers crus* must reach eleven and a half percent natural alcohol, and town wines must reach eleven.

In sum, the wines of the Côte Chalonnaise are similar to, though somewhat lighter than, those of the Côte de Beaune. Consequently both reds and whites are good warm-weather Burgundies. Being made from the noble Pinot grape they both have a certain elegance that makes them good companions for subtly flavored dishes. As the area is not widely known outside of France, the wines are a good value. However, as in all wines of somewhat regional character, there will be variances resulting from the technique and honor of the vintner.

The Maconnais region takes its name from Macon, a rather pretty city of some thirty thousand on the banks of the river Saône in southern Burgundy. The boundaries of the Maconnais are essentially etched in by two rivers—the Saône, which makes up the eastern frontier, and the Grosne, which meanders around the other three sides. Grosne, incidentally, is pronounced *groan,* quite unsuitable considering the beauty of the paysage it wanders through. This countryside is one of rolling hills, small streams, fields, hamlets, forests, and vineyards. It is good hunting country, and in the fall, after the vintage is made, the *vignerons* go out with shotguns and their trusty Brittany Spaniels to collect a little of nature's delicious provender to serve along with their wine.

Game is not the only form of meat that the Maconnais provides. The intense verdure is spangled with herds of passive Charolais cattle, bulky white forms dotted about the greenery as in nineteenth-century paintings. Short of leg and full of body, they look from a distance like huge, ivory-colored pigs. They seem to do nothing all day but munch the grass with benign expressions on their faces. The Charolais cattle may be considered natives of the region, as the town of Charolles lies just a few miles to the west. It was here, about a hundred years ago, that local breeders crossed Alpine cattle from the Jura with Durham bulls from England and came up with the Charolais, a breed whose fame is now sweeping the earth. The reasons for this notoriety are deserved and several. First, the Charolais have been remarkably hardy, adapting themselves with ease to nearly every environment where they have been placed. Second, they seem to have powerful genes, as whenever they are crossed with other cattle the offspring have many of the Charolais' characteristics. They thus make excellent herd improvers in poor countries where cattle have become stumpy and degenerate. But it is in terms of meat that the Charolais are most extraordinary. Their meat-per-pound-of-animal ratio is phenomenally high, making them much sought after by beef raisers. Moreover, the meat they produce is extremely lean, with almost no fat in, or even around, the tissue. It is therefore much desired by waistline watchers in this cholesterol-conscious age. Even better, the meat is very good, and the chefs of the region take justifiable pride in using Charolais steaks as the basis for some of the best local dishes.

Beginning in the northern part of the Maconnais, the first town of any consequence is Tournus, known to the ancient Romans as Trenorchium. Here, in 179 A.D., the martyrdom of Saint Valerian took place. For this reason Tournus became a church center of considerable importance in the early Middle Ages. The town itself is a pretty place with a kind of soothing charm that seems to emanate from old stones. Admirers of medieval architecture will find it a treasure trove. It is the site of one of the earliest Burgundian-Romanesque churches, Saint-Philibert, whose construction began in the ninth century. I must admit that my own admiration for the Burgundian-Romanesque is not boundless; I prefer the audacity of the Gothic or the more massive tranquillity of the pure Roman. However, Tournus does not disappoint even in this respect. Little architectural curios from nearly every period are scattered throughout the town, which also contains two museums —one dedicated to local Burgundian customs and costumes, the other to the eighteenth-century painter Jean Baptiste Greuze.

But architecture and history must batten on some more solid substance, and Tournus provides this, too. Right off the main street and a pebble's throw from the Eglise de Saint-Philibert is the Greuze, a delightful little restaurant run by Monsieur Ducloux. It has excellent food and charming décor. Specialties include *feuilleté de brochet à la Greuze,* a pastry shell filled with pike; *omelette aux queues d'écrevisses,* an omelet filled with crayfish tails; and *côte de boeuf à la moëlle,* a Charolais steak with a marrow dressing. If one is in luck one may run across *la pochouse,* a specialty of all the towns bordering on the river Saône. It is a sort of freshwater bouillabaisse made with white wine, perch, pike, freshwater eels, carp, and sundry other denizens of the Saône. It is perfection itself when washed down with a good white Viré or a Pouilly-Fuissé. The Greuze has a few rooms, or if it is filled up, another comfortable hotel with a good restaurant, Le Sauvage, is a short stroll away.

The vineyard country begins inland from Tournus and runs southward toward Macon. Both reds and whites are produced here, the whites made from the Pinot Chardonnay, and grown in calciferous soil, the bulk of the reds made from the Gamay Noir *à jus blanc* and grown in granitic soil. The whites of Macon have a greater reputation than the reds, the most famous of them, Pouilly-Fuissé, being known wherever wine lovers gather. However, the reds should not be ignored. They may not be grand wines in the style of the noble seigneurs of the Côte d'Or, but they can be very agreeable and easy to take. They are similar in many respects to the wines of Beaujolais, which is not surprising as they are made from the same grape on a similar kind of soil. They lack perhaps a little of the fruitiness of a typical Beaujolais, but nevertheless the best Macon Supérieur rouge is equal to a good Beaujolais, and a good Macon Supérieur rouge is on a par with a normal Beaujolais.

Beaujolais has lately enjoyed an enormous increase in popularity, and its price has consequently begun to rise. Moreover, some Beaujolais has begun to appear on the market that might more pleasantly have stayed at home. By contrast, the lesser-known Maconnais produces a host of good, inexpensive little table wines that would be good choices for the shrewd and thrifty oenophile. However, as with all regional wines, there is good, bad, and indifferent Macon, so choose the name of the shipper or importer carefully.

The vineyards running south from Tournus produce mainly red wines, though pockets of whites are scattered through the area. The best and most famous whites are found around the town of Viré, halfway between Tournus and Macon. After Viré come the wines from three nearby communes—Chardonnay, Lugny, and Clessé. All, of course, are made from the noble Chardonnay grape, and they show it. They are dry, yet quite fruity, resembling in many ways their cousins of Pouilly-Fuissé to the south.

Close to Viré on Route Nationale 6 is the tiny town of Fleurville, population 340. In spite of its size, Fleurville is the site of a good little restaurant, the Chanel, whose specialties include *grenouilles sautées fines herbes* and *terrine de volaille truffée*. Both are excellently irrigated by a good white Viré. As the vineyards lie a scant two miles to the west, this is the place to try the wine.

About fifteen miles west of Viré is Cluny, famed as the greatest monastic center of the early Middle Ages. It was the mother abbey of the extraordinarily powerful order of the Benedictines, and for a while its abbot general was the *éminence grise* behind the papal throne. Reflecting this, the church of the abbey was for several centuries the largest in Christendom, bigger even than the one in Rome. By the eighteenth century, however, the order had lost much of its power. The French Revolution delivered it its *coup de grâce,* and the entire property was declared a *bien national* and sold to the highest bidders. These, alas, turned out to be only speculators who wanted to buy it for the stone it contained. The next twenty years witnessed one of the saddest and most deliberate acts of vandalism in the history of architecture. The magnificent church, which even after Saint Peter's had been built was still the second largest in Europe, was used as a quarry and torn down stone by stone. Finally, in 1823, this astonishing display of petit-bourgeois philistinism was stopped, and what was left stands today. Paltry compared to what it once was, it is still impressive and well worth a visit if one is in the neighborhood.

If hunger strikes, there is a good restaurant at the Hôtel Moderne near the station just outside of town. It is run by Monsieur Chanuet. The specialties include *quenelles de brochet polonaise*—that delicious concoction of pounded and sieved pike mixed with the lightest of doughs and cooked until it becomes the soft and fluffy essence of fish flavor—and *canard à l'orange*. Wines include Pouilly-Fuissé and Juliénas.

Between Cluny and the twin towns of Pouilly and Fuissé lie about fifteen miles of the most delightful pastoral countryside on earth. Midway is the little village of Milly-Lamartine, where Alphonse Prat de Lamartine lived from his childhood in the 1790s until 1860. Lamartine was a nobleman, officer of the Guard, democrat, deputy from Macon, and, finally, Minister of Foreign Affairs in the short-lived Republic of 1848. But France is a country that most honors literary achievement, so that, despite this rather impressive display of public activity, Lamartine is best known as a poet. His style was romantic in the Wordsworthian vein, and his descriptions of the land around Milly and Pouilly are touched with a kind of magic that only a generation of un-ashamed adorers of nature could create. His poetry, moreover, is extraordinarily evocative of the land, so I trust it is forgivable if I present a few of his lines, clumsily translated by me from his *"Milly ou La Terre Natale."*

> *Mountains veiled by autumnal mists,*
> *Valleys carpeted by morning frosts,*
> *Willows from which those who prune*
> *Have plucked their crowns of leaves:*
> *In the distance ancient towers,*
> *Gilded by light of evening—*
> *Walls blackened by years, hillsides and footpaths,*
> *A spring where shepherds stoop and in their turn,*
> *Savor sip by sip its pure and limpid waters. . . .*
> *These heaths, these fields, these vines and pastures,*
> *All raise memories, the dear ghosts of times gone by.*

Just below Milly is the region of Pouilly-Fuissé, one of the most famous white-wine areas of France. The grape is the Chardonnay, and the soil is calciferous. The wine may come from any one of five communes: Pouilly, Fuissé, Solutré, Chaintré, and Vergisson. The region is marked by a huge, prow-shaped cliff at Solutré. Below it are the remains of a Stone Age community that is one of the oldest in France. Directly beneath the prow is a huge equine ossuary—apparently the ancient inhabitants used it as a primitive but effective slaughterhouse. Wild horses were trapped and run off the edge of the cliff, into the waiting stewpots of Madame Caveman below. The French middle classes have always had a liking for *filet de cheval*. Apparently it was a taste they developed early.

Whether all these bones add a certain requisite calcium to the soil I do not know. However, the Chardonnay seems to thrive here, and the wine is delicious. It is firm, dry, fruity—typical of a good white Burgundy. It is not only good, it is copious—the region produces almost 200,000 cases in an average harvest. All wines to be classified Pouilly-Fuissé must reach a minimum alco-holic strength of eleven percent, and twelve for first growths. No more than 396 gallons may be produced per acre.

Immediately adjacent to the communes that make up Pouilly-Fuissé are the townships of Pouilly-Loché and Pouilly-Vinzelles. The laws governing the production of their wines are precisely those that govern the wines from Pouilly-Fuissé. They are thus very similar, though some oenophiles maintain that they are a little lighter, mature more rapidly, and die earlier. In any case, all the wines should be consumed when the freshness of youth is still on them. Though not as magnificent as the lordly whites of the Côte de Beaune, they are still splendid and one of the best buys in white Burgundy. The usual word of caution, however. Though the wines of Pouilly-Fuissé, Vinzelles, and Loché are quite tightly controlled, they still verge on being regional wines, so know the reputation of the shipper or importer.

The hungry gourmet touring Pouilly-Fuissé may turn toward Macon a short three miles away, or, if he can contain his appetite, go seven miles across the river Saône to Thoissey. In Macon are several comfortable hostelries and one rather good restaurant, the Auberge Bressane, run by Monsieur Duret. Specialties include *poularde Marguerite de Bourgogne* and *écrevisses.*

In Thoissey, which lies about ten miles south of Macon on the east bank of the river, is the Chapon Fin, a splendid and comfortable little hotel-restaurant run by Monsieur and Madame Paul Blanc, chef and chatelaine. Monsieur Blanc is not only an excellent chef but he looks it, as he has the rotund and ruddy form of one who obviously enjoys sampling his own work. The Blanc family is well known gastronomically in the region. Their main rival is the excellent Chez la Mère Blanc at Vonnas, twelve miles to the northeast. Family rivalries are not always very pleasant to behold, but in this case one doesn't behold them; one tastes them, and they are very agreeable indeed.

Specialties of the Chapon Fin include *poularde de Bresse aux morilles,* the incomparable chicken of the region served with a delicate mushroom sauce; and *crêpes Parmentier,* a deliciously light potato pancake. As the brother of Madame Blanc is a leading Charolais raiser, the beef is very good, too. The wine list has a broad coverage of all the best regional growths and a number of fine wines from the rest of France. However, a word of warning to the budget minded: the Chapon Fin is, as all things of known excellence, not especially cheap. Reservations had better be made ahead of time as the Chapon Fin is deservedly popular.

Beaujolais

The traveler touring France usually visits Paris, and then whisks south to Cannes, Antibes, or Saint-Tropez. Finally, sated with a life just as expensive and not much different from the one he left at home, he returns, having "done" the country. And he probably will have been disappointed. He may have wanted peace, good food, and rustic charm; instead he spent days in the clutter and diesel fumes of traffic, and then a hectic week on the Côte d'Azur. It is ironic that the things he sought in France are readily available.

Somehow, an unintentional secret seems to have been kept from most touring foreigners. Just a couple of kilometers off the great Routes Nationales an entirely different countryside begins—a land of pastoral simplicity crisscrossed by small but beautifully maintained secondary roads, a country of good, inexpensive little restaurants and, with a little luck, excellent regional wines.

Take Beaujolais for example. Between Macon and Lyon are the Paris-Marseilles Autoroute and Route Nationale 6, two of the main north-south traffic arteries of France, forty-five-mile-long lines marked by the roar of speeding vehicles and the haze of carbon monoxide. But just a mile to the west is a region few people see: a rolling landscape of vineyards, charming little villages, and numerous wine cellars open to the public where one may stop to sample the delicious local wines.

Beaujolais—even the name has a melodious ring. Its history begins over a thousand years ago, when it was established as a minor province to serve as a buffer between the warring states of Lyon and Macon. Beaujolais prospered mightily during the Middle Ages, an island of peace in a sea of endemic war. It was

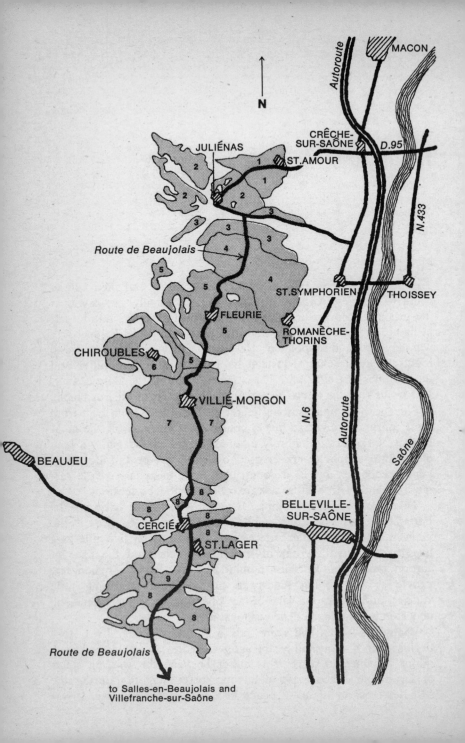

then that the *gens de Beaujolais* began to be noticed for their good-humored practicality, a trait vividly described by Gabriel Chevalier in his amusing books about Clochemerle.

This characteristic is well illustrated by a tale passed down from generation to generation. It concerns a fourteenth-century ruler of Beaujolais, a noble *sieur* who held court in Beaujeu, the ancient capital. One day his calm was shattered by the thunder of galloping hooves in his courtyard, followed moments later by a messenger sounding the alarm. It seemed that a band of mercenary soldiers had seized the town of Anse and were putting it to sack. The *sieur* was outraged. Calling for armor and horse, he set forth to the blast of trumpets and the roll of drums, summoning his peasantry to arms as he proceeded. The mercenaries, astonished at the rapidity of his approach, hastily barricaded themselves within the town's walls and prepared to defend their lives.

The *sieur* quickly surrounded Anse, and, swearing vengeance, prepared to destroy it and the looters within. But since he was from Beaujolais and inclined more to practicality than fanaticism, he had a second thought. If he destroyed his own town just to get the rabble out, he would have the double expense of razing it and rebuilding it. A parley was sounded. The *sieur* pointed out to the trapped mercenaries that to destroy them would inflict a double expense on his treasury. Consequently he had an estimate made of the cost of razing the fort. This sum would be given to the trapped plunderers provided they left both the town and Beau-

---

DAY 9
Itinerary p. 22

Route de Beaujolais

Michelin Regional Map 73
Michelin Guide Vert *Bourgogne*

CLASSIFIED GROWTHS

1	Saint-Amour
2	Juliénas
3	Chénas
4	Moulin-à-Vent
5	Fleurie
6	Chiroubles
7	Morgon
8	Brouilly
9	Côte-de-Brouilly

jolais, and never returned. As everyone stood to gain—the mercenaries their lives and a little money, the *sieur* the cost of reconstructing his demolished stronghold—the portcullis soon went up and everyone trotted happily on his way.

In most countries children are taught to admire the bloody deeds of their ancestors. In Beaujolais this tale is passed on as the triumph of good-natured common sense over vainglory.

My most protracted experience in Beaujolais took place some years ago. Arriving in the hamlet of Chervinges with wife and child, two Pekingeses, a small Hillman convertible, and an old London taxicab, I rented a splendidly broken-down old manor of the Charles Addams variety—high-ceilinged and dark, with a bathroom that, even by Beaujolais standards, was deemed primitive. The summer decided to add to the ambience by being little more than a succession of rainy days. Gloominess seemed triumphant, and the whole scene might have been too depressing had I not made a few discoveries.

Among them was my neighbor, Monsieur Regie Jousse, and his *copain,* a huge, mustachioed old man, *le père* Large. Monsieur Jousse had a *cave* directly adjacent to the manor. It contained, as I recall, thirty-two *fûts,* or good-sized barrels, of red wine.

Every morning at ten I heard a knock at the door, and there would be Regie Jousse and *le père* Large asking me to help them dispel a hideous doubt. They had the nasty feeling that some of the wine might have turned sour during the night. There was only one way to check and that was to try a glass from all thirty-two casks. Needless to say, by lunchtime I was awash with good spirits and Beaujolais. The summer, in spite of the rain, drifted by in a remarkably benign manner.

Beaujolais is the democracy par excellence of winedom, with most of the *vignerons* either owning or having an interest in the vineyards they work. The result is a kind of jovial independence and lusty good humor that by some miracle transfers itself to the wine. To taste it is to know something about the ease, the pleasantness, and the bonhomie of the country. The inhabitants of Beaujolais have charm and generosity, qualities reflected in their cuisine as well as their wine.

Gastronomically, Beaujolais is considered part of the *pays lyonnais,* thought by most epicures to be the greatest in France. Lyon itself is the Olympus of gastronomy, the city and its surrounding region spangled with two- and three-star restaurants. The area abounds with gustatory raw materials. A short distance to the northwest is Charolles, home of the white Charolais cattle. Just across the river Saône is the province of Bresse, renowned for its *poulardes de Bresse,* its eggs, cream, and butter, and also its excellent, somewhat Gorgonzola-like cow's-milk blue cheese, the *Bresse bleu.* Beaujolais produces good, tart, white cheeses made of goat's milk, called *chèvres* or *chevretons.* And as if this weren't enough to satisfy the turophile, the nearby Alps contribute their own supernal Reblochon, Tome, and Gruyère.

The Saône, which is the eastern boundary of Beaujolais, teems with freshwater fish including eels, crayfish, perch, and carp, all of which go into the delicious fish stew, the *pochouse.* The pike, or *brochet,* makes its gastronomic contribution in the form of the subtle *quenelle de brochet.* The uplands of Beaujolais are dotted with fat sheep, and every barnyard seems to have a pig or two, the basis for the splendid *charcuterie* of the region. Beaujolais is a trencherman's paradise.

Not surprisingly, the region has long been freckled with the *Guide Michelin*'s difficult-to-get restaurant stars, and now with the recommendations of the *Guide Kléber* as well. Near Beaujolais's northern boundary, at the town of Romanèche-Thorins, is the hotel-restaurant Maritonnes, where Monsieur Fauvin serves superb *quenelles de brochet* as well as *grenouilles sautées,* both admirable washed down with a white Macon or Pouilly-Fuissé.

Not far from Romanèche is the village of Chénas, one of the most famous vineyard centers of Beaujolais. At the Restaurant Robin, Monsieur Robin combines two local specialties—*poularde de Bresse* and Beaujolais—to produce a caponized hen in red wine, a dish splendidly accompanied by the agreeable wines from the neighboring vineyards. The restaurant itself is a pleasant little country inn looking out over the vineyards, a delightful stopover spot for a midday meal. It is a short way outside of Chénas on the scenic Route de Beaujolais, road number D 68.

A few miles to the south on the banks of the Saône is the pretty town of Belleville, where the simple but good hotel-restaurant Beaujolais offers *coq au vin* and *écrevisses à la crème,* crayfish served in a cream sauce, a delectable morsel perfectly accompanied by a dry white wine of Pouilly-Fuissé.

But by far the most famous local restaurant lies just south of Beaujolais in Collonges-au-Mont-d'Or, a village about five miles north of Lyon. It is called the Auberge Paul Bocuse, after its owner and creator, and it is one of the dozen restaurants in France to which the *Michelin* gives its supreme accolade of three stars. To understand what this means, one can do no better than quote the *Michelin* itself, a guide usually known for the brevity and restraint of its prose. Three stars means "one of the best tables in France: worth a special journey; memorable meals, the glory of French cooking, the best wines, faultless service." The Bocuse is all of these.

In this temple of gastronomy the menu will list such specialties as *terrine de grives aux baies de genièvre* (a terrine made of thrushes and juniper berries); *loup en croûte farci d'une mousse de homard sauce choron* (a famous Mediterranean fish, stuffed with lobster mousse, baked in cloudlike pastry, and served with a classic sauce); or *carré d'agneau à la broche aux herbes de Provence* (an aromatic shoulder of lamb cooked on a spit). The cellar contains a cross section of the finest French vintages, with special emphasis on the wines of Beaujolais. Tables, of course, should be reserved. The Auberge is closed for two weeks in mid-August.

However, Beaujolais is not known primarily for its restaurants, its amusing inhabitants, or even its charming countryside. It is known for its wines. As a province it is rather hard to define, for its geographical outline does not exactly coincide with its viticultural one. Geographically, Beaujolais is bound on the north by a brook with the rather ominous name of La Mauvaise. To the west and south its frontiers are a stream called the Azergues; and to the east lie the broad, somnolent waters of the Saône. Topographically, Beaujolais is the eastern slope of a thirty-three-hundred-foot-high massif, the Monts de Beaujolais, which falls off in a gentle curve to the basin of the Saône. Its climate is largely a result of these mountains, as they stop the winds from the northwest, guaranteeing Beaujolais a winter several degrees warmer than the lands on the opposite side.

The landscape, too, is dominated by the mountains. Although the best vineyards are on the rolling flats sloping off toward the Saône, the countryside immediately behind these vineyards is well worth seeing. There are charming little valleys with streams running through them like sinuous veins of silver, and winding roads that climb up through forests of oak and pine and then break out at unexpected moments into spectacular natural terraces. These look out over nearby villages, castles, and vineyards, the Saône in the middle ground, and the faraway escarpment of the Jura Mountains.

Beaujolais has a surprisingly high density of population for a rural area. It is not at all like most other agricultural regions of France where farmers, out of some atavistic fear of bygone wars and plunderings, still prefer the huddled safety of towns at night, and leave the countryside bare of farms. Here, barns and hamlets are sprinkled liberally throughout the landscape. The buildings are usually made of terra-cotta-colored stone which, when combined with the brownish-red tiles of the roofs, makes the scene seem almost Tuscan. Many of them are covered with vines, and around them drifts the delicious smell of wine.

The wine region permitted to be called Beaujolais actually starts a little to the north of the province's geographical limits. It begins just south of Pouilly-Fuissé, where the calciferous soil so beneficent to the Chardonnay grape shifts to granitic—Gamay country. The characteristics of a Beaujolais wine are smoothness and fruitiness. It is not a wine to reflect upon; it is a wine that refreshes. It is not a philosophical *grand seigneur;* it is a gay, charming companion. One sips a great Burgundy; one drinks a Beaujolais. One now encounters the pronounced difference in taste between a Beaujolais and a red wine from Burgundy proper —the Côte d'Or and Chalonnais—that is due mainly to the type of grape used in each. The Pinot Noir of the best northern Burgundies has been replaced by Beaujolais's Petit Gamay, or Gamay Noir *à jus blanc.* It is an excellent little wine. (Incidentally, in California the Gamay Noir *à jus blanc* is known as the Gamay Beaujolais, not the Gamay.) It makes wines that are full, fruity, and joyous, and in some instances have considerable finesse. Moreover, its gallon-per-acre ratio is far higher than that of the Pinot. Even better, from the *vigneron*'s point of view, is the fact that the wines are extraordinarily quick to mature—the lesser Beaujolais being ready to drink as carafe wines before the year is out. This, however, only applies to lesser wines that are not bottled. A good vintage Beaujolais in bottle needs about two years to bring out its best qualities.

The most renowned wines come from the northern half of the region. There are nine first-rank villages or vineyard areas allowed to call themselves by their place names alone—Saint-Amour, Juliénas, Chénas, Moulin-à-Vent, Fleurie, Chiroubles, Morgon, the Côte-de-Brouilly, and Brouilly. The car-borne oenophile can easily visit these, as they all lie on or just off the delightful Route de Beaujolais. At every famous wine center is a tasting shed where the visiting wine lover can sample the region's provender. It is all free, though contributions are certainly not shunned. There can be few more pleasant ways of spending a summer afternoon than drinking one's way through Beaujolais.

By taking Route Nationale N-6 south from Macon for about three miles, one comes to the village of Crêches. Turning right on D 31, one shortly runs into the Route de Beaujolais. From then on the road is well marked as it winds through hamlets and vineyards.

The first town is Saint-Amour, "holy love," and its name is descriptive of the wine. It is a gentle, soft, and caressing wine, probably the most famous example being the vineyard of Champs Grillés. The vineyards of the village produce close to 800,000 bottles of wine per year.

About a mile southwest of Saint-Amour is Juliénas, one of the most famous villages in Beaujolais. Some of the oldest and greatest admirers of Beaujolais are the Swiss, and Juliénas seems to be their favorite wine. It is more tannic than a Saint-Amour, richer in *sève,* and therefore usually needs a little more time to mature but then reaches a greater height. Juliénas has two pleasant little rustic restaurants, the Coq au Vin and Chez la Rose, both at the marketplace in the center of town. The best-known vineyards of Juliénas are Les Mouilles, Bucherat, Les Fouillouses, and Château des Capitans. The total production of the vineyards of Juliénas is about 1,800,000 bottles yearly.

A little over a mile south of Juliénas is Chénas, a pretty village just outside of which is the Restaurant Robin mentioned earlier. The wine of Chénas is one of the richest and fullest of Beaujolais, and about 600,000 bottles of it are produced per year. About three-quarters of the best vineyards of Chénas are not called Chénas; they are named Moulin-à-Vent, meaning windmill, and the region is so named because of an old windmill that crowns a hillock there. Half the vineyards that surround it lie in the village of Chénas, the other half in the town of Romanèche-Thorins. All are excellent. Moulin-à-Vent produces full, vigorous, and fairly heavy wines thought to be the finest of the region by many Beaujolais lovers. The best-known vineyards are Le Carquelin, La Rochelle, Les Caves, Les Verillats, Le Champ de Cour, Les Combes, and Rochegrès. The average production of Moulin-à-Vent is about 2,500,000 bottles a year.

Bordering Moulin-à-Vent to the southwest is the commune of Fleurie, and the vineyard that many believe to be the very best in Beaujolais. It is called the Clos de la Roillette, referred to locally as the "Clos de Vougeot" of Beaujolais. Other fine vineyards include Au Morier, Le Point du Jour, Au Garant, and Poncié—all close to the Moulin-à-Vent border—and La Chapelle du Bois, Champagne, and Roches farther off to the southwest. The wines of Fleurie are perhaps a little softer, lighter, and fruitier than those of Moulin-à-Vent. "The wines of Fleurie are flowery" is an easy and reasonably accurate jingle to help one remember. The total production of Fleurie's vineyards is in the neighborhood of 2,250,000 bottles a year.

Immediately southwest of Fleurie is the tiny town of Chiroubles, the most famous vineyard of which is probably Bel-Air, with a yearly production of just under a million bottles. Chiroubles is a quickly maturing, fresh, fruity wine that comes close to being typical of what one hopes a good Beaujolais will be.

Directly south of Chiroubles and Fleurie is Morgon, which produces wines that are some of the grandest and slowest to mature of all the Beaujolais. They are often compared with the wines of the Côte d'Or. Though there is a marked difference of flavor, the comparison is not entirely unjust, as a Morgon, which takes time to develop, has much of the style of its northern cousins. The area that surrounds the towns of Villié and Morgon is also one of the most generous of Beaujolais, producing close to 2,500,000 bottles in an average year.

Driving south from Morgon one soon runs into a fifteen-hundred-foot-high mountain with a chapel on the summit. In a circle around its base are five little towns: Saint-Lager, Charentay, Odenas, Quincié, and Cercié. The mountain, a landmark and navigational aid for those wandering through the tiny byways of Beaujolais, is splendidly conspicuous. It is the Mont de Brouilly.

The wines from around the mountain are divided into two groups—those from the slopes of the mountain itself, called Côte de Brouilly, and those from selected vineyards in the five towns at the base of the mountain. The latter wines are called simply Brouilly. The Côte de Brouilly is the bigger wine of the two, and by law it must attain one-half percent more natural alcohol than Brouilly, or indeed than any of the other seven top Beaujolais vineyard areas. The wines of the Côte de Brouilly are thus robust, full, and solid, ideal companions for game birds and beef. Those of Brouilly are lighter, fruitier, and subtler—excellent complements for lamb, roast chicken, turkey, or domestic duck. The average production of the Côte de Brouilly is about 750,000 bottles a year; of Brouilly about 3,600,000 bottles.

The classification of the wines of Beaujolais is similar in structure to that of the wines of the Côte d'Or. The major difference is that the Gamay Noir *à jus blanc* here produces considerably more juice than the Pinot Noir used on the Côte d'Or, and the amount of wine permitted to be made from each vineyard in Beaujolais is correspondingly higher. The classification of Beaujolais is as follows:

The highest category is that of the Crus de Beaujolais or name vineyards—the most famous having been cited above. These vineyards are not allowed to produce more than 352 gallons of wine per acre, and the wine must reach a natural alcoholic strength of eleven percent.

The Côte de Brouilly vineyards are permitted to make a maximum of 352 gallons of wine per acre, and the wine must reach a natural alcoholic strength of ten and a half percent.

Eight first-rank vineyard *areas* are also allowed to be called by their name alone, without having to preface it with the word Beaujolais. The names are those of the towns encountered above along the Route de Beaujolais (Saint-Amour, Juliénas, Chénas, Moulin-à-Vent, Fleurie, Chiroubles, Morgon, and Brouilly). These towns or regions may produce no more than 352 gallons of wine per acre, and this wine must reach ten percent natural alcohol. The total production of all eight towns is about fifteen million bottles per year.

The third category, Beaujolais, followed by the name of a town, or "Beaujolais-Villages" must come from the communes of Juliénas, Jullié, Émeringes, Chénas, Fleurie, Chiroubles, Lancié, Villié-Morgon, Lantignié, Beaujeu, Régnié, Durette, Cercié, Quincié, Saint-Lager, Odenas, Charentay, Saint-Étienne-la-Varenne, Vaux, Le Perréon, Saint-Étienne-des-Oullières, Blancé, Arbuissonass, Salles, Saint-Julien, Montmelas, Rivolet, and Denicé—all in the *département* of the Rhône, or from Beaujolais proper.

Also in this category are some vineyards in the *département* of Saône-et-Loire. They are classified as Beaujolais in spite of the fact that they fall just over the boundary of the Maconnais— Leynes, Saint-Amour-Bellevue, La Chapelle-de-Guinchay, Romanèche, Pruzilly, Chanes, Saint-Vérand, and Saint-Symphorien-d'Ancelles. These may produce no more than 396 gallons per acre, and the wine must reach ten percent natural alcohol. The average annual production is thirteen million bottles.

It will be noticed that a number of communes in the second category are duplicated in the third. The reason is that if a wine maker chooses to make more than 352 gallons per acre, he loses his right to the higher. However, if he chooses to make up to 396 gallons per acre he still may use the same name in the third category. Thus, an owner of a vineyard in Fleurie may call the wine Fleurie if he makes no more than 352 gallons per acre, and

Beaujolais-Fleurie or Beaujolais-Villages (the latter, however, being the name customarily used) if he makes up to 396 gallons per acre.

Beaujolais Supérieur may come from a broader region than Beaujolais-Villages, though the standard of production is the same: no more than 396 gallons of wine per acre, and a natural alcoholic strength of ten percent. The average production is about 3,300,000 bottles per year.

Beaujolais must come from vineyards in the province that produce no more than 440 gallons of wine per acre, and reach a natural alcoholic strength of nine percent. About thirty-three million bottles of Beaujolais are produced per year.

Generally speaking, all the best vineyards in Beaujolais are in the northern half of the province and the vineyards of Brouilly mark their southernmost limit. Beaujolais-Villages extends its borders for six or seven miles below Brouilly. South of that is the country where most of the ordinary Beaujolais comes from— good, quick-maturing, fruity little wines of the last two categories that are the delight of the bistros of Paris and Lyon. Their better exemplars are bottled and shipped all over the world and are beloved as among the easiest and most amiable red wines to drink under any condition. They go well with nearly any food that demands a red wine. They are thus like a perfect friend: easy to take in large quantities and always agreeable.

A small amount of not very distinguished white wine is produced in Beaujolais. The vast majority is red. The classifications above pertain to red wine only.

The Rhône

Northern & Central Sections

The Rhône starts as a trickle of melting ice high up near the six-thousand-foot Furka Pass in southeastern Switzerland. Hitting the valley floor, it gains momentum and turns into a tumultuous, iron-gray stream as it heads westward into Lake Geneva. The lake, volumetrically the largest in western Europe, is little more than the Rhône naturally dammed up in an Alpine pocket. At Geneva, the river finds its outlet. With the manner of an impetuous parvenu, it brusquely shoulders its way through the rather dowdy and genteel center of town, past the bonbon shops, banks, hotels, and *horlogeries*. Then it tumbles through a series of precipitously falling cataracts into France.

It is by now a swirling rush of water as it heads toward the staid old capital of French gastronomy, Lyon. There it runs into the Saône, changes direction by ninety degrees, and finally sets forth toward the distant warmth of the Mediterranean. In its 160-mile run toward the sea, the Rhône sweeps through the most ancient part of France. It was at its mouth, well over 2,500 years ago, that Greek traders and settlers established a colony, Massalia, or, as it is called today, Marseille.

The Hellenes were by nature high-spirited and argumentive, but one thing they all agreed upon, as the Dionysian revels and the *Symposium* illustrate, was the need for good wine, and lots of it. Without doubt they tried to import their favorites from Chios and Lesbos. But as those who have sailed the Gulf of

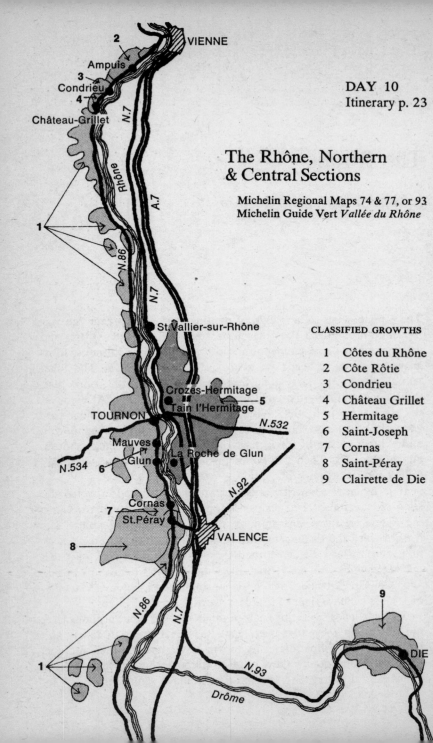

Lion know, the weather can be quite uneven. In the valley of the Rhône blows the mistral, a wind that comes cannonballing down the river, erupting onto the unsuspecting waters of the Mediterranean like a Miura skidding out into the sands of a bullring. Any boat unlucky enough to get in the mistral's path will have very rough going, if it survives at all. Consequently, the Greeks must have found their wine shipments arriving intermittently at best. And, shipped as wine was then in none-too-well sealed amphorae, then shaken thoroughly in the holds of the battered biremes, the flavor, nuance, and bouquet of what did arrive must have left something to be desired. It was a condition that had to be rectified.

The Greeks were nothing if not enterprising, and so sometime around the year 600 B.C. the first vines began to grow on the slopes of the hills above Massalia. Their initial produce was probably greeted with derision by the established oenophiles of the colony. But as in many other places, the laughter soon turned to smiles of contentment as the right grapes were found for the new soil. Dionysius may have been Greek, but his vines found French earth powerfully sympathetic.

The Rhône valley has always been the highway between the Mediterranean world and northern Europe. It is the only major

---

RESTAURANT-HOTELS

Condrieu (Rhône)   **Hôtel Beau Rivage   p. 23, p. 152
Les Roches-de-Condrieu   Bellevue (tel. 85.51.42; closed
    (Rhône)   1 week in early Aug.)   p. 153
Saint-Vallier-sur-Rhône   *Restaurant Célérier (114, av.
    (Drôme)   J.-Jaurès; tel. 3)

RESTAURANTS

Vienne (Isère)   ***La Pyramide   p. 23, p. 149
Saint-Romain-en-Gal   *Chez René (tel. 85.12.72; closed
    (Rhône)   mid-July to mid-Aug.)

HOTEL

Vienne   La Résidence de la Pyramide
                                       p. 23

break in the barrier of mountains that extends across the Balkans, northern Italy, and France. Greek traders, exchanging their ceramics and cloth for Celtic iron, amber, and furs, introduced the beer- and mead-swilling northerners to the glory of wine. Thus the Rhône, being partially Hellenized, became the first of France's vineyard areas. And, in fact, the Viognier, one of the great grapes still used in the Rhône valley, is probably a descendant of a Hellenic vine.

By the second century B.C., the Greek colony of Massalia was waxing sleek and fat, too much so for its own good. The Gauls eyed its rich markets, merchants' houses, and well-ordered countryside like a fox watching a plump goose. They began to attack, and the Greeks, a thousand miles away from their related city-states, called on the burgeoning power of Rome for assistance. Thus two generations before Caesar this part of France came under Roman rule. The Romans called it their "Provincia," from which the modern word Provence derives.

The Romans were great builders, and during their eight centuries' stay they crisscrossed the province with roads and aqueducts. Most of the great towns of the Rhône valley were built by them. Nîmes, Arles, Avignon, Orange, Valence, Vienne, Lyon—all have Roman foundations. Scattered over the countryside are walls, triumphal arches, and sections of aqueducts—ghostly reminders of the glory that once was Rome's.

After the Empire collapsed under the waves of Barbarian assault, Provence was one of the first islands to emerge from the swirling waters. For a thousand years it was to be the heart of one of the most brilliant cultures of Christendom. Its language was chosen as the perfect mode for poets and troubadours. Its code of chivalry was aped by ruder northern races. Its *chansons de geste* and *chansons d'amour* cast a romantic thrall on nations that had hitherto only thought of mayhem and loot. And though Provence was dismembered and absorbed by its more powerful neighbor centuries ago, a vestige of the language still exists in southern France and in northeastern Spain in the form of Catalan. Even today, Provence may be described as a country within a country. In character, outlook, architecture, gastronomy, even in the quality of its light, it differs markedly from the rest of France. The ghost of the banished civilization lives on where once it throve, in the form of a contagious vitality, a harmonious sense of beauty and human values, and a certain *douceur de vie*. Small wonder that so many painters have chosen it as their ideal habitat.

More interesting to the oenophile and gourmet is that the valley is one of the gastronomic centers of France. Belley, the town where Brillat-Savarin was born, lies between Lyon and Geneva. Lyon itself is considered *the* culinary center of France. The *Michelin* has scattered over twenty stars on its restaurants, more than any other city in France except Paris, which is of course eight times Lyon's size.

Lyon is a prosperous, bourgeois city, not the most swinging sort of place perhaps, but one that likes its comforts. A meal of fewer than five courses is considered a snack, and the helpings are hearty. The cooking is sublime, as are the raw materials. Crayfish, pike, carp, and trout abound in the nearby rivers. What is perhaps the most delicious, the *omble chevalier* or char, is dragged up from the deep waters of the lakes near Annecy. Just to the north lies the Charolais with its peerless beef, Bresse with its *poulardes,* the Saône with its frogs. To the west is the Auvergne with its splendid sheep. As for cheeses, what turophile can refrain from smacking his lips in contemplating such provender? Tome de Savoie, Reblochon, Gruyère, Bleu de Bresse, Chevrotin, Bleu d'Auvergne, and on and on—a parade of cheeses whose renown stretches far beyond their locales.

The most Olympian eatery in the Rhône valley is in the old Roman city of Vienne, twenty miles south of Lyon. It is called La Pyramide. Here, between the two world wars, the late Fernand Point established himself as one of the legendary masters of French cuisine. Choosing what at first seemed an out-of-the-way spot to make his gastronomic paradise, he soon gathered all the elite of an era when only the rich and fashionable had cars with which to stop off for a meal on their way between Paris and the Côte d'Azur. Even delegations going to and from Geneva. the seat of the League of Nations, would make a long detour to calm their nerves and appetites at his temple of gastronomy. I am told by Marc Chevillot, owner of the Hôtel de la Poste at Beaune, who as a young boy was apprenticed to Monsieur Point, that once when the President of the Republic, Albert Lebrun, and the Foreign Minister, Aristide Briand, telephoned from Geneva that they would like to stop off for lunch, Monsieur Point did not bat an eyelash. When the government cortege arrived with its usual bustle of bodyguards, chauffeurs, and secretaries, they seemed to expect Monsieur Point to go down to the gate and welcome the President there. Not at all. Monsieur Point took up his station at the top of the steps at the entrance to the Pyramide. After all, it was not he who had telephoned the President of the Republic to come admire his work. For a moment it looked as though there would be a sticky problem of protocol. But Monsieur Lebrun and Monsieur Briand, being French and cognizant of the gastronomic glory Monsieur Point's genius had bestowed upon their country, stepped up and presented their homages with pleasure, introducing themselves as sovereigns of one realm honored to meet a sovereign of another. Anyone, after all, might become President of the Republic. There was only one Fernand Point.

I remember Monsieur Point rather well. He was a large, roundish man, as befits a culinary genius who enjoys his own art. In fact *embonpoint* seems to describe him so perfectly that one must wonder if the word didn't derive from his name. My first meeting with him was in 1948, when, as a stripling, I was taken on one of my family's annual wine tours. We were accompanied by Geoffrey Parsons, Sr., then editor of the late *Herald Tribune*. We were joined at Vienne by Geoffrey, Jr., then editor of the Paris edition of the *Tribune,* and his wife, Drue, to celebrate old Geoffrey's wedding anniversary. Monsieur Point had been advised a few days earlier of the event, and so had prepared a little something special. When we arrived, Monsieur Point invited my father down into his cellar to help pick the wines—a signal honor —and then began the most superb meal I have ever eaten. We sat down at one and rose at seven. To describe the meal would take a small volume, but perhaps some indication of it may be garnered from the bottles that were opened: Château Grillet '45; Meursault-Perrières, estate-bottled M. Ropiteau, '37; Mouton-Rothschild '29 in magnums; Côte Rôtie "Brune et Blonde," estate-bottled Chapoutier, '29; Richebourg, *vieux cépages,* estate-bottled, Domaine de la Romanée-Conti, '34; Château d'Yquem, '29; Champagne Perrier-Jouet, Brut, '28; and Grande Fine Champagne Cognac *nature.*

This was truly gastronomy at its most heroic, and I am ashamed to say that my eighteen-year-old constitution, accustomed to normal American fare, broke down completely under the barrage of priceless wines and viands. I enjoyed every moment of the feast, and spent the next week in purgatory whimpering for soda mints and Perrier.

Monsieur Point died in the late fifties, sending a shudder of sorrow throughout the gastronomic world. There was suddenly an impossible void that ached to be filled. Luckily, the doughty Madame Point, her chef, sommelier, and waiters understood and rose to the occasion. The restaurant was kept open. The meals were presented exactly as when the *maître* supervised in the kitchen. The peerlessly high standard of the cellar was maintained. Of late, however, the restaurant seems to have begun to wind down. After so many years, even a monument to the greatest of men begins to take on the musty feeling of a museum. Though the Pyramide to this day is still rated as one of France's finest restaurants, this is, I'm afraid, more a question of nostalgia than of reality.

Across the river from La Pyramide, a few kilometers downstream, is the village of Ampuis. Clambering above it on little hillside terraces reminiscent of the Moselle lies one of the most famous red-wine vineyards in France, the Côte Rôtie. The Côte Rôtie means literally the "roasted slope," and so indeed it is. The steep hillside faces southeast, absorbing the full power of the sun. The Côte Rôtie is divided into two sections, La Brune and La Blonde, thus named perhaps because the soil of one is lighter than that of the other. However, there is a romantic legend giving another explanation. Once upon a time the vineyard was owned by a noble named Maugiron, who had two daughters—one dark, full bosomed, and fiery; the other delicate, restrained, and blond. When he died his estate was divided between them, and curiously enough each wine took on the characteristics of its respective mistress.

The wines of each section lack a little something on their own, but when they are blended together each balances the other beautifully. The result is a velvety, full wine that is at the same time delicate and subtle. The bouquet is strong and distinctive, with a flavor many find reminiscent of raspberries, truffles, or violets. What this comes from is a matter of some conjecture. There are two grape types that go into the making of a Côte Rôtie. One is the Syrah, or, as it is sometimes called, the Sérine, a vine allegedly brought back from the Middle East during the Crusades by a knight named Gaspard de Sterimberg. This is one of the red-wine grapes par excellence of the Rhône valley, being also the basic grape of the splendid red Hermitages. However, all by itself it does produce a rather heavy, thick, slow-to-mature must, and so the vintners of the Côte Rôtie are permitted by law to add anywhere up to twenty percent of a white wine grape, the Viognier. The amount of this admixture is one of the determining factors in the fullness of a Côte Rôtie.

In general the wines of the Côte Rôtie are palatable after four years, and are remarkably long-lived thereafter. A good wine kept in a quiet place can still be perfect after fifty years. Many consider these among the finest red wines of France, and they are certainly among the greatest of the Rhône. They are sumptuous, voluptuous wines, with an almost Byzantine luxury to their bouquet. They go well with all red meat and game. Quantity is severely limited, the total production being only about twelve thousand cases per year.

A little farther south, at the base of the same chain of hills, is the village of Condrieu. In it, with a terrace looking right out on the river, is a charming hotel-restaurant, the Hôtel Beau Rivage. There, one may have a splendid *mousse de brochet aux queues d'écrevisses,* with the lovely white wine of the village, following it with a *volaille de Bresse au poivre vert,* and a fine Côte Rôtie. Host and hostess, Monsieur and Madame Castaing, earned for their restaurant the crown of *grande cuisine* from *Kléber* and two stars from *Michelin.*

The slopes of the hillside behind Condrieu are garlanded with vines. Actually, the vineyards extend into two neighboring communes, Vérin and Saint-Michel. Nevertheless, all the white wine produced is entitled to the appellation of Condrieu. Made from the Viognier grape, it is something of a chameleon of wines, its character changing quite radically from year to year. Usually, however, it is a full-bodied, medium-dry wine of considerable bouquet, and the slight *goût de terroir,* or taste of the earth, common to many whites of the Rhône valley. At best, it is an excellent wine, one that serves admirably as companion to the Rhône's freshwater fish. Production is tiny, however, well under a thousand cases per year, and, as most of it is consumed on the spot, chances of running across it are slim.

Just downriver is a vineyard that has the odd honor of having the smallest Appellation Contrôlée in France. Its production is minuscule, about a hundred and fifty cases a year. It is called Château Grillet and is owned by the Gachet family. The white wine, like that of nearby Condrieu, is made from the Viognier grape, and is high in alcohol, full in body and bouquet, and dry in flavor. Because of the extreme shortage of this wine, it too is difficult to find outside of the immediate environs, but it is greatly appreciated by local oenophiles.

With that our tour of the upper end of the Rhône valley ends. But before moving on, mention should be made of an excellent and inexpensive little restaurant at Les Roches-de-Condrieu, one mile from Condrieu and eight downriver from Vienne. It is called by the rather prosaic name of Bellevue, and though its décor is not perhaps the most enchanting in the world, the rooms are immaculate and inexpensive and the food is delicious. The wine list is excellent, with fine examples of the locale's best. It is, after what you may have been through at Vienne and Condrieu, a good spot to sample the local cuisine and wines without feeling that somehow an army of gypsies has gotten loose in your bank vault.

The gallant *fin bec* Henri IV remarked, "*Bonne cuisine et bon vin, c'est le paradis sur terre.*" If this is true, then the valley of the Rhône must be the closest thing to heaven on earth. At its head lies Lyon, undisputed monarch of the *cuisine au beurre,* and at its base Provence, with a cookery tradition that goes back 2,500 years to its first Greek and Phoenician settlers. There the olive is the tree of life, providing food, shade, wood, and oil. Thus within a 150-mile stretch of river lie the archetypes of the north European and the Mediterranean cuisines.

But food was only half of Henri's formula for the terrestrial paradise. The other half—wine—the Rhône also produces in plenty. Without any doubt the top vineyards of the Rhône are among the finest in France. Better than that, a good Rhône carrying the name of a reputable grower or importer is about the best value in the wine world today. Snobbism has sent the prices of the first Bordeaux and Burgundy vineyards spiraling upward, pushed partially by neophyte wine enthusiasts impressed, or eager to impress, with the well-publicized names of these excellent vineyards.

In the nineteenth century, before tastes were as conditioned by mass communications, the Rhône was recognized as one of the three great areas of French wine making. The best of Hermitage was put right alongside the cream of Bordeaux and Burgundy in a gentleman's cellar. This was as it ought to be. But the Rhône has been slow in flaunting its charms to the world of twentieth-century communications. There are so far no "Compagnons de la Côte Rôtie" or "Chevaliers d'Hermitage," to be regaled with good food, drink, and song in some well-staged medieval château. Thus the press knows very little about them. The result of this rather shortsighted public relations policy may be bad for the Rhône growers, but it is excellent for the true oenophile. These splendid vintages of the Rhône remain at half the cost of vintages of similar quality from their sister regions.

The vineyards of Hermitage cover the southern flank of a huge moundlike mountain on the east bank of the Rhône, about fifty

---

RESTAURANT-HOTEL
Valence (Drôme)

**Hôtel-Restaurant Pic   p. 23, p. 158

RESTAURANTS
Tain-l'Hermitage (Drôme)

Restaurant Chabert (49, av. J.-Jaurès; tel. 10.34—closed June)   p. 157

Cabaret du Vivarais (23, av. F.-Roosevelt; tel. 11.21) p. 158

miles south of Lyon. The steep hillside is terraced like some giant's staircase, the retaining walls serving as billboards for some of Hermitage's more famous growers: Chapoutier, Jaboulet, and Jaboulet-Vercherre. Below, pinioned between the hill and the river, lies the tiny town of Tain. Opposite, across the river, is its twin, Tournon.

How Hermitage, or Ermitage, as it is sometimes spelled, got its name is a rather amusing legend. In olden days, when Provence was the center of Christendom and its every valley echoed with the romantic entreaties of knightly troubadours, when jousts were fought at the drop of a handkerchief and no lady's desire went unrequited, one noble gentleman stood out as being dissatisfied. Gaspard de Sterimberg, courtier of Queen Blanche of Castille, was bored. For Gaspard had done everything. He had crusaded; he had jousted in tournament and fought in war; he had sung all the *chansons* he wanted to sing; he had conquered too many times in love. And then, as ennui overwhelmed him, he decided, like so many of his spiritual confreres centuries later, to give the whole thing up, to quit the rat race.

Accordingly, one day in 1225 he mounted his charger and set forth up the valley of the Rhône in search of some lonely hill, one near enough civilization so that he could watch it pass by, one far enough away so that it would not bother him. In his saddlebags he allegedly carried a few cuttings of the Syrah vine acquired on a Crusade to the Holy Land. Up the banks of the turbulent Rhône he rode, searching the hills on both sides for some likely spot to retreat. Finally, above the village of Tain he saw his hill—one thousand feet high, austere, rocky, and removed. He tethered his horse and began to construct a hut on the foundations of a tiny, ruined Roman temple. This he dubbed his "hermitage."

But Gaspard's tale did not end with this dive into seclusion. He was an energetic soul, and immediately on building his shelter he made clearings on the hillside. There he planted his Syrah vines. These prospered mightily, producing ultimately such full-bodied *bouqueté* red wine that Gaspard has earned his niche in history as one of winedom's great benefactors. In this skeptical age, much of this tale has come under cold scrutiny. However, Napoleon defined history as "a fable commonly agreed upon." As

Gaspard has become a firm part of the Rhône's folklore, he must, in the Napoleonic sense at least, be accepted as a historical figure. True or not, today's Hermitage vineyards follow the slope where Gaspard's hut once was. A small chapel now marks the spot.

Describing the wines of Hermitage, the late George Saintsbury, the distinguished English wine lover and critic, wrote that they were "the manliest of wines," and they are just that. Both the red, to which he referred, and the white are full-bodied, vigorous, and flavorful. The red makes a splendid companion for all forms of beef and game; the white elegantly squires veal, pork, ham, creamed fowl, and seafood.

The red Hermitage is still primarily made from the same Syrah grape that Gaspard supposedly brought from the Holy Land. However, the Syrah, though splendid, can produce in the stony soil of the Hermitage mountain a wine that is a little coarse. Consequently the Hermitage vintner is allowed by law to add anywhere up to fifteen percent of the juice of the Marsanne and Roussanne, both white grapes, to lend the wine a certain elegance and finesse. The result is magnificent.

A good red Hermitage needs at least five years before the first bottle is uncorked, but its staying power is phenomenal. It is not at all odd to find a Hermitage that is still in fine shape at fifty. When young it is ruby red in color, but as it ages it turns a more russet hue, until finally in old age it is the color of a clear garnet.

A good white Hermitage, made from the Marsanne and Roussanne grapes, is full, dry, fruity when young, elegant as it ages, big in body and bouquet. It is one of the few white wines that can stand up at a tasting to the great white Burgundies, and it is half their price.

Not far from the Hermitage mountain are two other Appellations Contrôlées that produce wines of a similar type. The first is just to the north of Hermitage on the same bank of the river. It is called Crozes-Hermitage, and produces reds and whites made in exactly the same manner and from precisely the same grapes as Hermitage itself. Not surprisingly, the result is very like Hermitage, though the wine of Crozes is apt to be a little less nuancé, a little coarser than its neighbor.

Nestled at the foot of the Hermitage mountain is Tain. Directly across the river from it, connected by the world's first modern suspension bridge, lies Tournon. The bridge is no longer open to traffic, as there is another more modern one downstream. Built in 1826 by a French engineer named Marc Seguin, it was the model and inspiration for Roebling's masterpiece, the Brooklyn Bridge, which was put up fifty years later.

Tournon is also known as a place of temporary residence for one of France's great nineteenth-century poets. In his youth, Stéphane Mallarmé taught English in Tournon's lycée, then went on to fame in Paris as a translator of Poe, host of one of the capital's most fashionable and most literary salons, and a philosopher-poet. His philosophy, summed up by Jean-Paul Sartre as "truth is nothingness," served as a springboard for the postwar Existentialist movement stirring Sartre and, by extension, Simone de Beauvoir, to produce several epics of their own.

Tournon is a pretty town, far lovelier than Tain. Rising above it is a charming little sixteenth-century fort with flower-strewn parapets overlooking the town, the river, and Tain on the opposite banks. All around is an amphitheater of vines.

Behind Tournon is a steep escarpment that is similar geologically and climatically to the Hermitage slope on the opposite side of the river. Like the Hermitage, it is covered with vines. A few years ago this region was honored with a new Appellation Contrôlée called Saint-Joseph. The wines from it are also made much as those of Hermitage, except that the red wine must come one hundred percent from Syrah grapes. Though lacking some of the grandeur of the red and white Hermitages, a good Saint-Joseph can be a remarkably fine bottle of wine. And at a price about twenty-five percent lower than the Hermitages, it is one of the best values in the wine world today.

For the hungry gourmet nosing through the vines of Hermitage and Saint-Joseph, Tain has two small but excellent restaurants. Needless to say their wine lists show a good cross section of the best local provender. First is the Restaurant Chabert. The décor is straight small-town French restaurant. No nonsense about it. One goes to sample the cuisine, not look at the walls. The *écrevisses flambées au Noilly,* washed down with a good white Hermitage, followed by a *pintadeau farci et rôti aux aromates,* irrigated by a mature red Hermitage, make up for the lack of decorator frills.

A little farther down the same street (which is really part of Route Nationale 7) is the Cabaret du Vivarais, another establishment where the décor is not entirely to my taste, but whose *coq au vin d'Hermitage* served with a good red bottle of the same easily makes up for any visual shortcomings.

On the west bank of the Rhône about seven miles downriver from Hermitage opposite the old Roman town of Valence lie the twin vineyard areas of Cornas and Saint-Péray. Cornas is known for its red wine, which is similar to those of Hermitage, Crozes, and Saint-Joseph. Like Saint-Joseph it must be made wholly from the Syrah grape. Cornas is apt to be rough when young, but as it matures it loses its coarseness and becomes somewhat like a less sophisticated Hermitage. It is not a great wine, but a very good one if made by a reputable vintner. Like Saint-Joseph it is remarkably inexpensive.

The village of Saint-Péray is to the south of Cornas. It is rather well known for its white wine, made like its neighbors from the Roussanne (or as it is called here, the Roussette) and the Marsanne grapes. In character it is like a lesser white Hermitage. Saint-Péray is also known for a very agreeable sparkling white wine, also made from the Roussette and Marsanne. It is more full bodied, fruitier, and more flowery than a Champagne. Though it may lack some of Champagne's elegance, it is nevertheless one of France's best sparkling wines.

Valence is directly across the river from Saint-Péray. It is a center of some importance, a bishopric, and, more to the gourmet's interest, home to one of the best-known gastronomic shrines south of Lyon. The Hôtel-Restaurant Pic is just south of the city and has been known to a generation of *fins becs* for the excellence of its cuisine. It is graced with two *Michelin* stars. The *Michelin* makes it clear that the number of stars it issues depends on the area where the restaurant is located. A star or two stars do not have the same value all over France. In a region of culinary mediocrity, a very good but not necessarily superlative restaurant will get two stars; but where the cooking is good, a restaurant will have to reach to much higher eminence to earn those two stars. As Valence lies within the purlieus of Lyon, the elysium of French gastronomy, its Restaurant Pic is indeed eminent and richly deserves the *Guide Kléber's* additional rating of a restaurant of *grande cuisine*. *Spécialités* include a *gratin de queues d'écrevisses* made from delicate local crayfish and a *coquelet de Bresse au pistil*. The former is splendidly accompanied by a good white Hermitage; the latter by a red Hermitage or a Saint-Joseph. There can be no finer way of ending the meal than with one of the splendid melons of nearby Cavaillon and a bottle of cool, sparkling Saint-Péray from across the river. The restaurant has a lovely shaded garden for those who like to dine alfresco. Pic is closed in August.

Before ending this chapter, perhaps we should raise a glass to Gaspard de Sterimberg. Seven centuries have passed since he took to his hill of solitude—a time in which the world has grown more populated, frenzied, and complex. When we soften our sorrows or heighten our pleasures with a few goblets of his splendid Hermitage, it seems only just that we should propose a toast to that odd and world-weary knight who, five centuries before Candide, retired to cultivate his own garden, and by so doing left us forever in his debt.

The Rhône

Southern Section

Historically the mouth of the Rhône is the most ancient part of France. Over three thousand years ago Phoenician ships nosed along the Mediterranean coast bartering pottery, textiles, and bronze for amber and furs brought down the river by the rude Celts from the interior. Five hundred years later Marseille was a bustling Greek colony, and the first vineyards of France were being planted to provide the Hellenes with their favorite beverage. Later the region echoed to the tramp of Roman Legionnaires on their way north to fight with Caesar. Small wonder that there is a special feeling of ancientness to this section of the country.

The apogee of Provençal culture was from the tenth to the fifteenth century. In the fourteenth century Provence and its center, Avignon, became the focal point of Christendom when in 1305 the College of Cardinals, after a deadlock of eleven months, finally decided to elect Bertrand de Got Pope Clement V. It was an astonishing choice, as de Got wasn't a cardinal but a bishop, and wasn't Italian but French. He was bibulous and a nationalist and is probably best remembered for having founded the vineyard in Bordeaux still known today as Château Pape-Clément. Of more earth-shaking consequence, he moved the seat of the Church from Rome to Avignon, the beginning of a sixty-five-year expatriation known in ecclesiastical history as the "Babylonian captivity."

During those six decades, Avignon tried to grow from a middle-sized Provençal city into the capital of Christendom. Its great walls bear testimony to this period, as do the now empty papal palace and its lovely gardens. Down below lie the broken remains of a bridge built during this time, the Pont Saint-Bénézet, of which children the world over sing

> Sur le pont d'Avignon, l'on y danse, l'on y danse;
> Sur le pont d'Avignon, l'on y danse tout en rond.

Bénézet is only a local saint, not one universally recognized by the Church. But his miracle was extraordinary enough. He was a peasant lad guarding sheep when one day he heard a voice from heaven tell him to go build a bridge across the river at Avignon. He protested that he was too small and inexperienced to take on such a chore, but the voice insisted, and so he went to Avignon to notify the Pope. There, he told the Pope that he needed his help to build a bridge. The Pope laughed and said he thought Bénézet was a bit small for such a task.

"Oh no," said Bénézet. "God has told me to build the bridge, and He will help me."

"Very well," said the Pope. "Start off by picking up that huge boulder over there, carry it down to the riverside, and we'll use it for a foundation."

Bénézet picked up the boulder with the greatest of ease, trotted down to the Rhône's banks, and dropped it where the Pope had told him. With that the Pope joined in the endeavor, and the Pont d'Avignon was on its way to becoming a nursery rhyme.

The popes were great builders of bridges and monumental buildings, not only within Avignon itself, but also around it. Avignon, like most medieval cities, was a pretty pestiferous place, especially in the summer. Hot weather has never really appealed to city dwellers, and the popes, like so many of their fellowmen before and since, longed for a little country air when the temperature began to sizzle. A palace in town was fine, but a palace in town plus a château in the country was obviously that much better. Looking around for a good site, they settled on a pleasant plateau overlooking the Rhône about ten miles upstream from Avignon. The locals dubbed this summer place rather unimaginatively "the Pope's New Palace"—Châteauneuf-du-Pape.

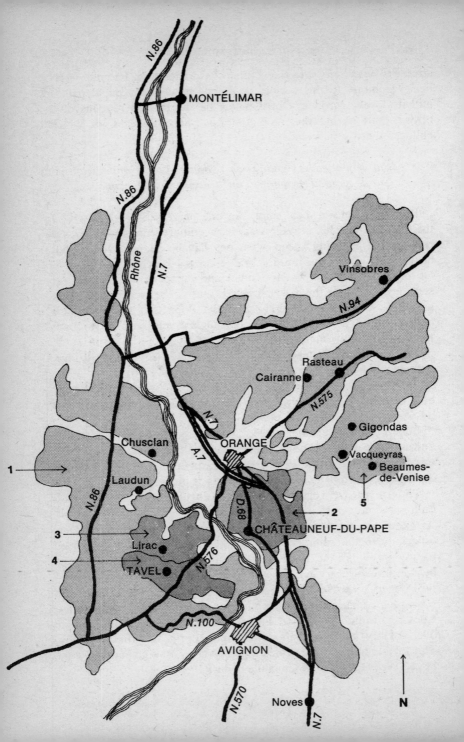

Which pope had the first vines planted here we do not know. It might have been Pope Clement himself, since he is known to have been such a great admirer of fine wine. But opinion seems to be that it was someone else, perhaps the energetic pope who succeeded him, John XXII. He rationalized and systemized church law and methods of taxation, finding enough spare time to dash off over sixty thousand letters. The amount of money that poured into the papal treasury while the Church was under his sway was staggering, so much so that the superstitious believed that he had found a way of turning lead into gold. Though this may be an exaggeration, certainly no wine lover would begrudge him praise for having discovered that the stony fields around his summer palace produced some of the world's most agreeable wines. This is alchemy of a much more rewarding kind.

After the popes returned to Rome, the vineyards remained prolific. But transportation being what it was in the Middle Ages, the wines were known only to a circle of local admirers. These conditions began to change after the Napoleonic Wars when canals and railroads began to spread their nets across the map of France. Specialties that had hitherto only been known regionally began to arrive in Paris. There they developed a more cosmopolitan reputation that carried them to the rest of the country, and indeed the world.

About this time a certain marquis owned some of Châteauneuf's finest vineyards. But apart from viticulture he had another passion. In an age of spectacular *roués* it was admitted by everyone that he had no equal. As a rakehell of style and spirit he was in a class by himself. In his youth his feats of debauchery were memorable,

---

DAY 11
Itinerary p. 24

The Rhône, Southern Section

Michelin Regional Maps 93, 80 & 83
Michelin Guide Vert *Provence*

CLASSIFIED GROWTHS

1 Côtes du Rhône
2 Châteauneuf-du-Pape
3 Lirac
4 Tavel
5 Beaumes de Venise

but this after all was only biologically natural. It was when he continued without break right into splendid old age that amused admiration turned to curiosity and envy. How did he manage to keep it up? At this the shrewd old man realized that he was his own best advertisement. He let it be known that his Châteauneuf-du-Pape was not only a glory to taste, but—and he stood as living proof—also a rejuvenator and aphrodisiac of remarkable potency. The fortunes of Châteauneuf-du-Pape were made.

RESTAURANT-HOTELS

Orange (Vaucluse)	*L'Arène (pl. Langes; tel. 34.10.95)
Villeneuve-lès-Avignon (Gard)	*Hostellerie Le Prieuré p. 24, p. 168
	*Hostellerie Provençale du Vieux Moulin (tel. 81.59.64) p. 168
Noves (Bouches-du-Rhône)	**Auberge de Noves (tel. 2.21 at Châteaurenard) p. 168

RESTAURANTS

Orange	*Le Provençal (27, rue République; tel. 34.01.89)
Châteauneuf-du-Pape (Vaucluse)	*La Mule du Pape p. 24, p. 166
	Mère Germaine (tel. 83.50.05) p. 166
Avignon (Vaucluse)	**Hiély-Lucullus (5, rue République; tel. 81.15.05— closed late June to mid-July) p. 168
	*Auberge de France (28, pl. Horloge; tel. 81.08.86—closed 2 weeks in mid-June) p. 168
Les Angles (Gard)	**Ermitage-Meissonnier (N. 100, 2 miles W of Avignon; tel. 81.44.08)

HOTEL

Avignon	Hôtel de l'Europe (12, pl. Crillon; tel. 81.41.36) p. 168

By the 1920s Châteauneuf-du-Pape was enjoying great popularity. Too great, in fact. Wines from all over the region began calling themselves by the magical name. The quality of course declined, and among the cognoscenti a bottle so labeled was looked upon with considerable skepticism. In 1923 a group of growers banded together under the leadership of the Baron Le Roy de Boiseaumarié and organized stringent safeguards to protect the region's name and wines. So successful were they that in 1936, when Senator Capus finally managed to have the French government create the Institut National des Appellations d'Origine, he used as his model the system devised in Châteauneuf-du-Pape a decade before.

Nowadays Châteauneuf-du-Pape must come from a strictly delimited area about six thousand acres in size that lies around the village. Each acre may produce no more than 374 gallons, a restriction that not only helps guarantee the name, but ensures that only the best grapes will be kept on the vines. Inferior ones are pruned off.

There is a tiny bit of white wine produced at Châteauneuf, full-bodied and dry, that goes well with pork, veal, or fowl.

The red makes up ninety-nine percent of Châteauneuf's production. It is made from a blend of different grape types, thirteen being permitted by law: Grenache, Clairette, Syrah, Mourvèdre, Picpoul, Terret Noir, Counoise, Muscardin, Vaccarèse, Picardan, Cinsault, Roussanne, and Bourboulenc. Usually, however, only four or so of these grape varietals are used, the exact mixture being the vintner's secret.

To be classified as Châteauneuf-du-Pape the wine must reach twelve-and-a-half percent natural alcohol, the highest of any Appellation Contrôlée in France. Wine coming from grapes grown during a good sunny season often reaches fourteen percent, making it one of the most potent of table wines.

The soil of Châteauneuf is unique. It is covered with large, smooth, water-washed stones showing that in some previous geological epoch the vineyards must have been beneath the surface of the Rhône. These rocks vary in size from a baked potato to a small football. They serve a purpose. In the daytime they reflect the hot Provençal sun onto the vines' leaves. At night they release their stored heat to keep the roots warm, guaranteeing a nearly ideal median temperature. The resultant wine is a splendid, full-bodied, fruity red that matures well and lives long. And, recently new methods of vinification have allowed the vintners of Châteauneuf to produce wines that are agreeable when young. These Châteauneufs are beginning to rival Beaujolais for the hearts and palates of those who like their red wines not too old.

In general it may be said that Châteauneuf-du-Pape, like Saint Bénézet, is a strong, vigorous, full-flavored wine, characteristics that make it an ideal companion for beef and game.

Among the best-known vineyards are Château Fortia, Château de Vaudieu, Domaine de la Nerthe, Clos-des-Papes, Château des Fines Roches, La Gardine, Mont-Rédon, La Solitude, Château Rayas, Clos Saint-Jean, Domaine de Nalys, Domaine des Sénéchaux, and Domaine de Saint-Préfert.

Châteauneuf-du-Pape is an agreeable little village to visit. Situated between Avignon and Orange, it huddles around the base of a large half-demolished tower that once was part of the papal château. Much of the town was destroyed in the religious wars of the sixteenth century, but what is left is old enough, and charming besides. Even better, Châteauneuf has an excellent restaurant, La Mule du Pape, situated in the town's main square. The *spécialités* include a splendid *moussaka provençale, feuilleté de truffes,* and a succulent *estouffade de boeuf.* The Mule is unfortunately closed during the month of August. However, directly across the square from it is another fine restaurant-hotel, the Mère Germaine, where the summertime trencherman can repair with pleasure from a hard day's contemplation of the vineyards. In both, needless to say, there is a good cross section of the region's wines.

Taking the road westward out of Châteauneuf-du-Pape one goes for a few kilometers through acres of beautifully tended vines. In the distance, looming up on the other bank of the Rhône, is the tower of Roquemaure—rock of the Moors—named after a fort held by the Saracens during the time of their occupation in the eighth century. One takes Route Nationale 576 through the village of Roquemaure and there, after a pleasant five-mile spin, finds the tiny town of Tavel. As any admirer of the prose of the late A. J. Liebling will remember, Tavel was one of his favorite wines. And though the placing of any rosé on so high a plane may cause some oenophiles to squint skeptically, few would disagree entirely with so eloquent an imbiber as Mr. Liebling. For even if Tavel is not the greatest wine, it is certainly among the best rosés.

The countryside around Tavel is spare and austere, rather like Spain or parts of California. Low hills and an occasional Provençal *mas* break the general monotony of the landscape. The village of Tavel is little more than a scattering of buildings around a fork in the road. Even smaller is Lirac, a hamlet a mile or so to the north, also known for its excellent rosés.

The rosés of Tavel, and to a lesser degree of Lirac, are full-flavored and hearty, redolent of the Provençal sun. To achieve their Appellation Contrôlée the wines must reach at least eleven percent natural alcohol, but in any normal year they will be well over that, nearer twelve-and-a-half. They, like the reds of Château-neuf-du-Pape, may be made from over half a dozen grape types. But the Grenache must dominate, and usually almost all of the wine is made from it. The resultant wine matures quickly. It is quite potable after a year, excellent after two or three, and generally begins to decline after five. A rosé, unlike a red, is only allowed to ferment with the grape skins for a few hours. The skins thus impart some of their color to the wine, but not much tannin, one of the elements that slows down the maturing of a wine. Having less tannin, rosés mature and die rapidly. Tavel and Lirac are excellent wines for summer luncheons. As they go well with everything, they are ideal companions for mixed buffets and picnics.

There are not many places for the hungry gourmet to sate himself in Tavel or Lirac. Tavel has one rather good inexpensive restaurant, the Hostellerie du Seigneur, which has a few rooms. However, if one wants more elegant accommodations, one must hie to other parts. Luckily Avignon and its outlying *banlieue* are a mere five miles away and rich territory for the traveler.

Closest to Tavel is the charming little thirteenth-century village of Villeneuve-lès-Avignon on the Tavel side of the Rhône where many of the cardinals chose to build their out-of-town palaces when Avignon was the papal capital. The west bank of the river was pretty and unoccupied, and within a short time an elegant little medieval town sprang up. It was soon speckled with chapels, cloisters, palaces, and even a rather impressive fortress, the Fort

Saint-André. Wine lovers will recognize the name of one of the town's prettier palaces, the Hôtel de Conti, once owned by the prince who also was the proprietor of Burgundy's great vineyard, La Romanée-Conti.

There are several pleasant spots to stay or dine in Villeneuve-lès-Avignon. One lovely hotel-restaurant lies in the shadow of an ancient priory, and is called, aptly enough, Le Prieuré. It isn't cheap, but its site is lovely and the food excellent. The host is Monsieur Mille, and his specialties include *carré d'agneau rôti aux herbes de Provence* and *sole au plat Pétrarque,* named after the great Italian poet who spent much of his time in Villeneuve-lès-Avignon lambasting the Avignon papacy.

The Hostellerie Provençale du Vieux Moulin is another pleasant hotel with a terrace overlooking the Rhône. The cuisine features *lotte à la camarguaise,* a local way of doing this succulent river fish, and *poulet sauté aux herbes de Provence.* The price is not too exalted.

Across the river in Avignon is the Hôtel de l'Europe, one of the best-known watering spots to the discriminating world traveler. A combination of impeccable service, a lovely sixteenth-century building, and a distinguished cuisine have earned it a great reputation. It is deservedly expensive. Two fine restaurants in town are the Hiély-Lucullus and the Auberge de France. The Hiély prides itself on two *Michelin* stars, *Kléber's* crown of *grande cuisine,* and specialties such as *petite marmite du pêcheur, agneau des Alpilles grillé sur feu de bois,* and *gratin de langouste de Corse.* The Auberge de France has earned one *Michelin* star with dishes such as *cassolette de truffe du Comtat* (in winter) and a truffle-stuffed pork tenderloin with the ringing Provençal name of *Poragnèu Coumtadino.* Reservations should be made at both restaurants. The Hiély is closed part of June and July.

Certainly no summary of the good restaurants around Avignon would be complete without a mention of the superb Auberge de Noves 13 kilometers southwest of the city. It is a lovely old inn made from a medieval *mas* and the view is lovely. It is tranquil and quiet, it has a pool and two *Michelin* stars, and it is luxurious and expensive.

Finally, to complete the roster of wines of the Rhône, the name Côte-du-Rhône alone on a label is an Appellation Contrôlée applying to strictly delimited areas along both banks of the Rhône which produce a good deal of red, white, and rosé wines. Good wine from these regions, that is to say wine shipped by a reputable shipper or imported by an honorable importer, is likely to be one of the finest buys today. The reds are full-bodied, vigorous, and hearty, the rosés refreshing, and the whites round, full, and dry. Sometimes the name of the subarea, such as Gigondas, Laudun, Vacqueyras, and Vinsobres for reds, whites, and rosés, and Chusclan for rosés will be mentioned on the bottle. These wines should be consistently inexpensive, and for what they are it will be money well spent. The reds go well with all beef and game, stews and casseroles; the whites with ham, veal, pork, and fowl; the rosés make admirable summer luncheon wines, delicious thirst quenchers on picnics, and also serve nicely when someone orders lobster, another orders beef, and the third orders veal. Rosés seem to go well with nearly everything.

Armagnac

Gascony is one of France's most ancient duchies. A rolling country of well-watered valleys, half-timbered market towns that seem to step straight out of the Middle Ages, woods, and vineyards, it provides welcome contrast for the traveler trying to avoid the extravagances of the twentieth century. To the south lies the high parapet of the Pyrenees, and beyond that, Spain. Westward is the forest of Landes and the Bay of Biscay. The northern boundary is traced roughly by the Dordogne, the river that streams out of the Massif Central, flows by the vineyards of Saint-Émilion and Pomerol, then joins the broad estuary of the Gironde just below Bordeaux for a rendezvous with the sea.

The word Gascony probably stems from a corruption of Basque, the name of the proud, industrious race that lives there. Who they are and where they came from, nobody knows. Their language is like no other. There is the romantic notion that they are the descendants of the lost Atlantis, mentioned in the *Critias* and *Timaeus* of Plato as having slid beneath the waves several millennia ago. But that, of course, is rather difficult to prove.

Though their past may be mysterious, the Basques have left a firm mark on the present. The women are noted for their beauty and the men for their drive and perfectionism. Gourmets who remember the late Henri Soulé, founder and dynamo of Le Pavillon, will recall the vigor with which he guarded his Olympian eminence, thereby setting a standard that has ever after served as a bench mark for the other *grands restaurants* on the American continent. Monsieur Soulé was a Basque.

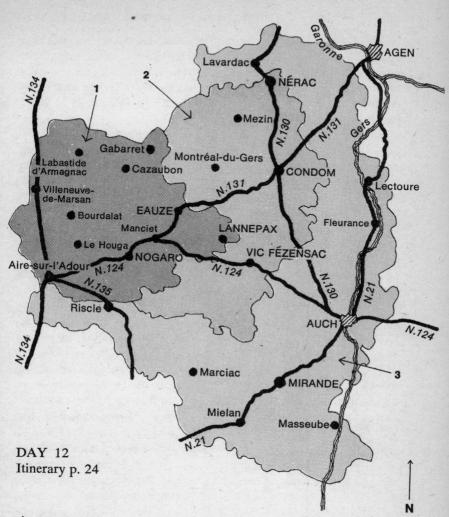

DAY 12
Itinerary p. 24

Armagnac

Michelin Regional Maps 79 & 82

1   Bas-Armagnac
2   Ténarèze
3   Haut-Armagnac

The Basque language, so unlike other European tongues, has contributed several words to the international vocabulary. One of them is *bizarre*. A bearded man in the Basque country is looked upon as potentially eccentric and foolhardy, a feeling shared by many Americans of conservative hue. Beard in Basque is *bizar;* hence anyone a little odd is "bizarre."

More interesting to those with culinary inclinations is the probable origin of bisque. Biscay, as in Bay of Biscay, is yet another form of Basque. Since time immemorial, Basques living on the bay's shore have had a special way of making a soup out of the local crustaceans. They cook them, purée them, and mix them with cream and the stock they were boiled in. They mash up their shells with a mortar and pestle and add this paste to the soup and simmer it to give it color and flavor, and finally strain out the residue of shells. The resultant smooth, coral broth, redolent of the shallow waters of the bay, was named after its inventors. Thus a bisque was born.

Gascony has kept its character as one of France's most individualistic provinces. The typical Gascon is reputed to be quick-witted, talkative, and not at all shy about broadcasting his virtues and his triumphs. In fact, the word gasconade, in both English and French, means an imaginative, high-flown, swashbuckling speech. Cyrano de Bergerac, archetypal son of the duchy, was a master of the gasconade, as were such famous literary and historical figures as d'Artagnan of *The Three Musketeers*, and "Le Vert Gallant," Henri IV.

At the very center of Gascony lies the old countship of

RESTAURANT-HOTELS

Auch (Gers)   **Hôtel de France   p. 25, 175
Villeneuve-de-Marsan   **Hôtel Darroze (Grande-Rue;
   (Landes)   tel. 2.07)   p. 174

RESTAURANTS

Carcassonne (Aude)   Le Sénéchal   p. 24
Condom (Gers)   *La Table des Cordeliers (av. Gén.-
                                    de-Gaulle; tel. 3.68)   p. 175

Armagnac. It is primarily remembered in history for its feud with Burgundy at the time of the English occupation in the fifteenth century, a vendetta that came close to making France lose her struggle for national survival. Nowadays Armagnac has a much more benevolent reputation. This stems from strong spirits too, in this case not human, but alcoholic. For within the confines of Armagnac is made a sublime irrigation: a brandy second only in fame to its northerly cousin, Cognac. In many ways Armagnac mirrors the character of the men who make it. It is a Gascon drink, and it has a full, jovial Gascon soul. Whereas Cognac is an elegant aristocrat, Armagnac is ruddy and forthright. The differences between the two stem from a host of factors: the type of grapes used; the soil; the climate; the method of distilling the wine; and the variety of the wood used in the maturing casks.

Cognac, as will be explained in a later chapter, is now made less by individual artisans than by half a dozen or so large brandy blenders and shippers. The advantage of this is that brandies of uniform quality are guaranteed, and the purchaser knows pretty well what to expect when he orders the product of one of the major firms. In Armagnac this is much less true. Though there are a few cooperatives and a scattering of medium-sized firms, the bulk of brandy making, maturing, and even selling is still in the hands of small farmers and local artisans. The result is something of a genial anarchy, splendid for those who like variety, who take pleasure in discovering what they like for themselves, and certainly for those who like to impress their less knowledgeable friends. But for the neophyte, the quantity of shippers and makers can cause considerable befuddlement.

The wine from which Armagnac is made comes primarily from the Folle Blanche grape, though the Saint-Émilion favored in Cognac is growing in popularity. Other widely used types include the Picpoul, a standard grape of the Midi, the Colombard, and the Jurançon. Permissible but not much used grapes are the Blanquette, Mauzac, Clairette, Meslier, and Plant de Grèce.

Cognac is swept by the damp, warm winds blowing off the Gulf Stream. The country is green, the atmosphere misty. In Armagnac one senses the proximity of Spain. The air is dry and the sun strong. In Cognac the best brandies come from grapes grown in calcareous soil. In Armagnac the reverse is true. The best Armagnac comes from the Bas-Armagnac, the westerly part of the province that lies between the towns of Villeneuve-de-Marsan and Eauze. The soil here is sandy. Second in the hierarchy of Armagnacs is that from Ténarèze, a reverse C-shaped piece of land embracing Bas-Armagnac from the east. Its center is Condom, and its earth is clay loam. Next is still a larger C that enfolds both Bas-Armagnac and Ténarèze. This is called Haut-Armagnac, and its capital is Auch. The soil here is like that of Cognac—chalky; but for some reason the brandy it produces isn't up to that of its two neighbors.

Distilling is different in the two areas also. In Cognac the pot still, which is essentially a huge teapot with a spiral exhaust, is used. The brandy has to be made in batches, and it is distilled twice. In Armagnac the brandy is made in a local variant of the Coffey still. The wine pours in one end and the brandy comes out the other of this gigantic double percolator, giving the machine its other name, the continuous still. Though it distills more alcohol from the wine than a single run of the pot still, the double run customary in Cognac causes that brandy to be lighter, more alcoholic, and less filled with the taste of the grape than Armagnac.

Last but not least in determining a brandy's character is the oak used to make the casks in which it matures. Armagnac is matured in barrels made from native trees rather than the oak of the Limousin used for Cognac.

The end result of all these processes is, in the case of Armagnac, a velvety, grapy, full-bouqueted brandy whose warming qualities make it the ideal potation for chilly winter evenings. It usually is bottled in a squat flagon not unlike the *Bocksbeutel* used for German Steinwein. The Armagnac bottle is no copy. This bottle has been used in the region for centuries, so long, in fact, that it is called the *basquaise*.

Armagnacs shipped into the United States include that of the Marquis de Caussade, the Marquis de Montesquiou, Larresingle, San Gil, and Bellows Fine Bas-Armagnac.

The towns central to each of the three regions of Armagnac offer an impressive trio of restaurants. At Villeneuve-de-Marsan is the Hôtel Darroze, with two *Michelin* stars, the crown of *grande cuisine* from *Kléber*, and regional specialties such as *foie gras* and *ortolans en barquette*. At Condom is La Table des Cordeliers, with one *Michelin* star, at which specialties are *foie gras au naturel parfumé au vieil Armagnac* and *oie en daube*. And at Auch is the Hôtel de France, with two stars and the crown of *grande cuisine*, where one may dine on *foie frai au poivre vert, daube gasconne,* and *glace aux pruneaux à l'Armagnac*.

The Winelands of Bordeaux

Bordeaux has the sixth largest population in France; it is the second largest city in area, and the greatest port in the southwestern part of the country. It is situated thirteen miles up the confluence of the Garonne and Dordogne rivers, and its harbor bustles with ships from the Middle and Far East, Africa, the Baltic, England, the Antilles, and America. Its name is therefore justified: Bordeaux, loosely translated, means "beside the waters." An oenophile, however, would protest that it might better be called "Borduvin," "on the banks of the river wine."

For Bordeaux is the capital of probably the greatest wine-producing region of France. Other vineyard areas match one or perhaps even two of Bordeaux's types, but no other region produces wines in such variety and quantity. The spectrum of Bordeaux's wines is complete—light, elegant reds as well as full, burly ones; even rosés and sparkling white wines made by the *méthode champenoise*. In every category, except perhaps the last, Bordeaux sets a standard of excellence that all may envy but few can match. This is not to say that all Bordeaux wine is good; there is a considerable amount of mediocre wine made in the *département* of the Gironde. But good Bordeaux set the standard for what wines of their types should be.

The only region that matches Bordeaux's reputation is Burgundy, whose regal reds and dry whites also set a standard for wines *sui generis*. However, the scope of Bordeaux is far greater. Burgundy does not produce any wines with the delicacy and finesse of a properly matured first-growth Haut-Médoc or Graves. It does not produce any liqueur wines to rival a Sauternes or a Barsac. And when it comes to quantity, there is no contest. In a good average year Bordeaux produces about five hundred million bottles of wine. All of Burgundy, including Maconnais and Beaujolais, makes only a little over a quarter as much.

The history of Bordeaux goes back over two thousand years. It was already a port of Celtic Gaul when the Romans took it in 55 B.C., but not, as far as we know, a wine center. The Romans named it Burdigala, and under them it became a flourishing city of some sixty thousand people. It was made the capital of the Roman province of Aquitania, and, as such, became a regional center of arts, architecture, and law. More important, the Romans brought with them their considerable knowledge of the cultivation of vines. During the twilight years of Roman rule, Bordeaux glowed with culture and oenology. Ausonius, the Latin poet and tutor of the Emperor Gratian, was a native Bordelais, and many of his finest lines extol the virtues of Bordeaux wines. And, though he traveled throughout the empire with the court, when the time came to retire he returned to his native *pays* to write poetry and raise vines. The present Château Ausone, which produces one of

---

RESTAURANTS

Bordeaux (Gironde)	Le Saint-James (2, Cours Intendance; tel. 52.59.79—closed Sat. & Sun., July–Sept; closed last 2 weeks in April & August and Mondays from Oct.–June) p. 183
	*Restaurant Dubern p. 26, p. 182
	*Restaurant Clavel (44, rue Ch.-Domercq; tel. 92.91.52—closed Aug.)
	La Toque Blanche (245, rue Turenne; tel. 48.97.86)

HOTEL

Bordeaux	La Normandie (7, Cours Trente-Juillet; tel. 52.16.80; telex 57, 481)

For restaurant-hotels and restaurants outside the city, see the following chapters on the regions of Bordeaux.

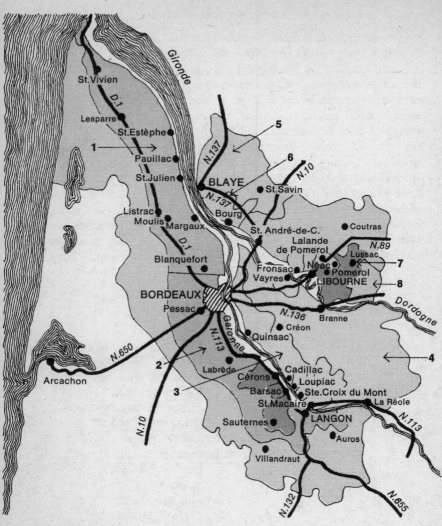

DAYS 13–15
Itinerary pp. 25–26

Bordeaux

Michelin Regional Map 71
Michelin Guide Vert *Côte de l'Atlantique*

the finest growths of Saint-Émilion, is said to have been built on the site of his country house.

Probably the greatest moment in the history of Bordeaux came in the twelfth century. Eleanor, the high-spirited duchess of Aquitaine, owned as her feudal fiefs all of southwestern France from the Spanish frontier to the Loire. In 1137 she married Louis VII of France and became his queen. But to her dismay she found him cold and extraordinarily religious. After thirteen years of matrimony she got fed up with the King's monasticism and his penchant for fighting distant Crusades. In an act that scandalized Christendom, she had her marriage annulled. She promptly married the lusty Henry Plantagenet, duke of Normandy and count of Anjou (to whom she bore three daughters and five sons—Richard the Lion-Hearted among them). This marriage was far more than a personal affront to her ex-husband. Henry Plantagenet had as his own personal fiefs all of northwestern France from the Loire to the English Channel. When the union between Eleanor and Henry was announced, everyone knew that a deadly political rivalry had begun between the king of the French and his two most powerful nobles. Eleanor and Henry controlled between them half of Louis' kingdom. And to add to Louis' troubles, in 1154 Henry became king of England as well. The next three hundred years were to witness almost continual war as the successive kings of France tried to regain their kingdoms.

PRINCIPAL REGIONS

1 Médoc
2 Graves
  Cérons
  Barsac
  Sauternes
  Bordeaux Saint-Macaire
  Sainte-Croix-du-Mont
  Loupiac
3 Premières Côtes de Bordeaux

4 Entre-Deux-Mers
  Graves de Vayres
5 Blayais
6 Bourgeais
  Fronsac
  Pomerol
  Lalande-de-Pomerol
  Néac
7 Saint-Émilion
8 Côtes de Castillon
  Bordeaux

The upshot of the wedding between Henry and Eleanor was that for three centuries Bordeaux was under English rule. It was an enjoyable time for the Bordelais. The English treated Bordeaux as one of the most honored cities of their realm, letting it have its own civic freedoms, and even its own parliament, called the *Jurade*. But more important from an oenophile's point of view was the birth of the Bordeaux wine trade. The English of that day were avid wine bibbers, and the incorporation of Bordeaux into their kingdom was a great stroke of luck for them, and for the Bordelais. The English dubbed the red wine of Bordeaux claret, and the name is still used today. It probably stems from *clairet*, the Languedoc term for a very light red wine, or perhaps a dark rosé would be more accurate. It is a term still employed in southern France, and in northern Spain where light reds are called *claretes*. If this etymology is correct, the claret of Bordeaux has changed considerably in the past eight hundred years, as it is now deep red in color.

During the centuries of English rule, the maritime wine trade between England, the North Sea countries, and Bordeaux became enormous. It was probably the largest operation of transportation and trade of the Middle Ages. Another term has come into the language because of it, the word "ton." A Bordeaux wine barrel, or *tonneau* as it is called, weighs a little over two thousand pounds, wine and barrel included. In the thirteenth century, when one wanted to describe the size of a ship, one said how many full wine barrels it could carry. Or to put it in maritime terminology, what "*tonneaux* burden" it could hold. *Tonneaux* was shortened to "tons," and the word has been a way of measuring the size of ships ever since.

English rule of Bordeaux ended in 1453 when John Talbot, first Earl of Shrewsbury, marshal of the king's armies, and constable of Aquitaine, was killed at the Battle of Castillon, twenty-five miles east of the city. After three centuries of relative freedom and prosperity, Bordeaux grudgingly fell back into the arms of mother France. The French, doubting the reliability of their new subjects, and for good reason, treated the city as occupied territory. Two forts were erected to dominate it, named derisively by the populace the Château Trompette and the Château du Hâ. The latter's curious name was given it when the king of

France, no great intellect, was told that the fortress was finished. The king as usual could think of nothing to say, so he simply murmured "*ha*." To the Bordelais this seemed indicative of the level of the French king's wit, and to commemorate his memorable remark they named his fortress after it. Both châteaux have now disappeared.

During the next few centuries, Bordeaux became known for its tendencies toward local autonomy and personal liberty. Constantly opposing the centralizing proclivities of the rather benevolently despotic kings, it was the scene of several revolts. It also gave birth to such great libertarian and humanistic writers as Michel de Montaigne in the sixteenth century, and the Baron de Montesquieu in the seventeenth.

During the seventeenth and eighteenth centuries, France began to develop an empire in India, Canada, and the Antilles, and Bordeaux prospered mightily as France's main Atlantic port. It also profited during the eighteenth century from an extraordinary series of "intendants," as the royal governors were called, each of whom seemed to have no other purpose than to make the city even more beautiful than his predecessor had left it. Bordeaux is greatly in their debt. It is a monument to one of mankind's most orderly architectural periods. Its *quais* and esplanades, its place de la Bourse and Grand Théâtre are all tributes to the graceful decorum of the eighteenth century.

The Revolution saw one of Bordeaux's finest and most tragic hours. Initially, the *Girondins*, as its delegates to the Estates-General at Paris were called, led the Revolution, and under their guidance a moderate federal republic, or possibly even a constitutional monarchy, seemed about to emerge. But they were overthrown by the radical Jacobins led by Robespierre, and the Revolution suddenly took a sharp and bloody turn. In the ensuing Terror, nearly all the prominent *Girondins* were hunted down and guillotined. With them died the hope of a moderate republic: Bonaparte with his imperial ambitions stood waiting in the wings.

Since then Bordeaux has settled down into a more provincial existence. It was occupied by the English again at the end of the Napoleonic Wars, when Wellington invaded France from Spain. It also became the temporary capital of the country when the government fled Paris in 1870, 1914, and 1940. Apart from these interludes, Bordeaux has concentrated on being a port and a center of gastronomy and wine.

Gastronomically, Bordeaux relies heavily on the sea. The oyster beds of Arcachon southwest of the city are among the most prolific in France, providing a local oyster called the *gravette*, as well as the elegant *plate* and the more common *portugaise*. The latter is by far the cheapest, and though poor ones can be unpleasant, properly raised *portugaises* have excellent texture and flavor. Their growth on the coast of France is literally accidental. In 1858 a Portuguese ship laden with oysters was shipwrecked at the mouth of the Gironde, and the bivalves were dumped back into the sea. They quickly made themselves at home and have been thriving in French waters ever since. *Portugaises* may be distinguished by their rough and crenellated shells, while the native *plates* are smoother and smaller.

Without doubt one of the world's finest oysters is a native French *plate* that has been allowed to grow at Marennes, a little north of the mouth of the Gironde. Of all French oysters, only the *belons* and *cancales* of Brittany can match them. Bordeaux is thus surrounded by superb oyster beds, so it is not surprising that the Bordelais have their own way of serving them. A dozen *portugaises* or *plates* are presented with a tiny grilled, rather spicy sausage between each of them. The juxtaposition of flavors is surprising and very good. There can be few finer ways of beginning a meal than with a dozen *plates de Marennes* and sausages washed down by a cool bottle of dry white Graves.

Shad and sturgeon also abound in the rivers near Bordeaux, and a rather good local caviar is made from the latter. A specialty from the pastures of the Landes and the Médoc is the *agneau pré-salé*, lamb that has fed on special grasses growing only in the flats near salt water. They give a delicious and subtle flavor to the meat. A *gigot* of lamb *pré-salé* is one of heaven's great gifts to the gourmet, and with a properly matured red wine of the Haut-Médoc it is divine.

Another great Bordelais dish is an *entrecôte marchand de vin grillée aux sarments*. This is a steak grilled over a fire made of vine shoots; when done to a turn it is covered with a sauce made of marrow, shallots, butter, red wine, carrots, onions, celery, salt, pepper, thyme, and bay. It is splendid, especially when accompanied by a good red wine of Saint-Émilion or Pomerol.

Bordeaux has a number of oases where the gourmet may satisfy his inner inclinations. One of them is the relatively new Le Saint-James, whose cuisine is under direction of possibly one of the new stars of French gastronomy, Jean-Marie Amat. His *specialités* include *Pigeon aux cèpes frais, cèpes* being the delicious, great, flat mushrooms that are a specialty of Bordeaux. Ducks are his delight. The Terrine de Canard is excellent, as is the duckling —*Caneton rôti au citron*—roasted with lemon.

Another most agreeable spot to dine is the charming Restaurant Dubern on the allées Tourny. The allées Tourny is not an alley in the English sense of the word, but a broad tree-lined esplanade ending at the place de la Comédie and the Grand Théâtre. One enters the Dubern through a sort of grotto filled with fine foods —a fancy-food shop downstairs beneath the restaurant proper. Specialties include *écrevisses bordelaise* (crayfish in a sauce of shallots and butter); *suprême de poularde Dubern* (capon served in a sauce of cream, butter, white wine, shallots, *foie gras*, and a little red pepper); and *bécasse au foie gras* (woodcock and *foie gras*). The wine list is excellent.

In general Bordeaux has a somewhat English feeling to it, which is not surprising as the English not only owned it for about three hundred years but have also been the dominant element in its wine trade. To this day many of the great châteaux and exporting firms are owned by Englishmen or their descendants. The society of Bordeaux is stratified along the lines of pre-First-World-War Britain. It is based on what is known locally as the *"noblesse de bouchon"*—the "nobility of the cork"—a combination of old family names, great châteaux and vineyards, and private wealth, in that order. This is most pronounced in the Médoc, Graves, and Sauternes—less so on the northern side of the Gironde and along the Dordogne. The ramifications of the system are extremely complicated. A title received from the Capetians, Valois, or Bourbons is more acceptable than one received from Napoleon I and III. Other factors enter. Not only is the amount of money important, but also whether it is new or old money, and how it was acquired. One senses that this is one of the few places in this last half of the twentieth century where Marcel Proust would have felt at home. And it would take his genius to unravel all the combinations of title, wealth, and land that make up the established pecking order.

In this way Bordeaux is quite different from most other vineyard areas in France. Only Champagne has family dynasties that are somewhat similar, but in a considerably less pronounced fashion. Whereas Burgundy is essentially a wine democracy where vineyard owners either work in their own vineyards, or at least are close to the soil, great Bordeaux vineyards are likely to be owned by old noble families, descendants of Napoleonic bankers, or wealthy foreigners. To own a château is not only a profitable enterprise, but it has the same cachet as owning a string of fine racehorses or an America's Cup winner. The great châteaux are run like corporations. They have *gérants* who take care of the business and the finances, *maîtres de chais* who are in charge of the vine raising and wine making, and a multitude of workers who live on or near the estates.

The vineyards of Bordeaux lie at nearly every compass point from the city. To the north are those of Bourg and Blaye, to the east those of Pomerol and Saint-Émilion, to the southeast Entre-Deux-Mers and the Premières Côtes de Bordeaux, to the south Sauternes and Barsac, to the southwest and west Graves, and to the northwest the Médoc and the Haut-Médoc.

Bordeaux produces almost a hundred million gallons of wine a year, nearly all of which is red and white. Although rosé production is growing, it is still minuscule in comparison.

The great red-wine regions of Bordeaux are the Haut-Médoc, Graves, Pomerol, and Saint-Émilion. Good red-wine areas are Bourg, Blaye, the Médoc, Saint-Macaire, Premières Côtes de Bordeaux, and Fronsac.

The great white-wine vineyards are in Graves, Sauternes, and in a subdivision of Sauternes around the town of Barsac. Lesser whites of good quality come from Cérons, Blaye, Saint-Macaire, Bourg, Entre-Deux-Mers, Loupiac, and Sainte-Croix-du-Mont.

The different characteristics of the wines from the great regions are quite pronounced. They are based on a combination of factors —the soil, grape types, time of picking, and methods of vinification among them. Bordeaux wines, both red and white, are made of a blend of grape varietals, and the proportion used of each has a great deal to do with what flavor the resultant wine will have.

In the Médoc and Haut-Médoc, where only red wine is made, and in Graves, the primary type of grape used is the Cabernet Sauvignon, with admixtures of the Cabernet Franc, Merlot, Petit Verdot, and sometimes the Malbec. Each château has its own recipe, and with some of them it is a closely guarded secret.

The Cabernet Sauvignon is without doubt one of the world's greatest red-wine grapes, and it is primarily because of its influence that the properly matured wines of the Haut-Médoc and Graves achieve an elegance, a delicacy, and a finesse that make them the finest wines of their type. However, the phrase "properly matured" must be stressed, for a young wine made from the Cabernet Sauvignon is hard and astringent. It takes a long time to mature but it can live to a phenomenally old age. A great Haut-Médoc or Graves will take at least ten years to mature and will probably still be good at sixty.

There are, of course, exceptions. The 1947s matured quickly, as did the 1950s and 1953s. The years 1958 and 1960, both considered "off" on vintage charts, nevertheless produced some very creditable and quickly maturing wines. However, in general, the '52s and '45s of great vineyards are in their prime now in the early seventies, as is another very late starter, 1928. Equally great is its sister, 1929, which matured rapidly but did not deteriorate. In general, to drink a Premier Grand Cru Haut-Médoc or Graves made within the decade is an abomination. The wines of Haut-Médoc and Graves should be held, and he who does so and keeps them the requisite number of years will be rewarded with one of the greatest delights in winedom.

The holding quality of wines using large amounts of Cabernet Sauvignon is due largely to tannin. A tannic taste in young bottles can be lessened by giving the wine plenty of time to "breathe" by pulling the cork a few hours before serving and letting air get in. Better yet, one may pour the wine into a large decanter leaving a broad surface open to air, and then keep the top off the decanter for a few hours. In extreme cases, astringent young clarets may be poured back and forth between decanters or pitchers for five or ten minutes, giving air a chance to mix in thoroughly. Air softens tannic acid, and this becomes in effect a way of forced aging.

Unfortunately, the pressures of trade, demanding quickly maturing wines, are compelling many growers to regard the mag-

nificent Cabernet Sauvignon with disfavor. In all but the greatest
châteaux there is a steady tendency toward lowering its percentage
so that wines may be put on the market sooner. Much of this is
because of the economic changes wrought in the past few decades.
Few people now have large cellars in which to keep wines. Most
people prefer to buy wines directly from a store and serve them
at the table that evening. As stores and wine merchants do not
like to carry large inventories, everything militates toward producing round, smooth, rapidly maturing wines. These may never
achieve the heights of the wines made from the Cabernet Sauvignon, but they are drinkable long before.

A wine of the Haut-Médoc, the Médoc, or Graves perfectly
accompanies beef, lamb, roast veal, and roast domestic fowl.

The red wines of Saint-Émilion and Pomerol are excellent and
in great vogue, as they have the sought-after characteristic of
being more quickly maturing than the reds from the banks of the
Garonne. The grapes primarily used are the Cabernet Franc and
the Merlot, varietals whose wines are less astringent when young
than those made from the Cabernet Sauvignon. They are full,
round, smooth, and hearty, and are sometimes called by the Bordelais the "Burgundies of Bordeaux." Though they lack the elegance and finesse of a properly matured Haut-Médoc, they don't
take as much time to mature. They are excellent with beef and
game.

The dry white wines of Bordeaux reach their acme in Graves.
The grapes used are the Sémillon and Sauvignon Blanc, the same
ones favored by Sauternes and Barsac. However, because of the
soil and the entirely different way of harvesting the grapes, the
wines are utterly different. A good white Graves is a full, dry wine
with a slight taste of the gravelly soil from which it comes. It
perfectly complements seafood, ham, pork, and creamed fowl.

Among the greatest dessert wines are those of Sauternes and
Barsac. Only the finest Rheingaus, such as the *Trockenbeerenaus-
lesen* of Schloss Johannisberg, Rauenthaler Baiken, or Kloster
Eberbach can come close to matching them. The grapes are the
same used to make dry white Graves—the Sémillon, Sauvignon,
and usually a little Muscadelle. But there is a great difference in
the final product because of very different harvesting methods,
which will be discussed in detail in the following chapter.

Sauternes & Graves

The quality of sweetness is not strained, certainly not in people, and it is getting difficult to find even in wine. For reasons known only to God and the advertising fraternity, a wave of pro-dry propaganda has swept the country. Dry beer and dry ginger ale are extolled as the best, and now some people are trying to apply this shibboleth to wine itself. This chapter is not directed to the likes of these. It is addressed to those of open mind, who admit that taste should have variety, and that praising one kind of beauty to the disadvantage of another leads to an impoverishment of aesthetic experience. In no case is this more true than in the appreciation of wine.

My first experience with the luscious sweet wines of Sauternes was rather disastrous. It took place over thirty years ago, when I was still a child. In the summer of 1936 my family, in a moment of soon-to-be-regretted bravado, decided to take my two older brothers and me on a grand tour of Europe. As we were aged fifteen, thirteen, and six, respectively, any unity of purpose or taste was out of the question. But war clouds were darkening every horizon that summer, and my parents thought that we had all

---

RESTAURANT-HOTELS

better go before Europe and its treasures were plunged in the cauldron of war.

Accordingly, all five of us were packed into a spanking new Lincoln Zephyr—a futuristic car in the 1930s—and this rolling bedlam toured England, northern France, Belgium, Germany, Burgundy, and Italy. From Italy we cut across the southern part of France to Saint-Jean-de-Luz on the Bay of Biscay, planning to end with a quick tour of the Spanish Basque provinces. But no sooner had we arrived at the Spanish frontier than Spain went up in flames as her civil war began. And so I spent a couple of weeks making sand castles on the beach of Saint-Jean-de-Luz to the distant thunder of antiaircraft batteries.

My father, a wine importer, took advantage of the pause to leave my brothers and me with a nanny and go up to Bordeaux with Mother to discuss business affairs with local château owners. As has just been noted in the previous chapter, Bordeaux wine families are the aristocrats of the wine world. With their great châteaux in the country and their *hôtels particuliers* in town, their retinues of servants and their incomparable cellars, they set a standard of elegance and hospitality that few can hope to match in this century. One day we children were called to one of the most distinguished *hôtels particuliers* in Bordeaux for a family luncheon. The head of this family was well known for the excellence of his table—a reputation that found him his *chef de cuisine*. The chef had quit the kitchens of the President of the Republic to come to a house where he felt his work would be more properly appreciated.

The setting of the luncheon was supernal. There was an enormous table for adults and another one for children, with footmen

---

DAY 13
Itinerary p. 25

Sauternes & Graves

Michelin Regional Maps 71 & 79
Michelin Guide Vert *Côte de
l'Atlantique*

GRAVES

SAUTERNES
BARSAC
CÉRONS

CLASSIFICATIONS, p. 191, p. 196

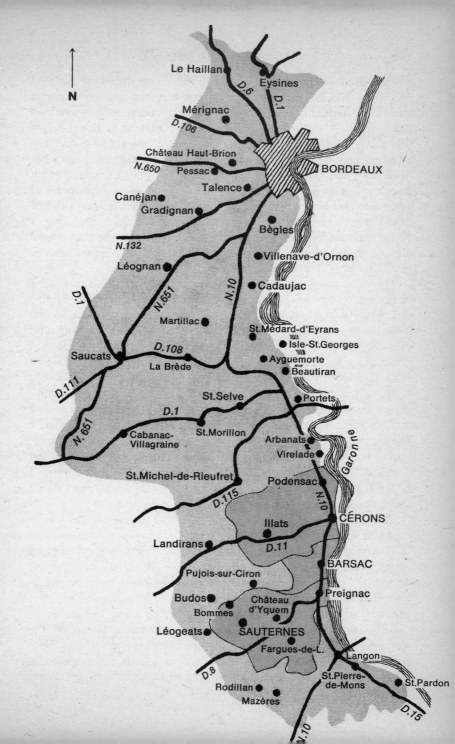

waiting against the wall. Because of this separation of tables I found myself, for the first time in my life, beyond the reach of immediate parental retribution. The first course was served—a *foie gras truffé en brioche*—and, as is the custom in Bordeaux, it was accompanied by a thick, luscious wine of the greatest vineyard in Sauternes, Château d'Yquem, probably a 1921. I couldn't believe my good fortune. Up to this point my only experience with Bacchus had been an occasional well-watered glass of rather tart red wine. But here I was, all by myself, with a crystalline bowl of liquid honey. I drank it with enthusiasm. Finishing the wine, I was captivated by the beauty of the glass, and knowing that crystal gives a pretty sound, I tapped it to hear it ring. Immediately a footman stepped forward to refill it.

This was too good to be true! Forgetting all about the pâté, I drank and rang again, and once more the glass was filled. By this time my six-year-old head was swimming deliciously, and I grew more boisterous. Forgetting all decorum, I began giggling and throwing bread at the other children. Then I felt the shadow of my mother looming over me. Calming myself quickly, I tried to feign sobriety by hastily addressing myself to the pâté. Suddenly I felt very queasy. I was quickly hustled off to the waiting nanny, who chastised me roundly for my precociously erring ways and took me squalling to the family's hotel. For twenty years after, I ascribed my resultant *gueule de bois* not to winey overindulgence, but to the pâté—a conventional enough excuse for an adult, but certainly rather advanced for a six-year-old. What is more, I *believed* it, so much so that a long time was to pass before I dared touch that exquisite delicacy again.

That experience, I might say, is the only unpleasant one I have ever had with Sauternes.

The wines of Sauternes come from a strictly delimited area about twenty miles southeast of Bordeaux on the left bank of the Garonne. The region is made up of five townships: Fargues, Preignac, Bommes, Barsac, and Sauternes itself. Altogether, Sauternes produces about 400,000 cases of wine during a good year.

From the five townships listed above come a dozen of the world's most famous wines. Their special character results from four factors: the soil in which the vines are grown, the grape types from which the wine is made, the way in which the grapes ripen, and the method of harvesting them. The soil of Sauternes, except for that of Barsac, is a combination of clay and sandy gravel. (The soil of Barsac is somewhat more calciferous.) The grape varietals from which Sauternes is made are the Sémillon, which accounts for about eighty percent of the wine, and the Sauvignon, which contributes about twenty percent. Usually a small amount of Muscadelle is added, though this is not a requisite.

But more than the soil and the grape type, it is the manner and time of picking that make Sauternes unique among French wines. There is a legend that explains how this came to be. In the Middle Ages it was customary for the feudal proprietor of a vineyard to set the date when the grape harvesting, the *vendange,* was to begin. It seems that just before picking time one of the great proprietors went off on a hunt and, running across a fair and complaisant young maid, had a leisurely dalliance at a considerable distance from his estate. This sort of good fortune doesn't happen every day, and he didn't return until well after the grapes should have been picked. By the time he appeared, the grapes were half-shriveled on the vine. His *vignerons* were furious, as it was obvious

---

CLASSIFIED GROWTHS OF SAUTERNES & BARSAC

Premier Grand Cru: Château d'Yquem (since 1855)

Deuxièmes Crus:

Premiers Crus:

	Château Myrat
	Château Doisy
Château La Tour-Blanche	Château Doisy-Daëm
Château Lafaurie-Peyraguey	Château Doisy-Védrines
Château Clos Haut-Peyraguey	Château d'Arches
Château de Rayne-Vigneau	Château Filhot
Château de Suduiraut	Château Broustet
Château Coutet	Château Nairac
Château Climens	Château Caillou
Château Guiraud	Château Suau
Château Rieussec	Château de Malle
Château Rabaud-Promis	Château Romer
Château Sigalas-Rabaud	Château Lamothe

that the vintage was ruined. But he ordered the grapes picked anyway, and to everyone's great surprise the result was a delicious, syrupy, nectarlike wine.

Whether the legend is true or not, it is indeed late harvesting that accounts for the sweetness of Sauternes. The grapes are left on the vines far longer than in other sections of France. As autumn wears on, the leaves of the vines are trimmed from the grapes so that the sun may shine on them and dehydrate them. About this time a mold called *Botrytis cinerea* begins to grow on the grape skins, consuming a great deal of the waterproofing element in them. It first appears as a faint cloudiness on the skin, and as it grows the grapes shrivel to an almost raisinlike state. This mold, called in French *pourriture noble,* or "noble mold," is probably the most important single reason that the wine of Sauternes is as it is.

All of the grapes are not gathered at the same time. As many as six pickings, over a period of two months, may be required in order that each grape be picked at the moment it attains the right degree of dehydration.

The result of this late picking and of the *pourriture noble* is a must, or grape juice, with an extremely high content of sugar, glycerine, and grape concentrate, and at the same time a low content of water. In the process of fermentation a good deal of the sugar is changed into alcohol. But at between thirteen and sixteen percent alcohol, the yeast that causes fermentation is killed, and because there is so much sugar in the must, a large amount remains over and above that converted into alcohol.

It is not only this residual sugar, however, that makes Sauternes unique. The liqueurlike quality of the wine also comes from the high amount of natural glycerin and concentrated grape essences. The glycerin gives it a viscous, thick, quick-silvery quality that few other wines have. The grape concentrate gives it a savor of enormous fruitiness and fullness. It is the quintessence of the grape. According to J. R. Roger of the Académie de Vin de France— no lover of understatement—Sauternes is "the most sumptuous of those white wines that are strictly natural: unctuous, velvety, liqueurish, highly perfumed, with a great strength that is, however, fine, elegant, and filled with nuances." After that description, further words from me would seem niggling.

"Bring me a flagon,/ Enough for a dragon,/ And fill it with

Château Yquem!" wrote A. P. Herbert in the song "Table for Two." Mr. Herbert's dragonly acquaintances must have had elegant taste for, of all the Sauternes, Yquem is considered the greatest. In the classification of Bordeaux wines in 1855, Château d'Yquem was the only one to be given the extraordinary honor of a category by itself, a position it has held ever since.

The château has been owned by the family of the Marquis de Lur-Saluces since 1785. In the Middle Ages it was the property of a family with the English name of Eichem and the castle was called the Château d'Eichem, later to be Frenchified into Château d'Yquem. One of the greatest French writers, and founder of the essay as a literary form, was Michel Eyquem de Montaigne. Although he did his writing in a tower some kilometers to the north, it was his family that owned the château.

It is a beauty. Constructed from the thirteenth to the fifteenth century, the château gracefully crowns a slope overlooking 230 acres of manicured vines. There is a feeling of agelessness about it, a link in this rather frenetic century with the beauty of the past and, one hopes, that of the future. Even the workers and artisans who cull the vines and make the magnificent wine seem to reinforce this sensation. I met there Monsieur Bureau, a superbly mustachioed *maître de chais* in charge of all the aspects of growing, making, and maturing wine, and a descendant of *vignerons* who have worked the estate steadily for over five hundred years.

The Château d'Yquem is within the limits of the town of Sauternes. In the same commune, a little to the south of the Château d'Yquem, lies the Château Guiraud. Perhaps not quite as exalted as its two famous neighbors is another excellent vineyard, the Château Filhot, owned by the Comtesse Durieu de Lacarelle, née Lur-Saluces. With vineyards such as this and Yquem, the Lur-Saluces family is rather well known in Sauternes.

In the town of Bommes, the most famous vineyard is probably the Château Rayne-Vigneau. This château, which produces one of the most memorable Sauternes, has a unique characteristic. The vineyard appears to be scattered with semiprecious stones. Agates, jasper, onyx, opal, amethysts, and even, it is said, a few sapphires have been found among the vines. In spite of the fact that more than twelve thousand of these stones have turned up, nobody dreams of tearing up the vines to harvest the gems—proof of the value the French attach to their vineyards.

Other well-known vineyards in Bommes are the Château La Tour Blanche, now an experimental agricultural station run by the government, the Château Rabaud, the Château Lafaurie-Peyraguey, and the Clos Haut-Peyraguey. In the town of Preignac, another rather grand Sauternes is produced, Château Suduiraut. Its reputation slipped a little during the twenties and thirties, but now, under a new owner, it has recovered much of its former grandeur.

In the town of Fargues is the Château Rieussec, an excellent vineyard. Its vines border on those of the Château d'Yquem, though they are in different townships. This wine is perhaps marginally less grand, liqueurish, and nuance-filled than its superlative neighbor, but nevertheless it is one of the finest Sauternes.

Without doubt, the only town that comes close to matching the reputation of Sauternes itself is Barsac, which lies to the north across a pretty little stream called the Ciron. Its fame is due to two splendid vineyards. One is the Château Coutet, the other the Château Climens. Perhaps because of the separation from the rest of the Sauternes area by the Ciron, the soil of Barsac is more calciferous. This makes the wine fractionally harder, with a pronounced, almost lemony aftertaste. The Château Coutet and the Château Climens both produce splendid wines, but to my taste Climens has the edge. It is a little fuller in flavor, a little subtler, perhaps a little more liqueurish. The characteristic many oenophiles seem to note in Barsac is its faint flavor of "rustiness."

Château Climens reminds me of one of the most memorable eating experiences of my life which took place in the early 1960s at the Restaurant de la Pyramide in Vienne, south of Lyons. We ended Madame Point's spectacular supper with the delicious little pastries and the four kinds of mousse famous at that fine old restaurant. The wines matched the empyreal quality of the food: a Pol Roger '52 as an apéritif, a Meursault-Perrières '52 with the *omble chevalier*, a Richebourg '45 with the *bécasse*, and a Château Climens '47 with the desserts. Of this galaxy of beautifully balanced wines and foods, the Climens leaves the most pronounced memory. It was a magnificent Sauternes. Its body and liqueurish quality sustained the desserts and added, at the same time, an ever-so-subtle almost lemony flavor to balance them. It was so good that we ordered another bottle and had it as a liquid, final dessert all by itself.

In this day and age of the dry-white-wine fetish, the self-styled Brahmins of taste have put us in a spurious dilemma. What wine can one serve with a sweet dessert? Even the dry-wine snob finds his gorge rising when he considers a bottle of Chablis with a *soufflé au Grand Marnier,* or a Brut Champagne with a mousse. A good meal, like an essay, should have a memorable ending. If it is to be a sweet one, there can be few better conclusions than a slightly chilled bottle of Sauternes.

A good base for the wandering wine-lover making a tour of the Sauternes region is the town of Bazas about twelve miles to the south. Here there is a comfortable, up-to-date hotel with a fine one-starred restaurant, the *Relais de Fompeyre.* The host, M. Mora, in spite of his Spanish name, sets an excellent table of regional *spécialités,* including a splendid *Lamproie à la Bordelaise,* and his own private *Purée de Palombe à la Bazadaise.* The hotel is impeccable, the food distinguished, and the cellar has a good cross-section of the region's wines, especially the much over-looked, often excellent, and usually inexpensive wines of Bourg on the north side of the Gironde opposite the Médoc. For the trencherman wishing to melt off a few of the calories he has picked up, the Relais de Fompeyre also has a tennis court and a pool, and even a largish garden if a bit of private jogging seems in order.

The address is: Relais de Fompeyre, Route de Mont-de-Marsan, Bazas, 33430 (Gironde). Telephone: Bazas (Gironde) 51.

Graves

To a teetotaler ruminating over a cup of water, the word Graves has a melancholy meaning. Not so for the wine lover. As he swirls his amber or ruby glass and thinks of Graves, a benign smile comes across his features, for to him the word has the happiest significance. It refers to an elixir, a wine coming from one of the largest and best vineyard areas of Bordeaux.

The region of Graves starts at the gates of Bordeaux and borders it on three sides—north, west, and south. The eastern edge of both Bordeaux and Graves is traced by the Garonne, a meandering stream that tumbles out of the Pyrenees, slows down as it passes Toulouse and Agen, and glides past the vineyards of Sauternes and Graves toward its juncture with the Dordogne and the Atlantic.

Graves is not enormous; it is a rather irregularly shaped rectangle about thirty miles long and six miles wide. Geographically Barsac and Sauternes are part of Graves, but their wines are quite different. Most white wines of Graves are far lighter and drier than the luscious dessert wines of Sauternes and Barsac. Consequently, wine maps show Sauternes-Barsac as an enclave in the southern part of Graves, not as part of the region itself.

The word Graves is related to the French *gravier*, meaning gravel, and to *grève*, the pebbly marl found on riverbanks. These

---

CLASSIFIED GROWTHS OF GRAVES (CHÂTEAUX)

Pessac:	Haut-Brion (since 1855)	red
	Pape Clément	red
Talence:	La Mission Haut-Brion	red
	La Tour Haut-Brion	red
	Laville Haut-Brion	white
Villenave d'Ornon:	Couhins	white
Léognan:	Haut-Bailly	red
	Carbonnieux	red & white
	Domaine de Chevalier	red & white
	Fieuzal	red
	Malartic-Lagravière	red & white
	Olivier	red & white
Martillac:	Smith-Haut-Lafitte	red
	Latour-Martillac	red & white
Cadaujac:	Bouscaut	red & white

terms are perfectly descriptive of the gravelly earth of the area, washed down by the Garonne's waters. To this pebbly soil the wine of Graves owes much of its character.

The region produces wines of nearly every type—red wines that come from communes just south and west of Bordeaux, medium-dry white wines that come from the same communes and from the center of Graves near the villages of Léognan and Labrède, and quite sweet, liqueurish white wines that come from around the town of Cérons, just north of Sauternes. (Cérons is in effect a district itself, but it is allowed to be called either Cérons or Graves.) Of the world's wine regions, few can match Graves' variety.

The red wines of Graves owe many of their qualities to the types of grapes used. In the best vineyards the varieties relied upon most heavily are the same ones used in the Médoc: Cabernet Sauvignon and Cabernet Franc, with admixtures of Merlot, Petit Verdot, and Malbec, the last two used sparingly. Consequently, the wines bear a considerable likeness to those of the Médoc, but they are fuller and burlier, or, as the Spanish say, more *macho*, or masculine.

Many of Bordeaux's best vineyards lie on the outskirts of the city, surrounded by suburban villas and apartment houses. As Bordeaux is the second largest city of France, the urban sprawl is considerable, with houses, shops, factories, and warehouses pouring out over the countryside and devouring field and vineyard. But the best vineyards are too valuable to be torn up, even by real-estate developers, so the visitor to Bordeaux is confronted with the anomalous sight of a row of buildings and shopwindows suddenly broken by acres of immaculately tended vines. It is a little like coming across a cattle ranch in Brooklyn.

Pessac and Talence, two of Bordeaux's greatest wine communes, are right on the edge of the city. Following the signs that point to Arcachon, a resort about forty miles to the southwest, one finds oneself, while apparently still in the city, at the gates of Château Haut-Brion. The view from the road is not extraordinary—a hundred acres of well-kept vines off to the right and the long sheds of *chais* where the wines are made and stored. But inside the property other sights unfold: a lovely sixteenth-century château surrounded by lawns and massive pines.

However picturesque Haut-Brion is, it is known primarily for its superlative wines. From the time of the earliest records, Haut-Brion has been a prominent name. The wine was a favorite of the Flemish in the fifteenth century and widely appreciated in England in the sixteenth and seventeenth centuries. Haut-Brion is ranked among the top four red-wine vineyards of Bordeaux according to the famed—or, some feel, notorious—Classification of 1855, which listed the greatest vineyards of the Médoc and Sauternes. In spite of the fact that Haut-Brion is a Graves and not grown in the Médoc at all, it was included in the listing. Even more extraordinary, of the sixty wines classified as *grands crus*, Haut-Brion was classified as one of the four *premiers grands crus* —at the very top of a list on which, geographically at least, it shouldn't even have been. Nevertheless, Haut-Brion is certainly among the top dozen or so red wines of France. It is also unique in that it is the only one of these paragons to be owned by an American, the well-known banker Clarence Dillon, father of Douglas Dillon, our former ambassador to France.

Among its distinguished owners was Talleyrand, Napoleon's Foreign Minister, and one of Europe's most far-seeing statesmen. "To keep one's head on one's shoulders" was no idle cliché during the time of the French Revolution. Talleyrand not only managed to do it, but almost inevitably came out on top. He was accused of betraying every king he ever served, except one— "the king of cheeses, Brie." This charge is a little unjust, as there was usually good reason for Talleyrand to withdraw before the fanatics followed their fantasies to bloodshed and disaster. However, the remark *is* just in stressing that Talleyrand was regarded as a leader of gourmets. Brillat-Savarin mentions him, and the stories told about his table are legendary.

When Talleyrand was sent as the representative of a defeated France to confront the victorious powers of England, Prussia, Austria, and Russia at the Congress of Vienna, he took with him Carême, France's finest chef, and asked the French government to provide him with free transportation for his wines—among them the splendid wines from the Château Haut-Brion, which he had owned a few years before.

At first, he was cold-shouldered by the victorious allies, but he soon turned the tables—literally. That is to say, he turned the conference table into the dining-room table. His soirées were so famous for their good food and drink and witty conversation that they became the social, and soon the political, center of the Congress. The rather boring morning conferences came to be mere preludes to the serious conversation at Monsieur de Talleyrand's evening gatherings. Needless to say, his wit and dexterity, aided by goodly doses of sublime wine and food, soon had the allies quarreling among themselves. The result was that Talleyrand, in spite of the embarrassing interruption of Napoleon's reappearance and subsequent defeat at Waterloo, walked away from the Congress of Vienna with more territory for France than she had had when the wars began. Where Napoleon and all his marshals failed, Talleyrand, with a strong assist from Carême and Haut-Brion, succeeded.

The name Haut-Brion is a curious one, and there is much theorizing as to its possible Irish origin. Perhaps there was a thirteenth-century Irish soldier named O'Bryan, who, when his battling days were over, settled down to another splendid Ibernian pursuit, a "cup o' the finest." Pepys, that famous and rather indiscreet diarist, mentions that on the tenth of April, 1663, he visited "the Royal Oak Tavern in Lombard Street . . . and here drank a sort of French wine called Ho Bryan that hath a good and most particular taste that I never met with." This is close to the Irish spelling, and though it is scarcely proof positive, it at least shows that Haut-Brion has been known and appreciated in the best circles for quite some time.

Haut-Brion is a superlative wine with the finesse of the finest Médocs, but with an underlying strength and savor that is astonishing. However, like any aristocrat, it does take its time to reveal itself. To drink a Château Haut-Brion that is less than ten years old is a pity. To open one that is less than five is, as Talleyrand observed over Napoleon's execution of the Duc d'Enghien, "worse than a crime, it is a blunder."

Haut-Brion produces a hundred *tonneaux*, or about ten thousand cases, of red wine during a good vintage year. It also produces about eight *tonneaux*—eight hundred cases—of a full-bodied, powerful, medium-dry white wine made from a combination of Sémillon and Sauvignon grapes. Though the white is perhaps not up to the quality of the red, it is interesting and, because of its scarce supply, in great demand as a curio.

The suburbs around Haut-Brion are spangled with châteaux

of renown. Pessac and Talence, though once different towns, are contiguous, and within their limits, cheek by jowl, are four more excellent vineyards: the châteaux La Mission Haut-Brion, Laville Haut-Brion, Latour Haut-Brion, and Pape Clément.

The wine of the Château La Mission Haut-Brion bears a strong resemblance to its illustrious neighbor and namesake, although it is somewhat lighter and quicker to mature. The vineyard produces about five thousand cases of red wine in a good average year. La Mission also produces fifteen *tonneaux* a year of excellent white wine, one of the finest of Graves, under the name of Château Laville Haut-Brion.

Before the French Revolution, the château was owned by a religious order called "The Preaching Fathers of the Mission," founded by Saint Vincent de Paul. The wine was a great favorite of the Duc de Richelieu, the eminent marshal, libertine, and gourmet who, when once told that God was against drink, pointed to his glass of Mission Haut-Brion and said, "If God had meant for us not to drink, then why did he make this wine so good?"

The Almighty seems to have had quite a lot to do with the château's past. In the *chai* is a statue of a mitered, bearded, wine-sozzled old man desperately clutching at a bunch of grapes. There is a legend that tells how Saint Vincent, the patron saint of *vignerons* and wine, was immediately whisked up to beyond the Pearly Gates after his death. He moped around with a rather blue look on his face for a few days and God, noticing it, asked him why he seemed so sad. Saint Vincent answered that he was unhappy not to have had a chance to say good-by to all his old friends, the *vignerons* of Burgundy, the Loire, Bordeaux, and so forth. God felt quite sorry for him, and so gave him special permission to go down and bid his friends adieu. When Saint Vincent did not return after a few weeks, God began worrying about him and sent a messenger to tell him that it was time to come back. Searching high and low, the emissary finally found Saint Vincent, filled with good humor and all-too-obviously plastered in the *chai* of the Mission Haut-Brion. The messenger told him that God thought it was time he returned to heaven, but Saint Vincent hiccuped and adamantly refused; he far preferred bibbing the excellent wine down below. When God heard this, He was furious, and saying "So be it!" changed Saint Vincent to stone. And there he is still, in the *chai* of La Mission Haut-Brion.

Under the same ownership is the adjacent vineyard of the Château Latour Haut-Brion, which produces fifteen hundred cases a year of wine that is quite similar to the reds of La Mission. The wines of all three Haut-Brion vineyards are classified as Grands Crus de Graves.

The last excellent vineyard in the neighborhood is Château Pape Clément, which produces an average of fifty *tonneaux* of *grand cru* red a year. It is one of the oldest vineyards in Graves, perhaps planted by Bertrand de Got, the thirteenth-century Archbishop of Bordeaux who was elected Pope Clement V in 1305, to everyone's great surprise, as he was neither a cardinal nor even an Italian. As mentioned in the chapter on the southernmost Rhônes, it was he who moved the Church from Rome to Avignon and possibly he who founded the vineyards at Châteauneuf-du-Pape.

Today, Clement V is not remembered as a pope of much stature, his memory being best preserved by the lovely vineyards he caused to be left behind. After his death, Château Pape Clément continued to be owned by the archbishops of Bordeaux until the French Revolution when the great Church-held vineyards were secularized. Today it is owned by Montagne and Company and is still one of the finest Graves, as befits its distinguished history.

All these vineyards are on the southwestern fringe of Bordeaux, none more than five miles from the center of the city. The inquisitive wine lover who visits them will probably want to end his tour with a bite to eat. Nothing could be easier. The five châteaux are a stone's throw from Route Nationale 650, the Arcachon road. A mile or so beyond Château Haut-Brion is one of Bordeaux's best and most pleasant hotel-restaurants, La Réserve. It is owned by Monsieur Flourens, who serves French food with special emphasis on the best Bordelais specialties, such as *lamproie bordelaise, coq sauté au vin de Graves*, and *steak en cocotte au fumet de poivre vert*. The wine list naturally has several examples of the finest local provender. As the setting is delightful and as the Bordelais appreciate it and the good food as much as anyone, it is wisest to phone ahead for a reservation. As it has comfortable bedrooms, it is also a good place to make one's base while exploring the vineyards around Bordeaux.

About five miles south of Bordeaux and within the limits of

the parish of Villenave d'Ornon lies the pretty Château Couhins. Like so many Graves vineyards, it produces both red and white wines—about twelve hundred cases a year of sound red, and about twice as much *grand cru* white.

Another excellent vineyard in the neighboring parish of Cadaujac is the Château Bouscaut. Producing about ten thousand cases of *grand cru* red, and five thousand cases of *grand cru* white, Bouscaut is owned by Monsieur Victor Place. The special qualities of the wines are due to the considerable amount of iron in the soil. The red wines are unique in Graves in that the grapes used are forty percent of Merlot, fifteen percent of Cabernet Franc, fifteen percent of Petit Verdot, fifteen percent of Malbec, and fifteen percent of Cabernet-Malbec, a hybrid developed by the proprietor.

Just to the north of Villenave and Cadaujac is Léognan, one of the more famous communes in Graves. Of the fourteen *grands crus* growths of Graves, six lie within its borders.

One of them is Château Carbonnieux, a splendid vineyard that produces about six thousand cases of *grand cru* red, and eight thousand cases of *grand cru* white during a good average year. The latter is especially appreciated as one of the finest examples of white Graves.

The foundations of the château date back to the fourteenth century, but the bulk of the present building was erected in the sixteenth century as a hunting lodge for the Duc d'Épernon, one of the favorite *mignons* of the bizarre king Henry III. Before the French Revolution it was the property of the Abbey of Sainte-Croix and worked by the Benedictines. There is a story that in the eighteenth century Barbary corsairs captured a French ship on which they found an attractive young Bordelaise. She was given as a present to the Sultan of Constantinople, who immediately installed her as the favorite of his harem. She rather enjoyed the whole affair, only missing the good wine of Bordeaux, which was forbidden under Moslem law as a dangerous drug. The Sultan was hopelessly smitten with her, and it disturbed him greatly to see her pining away. He contacted the Benedictines in Constantinople and asked if they had any wine. They offered the excellent white made by their brothers of Carbonnieux. The Sultan's Bordelaise was delighted, and she recovered so noticeably that the

Sultan decided to try some himself. He did and loved it. Not wanting to scandalize his subjects with his errant ways, he had subsequent shipments sent in, not as wine, but as "mineral water of Chateau Carbonnieux." What his servants thought of the mineral water's pale golden hue, the story fails to relate.

Another well-known vineyard of Léognan is Château Haut-Bailly, a newcomer by Bordeaux's standards. Planted only about a century ago, it was heavily capitalized during the last part of the nineteenth century—special drainage was built, only the best vines were planted—in short, it was a model vineyard. All the efforts have been worthwhile. Haut-Bailly produces a splendid if slowly maturing red wine but, alas, in very small quantities. Only about three thousand cases of the wine are forthcoming in a good average year. It is deservedly classified as a Grand Cru de Graves.

Nearby is the Domaine de Chevalier, one of the few Bordeaux vineyards not preceded by the word "château." It is considered one of the finest Graves, its excellent red being surpassed only by its superlative white. Both are produced in lamentably small quantities, however—three thousand cases of red and only four hundred of white.

There is also an excellent château in Léognan, the popular Château Olivier, which makes about two thousand cases of good red and ten thousand cases of equally fine dry white per year.

Two more classified growths in Léognan are the Château Malartic-Lagravière, which produces about twenty-five hundred cases of equally good red and white wines, and the Château Fieuzal, once the property of the La Rochefoucauld family, which produces about three thousand cases of very good classified red wine and a much smaller amount of pleasant but unclassified dry white wine.

Just south of Léognan, about seven miles from the center of Bordeaux, is the pretty Château Latour-Martillac, named after the tower in the middle of its court. The tower, said to date from the twelfth century, was built as an outlying defense for the Montesquieu family's Château de la Brède, two and a half miles to the southwest. The vineyards of Latour-Martillac produce about five thousand cases a year of very good red, and fifteen hundred of equally fine white. The wine is not always called Latour-

Martillac, but sometimes Château Kressmann-Latour after its owner, Monsieur Jean Kressmann.

These vineyards complete the list of classified growths of Graves. All of them fall in a belt that girds Bordeaux to the south and southwest—the nearest in the suburbs of Bordeaux itself, and the farthest only eight miles away. This is not only the region of the finest white Graves, but also the main region for all the reds. Very few vineyards south of Martillac produce red wines, and none that come up to the standard of those to the north of it.

Near the village of Labrède is a ravishing thirteenth-century château that seems to pop straight out of a storybook—with donjons, keeps, and conic towers, all shimmering in the wind-rippled moat that surrounds them. Anyone in the neighborhood should certainly stop by to look at it. It is quite literally as pretty as a picture. Here Charles de Secondat, Baron de la Brède et de Montesquieu, satirist, historian, and political theorist, was born in 1689. His major work, *L'Esprit des Lois*, a masterpiece discussing the philosophy and functioning of an ideal civilization and government, suggested several new ideas that profoundly influenced the subsequent forms of government in the west. Our own Founding Fathers were all schooled on Montesquieu's theories, and his doctrine of the necessity of a separation and balance between the executive, judicial, and legislative powers of government is graven into our Constitution.

Besides being a writer and philosopher, Montesquieu was an experienced *vigneron*. At La Brède he supervised some 125 acres of vineyards, and made a white wine which, though it didn't "come forth abundantly, what there was was good." He died at La Brède in 1755, but the château is still owned by one of his descendants, the Comtesse de Chabannes, and it still makes a good *vin blanc de Graves*.

The bulk of Graves stretches out southward from Labrède, and in this region much of the white wine for which Graves is so famous is made. Ask any Frenchman what is meant by Graves, and he will answer, "A medium-dry, full white wine," never thinking of the excellent but rare reds that come from the north. The reason for this is quite simple. The red wines generally are called by the name of their châteaux, rather than Graves.

Seven hundred thousand cases of Graves Supérieur, by definition white wines, are produced yearly, and another two hundred thousand cases of sweet dessert wine of Cérons. Red-wine production is under a fifth as much. The Graves Sec Supérieur is not a great wine but a very pleasant one. It is almost an all-purpose wine, as it goes well with ham and pork, creamed fowl and veal, fish and crustaceans.

Cérons is an enclave in Graves just to the north of Sauternes-Barsac. The white wines produced there range from the honeyed, liqueur wines similar to those of Sauternes, to rather cloying and bodiless wines that I do not find particularly commendable.

A red Graves makes a good companion for lamb and beef, game and roast fowl.

Médoc

To state it boldly, the Haut-Médoc is one of the two greatest red-wine producing regions in the world. If one considers quantity as well as quality, it is without peer. Only the Côte de Nuits in Burgundy has a number of vineyards whose reputation matches those of the Haut-Médoc, but these generally are thimblefuls of land compared to the Haut-Médoc's rolling acres.

The Médoc is a dagger-shaped piece of land jutting out into the water. The pommel starts just north of Bordeaux, and the blade runs fifty miles in a northwesterly direction until it reaches a tiny peninsula called the Pointe-de-Grave opposite the old Huguenot center of Royan. The countryside is flat—meadows and vineyards interspersed with châteaux and copses of trees. To the west the long gray combers of the Atlantic break on miles of sand dunes. To the east the broad estuary of the Gironde, often shrouded in fog, serves as a highway for shipment on its way to Bordeaux. Just across the mouth of the Gironde lie the famed oyster beds of Marennes.

In Roman times the Médoc was part of the province of Aquitania. *Aqua* being the Latin word for water, Aquitania thus meant "the land of the waters" because of the multitude of streams and rivers passing through it and the Atlantic, which made up its western boundary. The Médoc probably owes its name to the Latin phrase describing its geographical situation—*in medio aquae* —in the middle of water. *Medio aquae* changed to *mediac*, and from there it was a short step to Médoc.

Although all this may be grist for the philologists' mill, the wine lover really doesn't much care. For him what matters is not the origin of the Médoc, but what it offers which makes any true oenophile's heart—or, more accurately, his palate—thrill with anticipation. For the best red wines of the Médoc, if properly matured, are surely among the most elegant, subtle, and sophisticated to be found anywhere.

The vineyard country of the Médoc is a strip rarely more than eight miles wide running up the bank of the Gironde. The soil is mixed. Down by the riverbank it is an alluvial mud called *palus*, alternating with a clay known as *terreforte*, and though vines can be grown in it, the wine produced is not the best. A little higher up on the escarpment overlooking the river, however, the soil changes in quality. The land here is crisscrossed with creeks, called *jalles*, in the Médoc. It is on the patches of gravel between the *jalles* that the best vineyards are planted.

Almost all of the great vineyards lie in a belt between half a mile and three miles from the riverbank: in other words, far enough away so that the soil is not alluvial mud, yet near enough so that the river mist can mitigate the harshest rays of the sun, and the moisture in the atmosphere can level the extremes of temperature.

But the greatest contributors to the character of Médoc wines are the grape types from which they are made. First and most important is the Cabernet Sauvignon, already cited several times as one of the world's finest wine grapes. Although the wine it yields is astringent when young, it mellows with age into one of great elegance and finesse, yet with a quality that the French call *sève*—nearly untranslatable into English, our closest words to it being something like "vigor," or better, the slang word "guts." The end result is like an impeccable gentleman of the old school —gracious, sophisticated, witty and elegant, yet with a core of will that peeps out from behind the polished delicacy. All the best vineyards of the Médoc use a very high proportion of Cabernet Sauvignon, up to ninety percent in the case of Mouton-Rothschild.

RESTAURANT

Lesparre-Médoc (Gironde)   La Mare aux Grenouilles (tel. 3.46)

Another quite widely used grape is the Cabernet Franc. This type is in many ways similar to the Cabernet Sauvignon, except that it lacks a little of its *sève*, making up for this by having a fuller bouquet and being softer and rounder, especially when young. It is used in blending to cut some of the Cabernet Sauvignon's early harshness, and to make the wine less reserved and more generous.

A third varietal of growing popularity throughout the Bordelais is the Merlot. In recent years it has been adopted by a large number of small growers and châteaux because present conditions of trade and modern drinking habits demand a wine that matures quickly or is pleasant and soft to drink when young. Many of the growers of the Médoc, noticing the demand for such wines from Pomerol and Saint-Émilion, decided to try the grape type that thrives there—the Merlot. Unfortunately, although the grape produces an elegant and pleasant wine in Dordogne, the wine it produces in the Médoc seems to lack finesse. It makes a full and jolly enough wine—a good-hearted bourgeois—but it has neither the aristocratic asperity of a young Cabernet Sauvignon nor the elegance of a mature one.

A few years ago the Comité National des Appellations d'Origine in Bordeaux sent a warning to the growers of the Médoc that they might lose their rights to the Appellation Contrôlée unless they planted approximately seventy percent of Cabernet. This rather conditional advice caused quite a stir. Small growers felt that the only way they could keep up with market conditions was to cater to the taste of the times and produce softer, suppler, more quickly maturing wines. The Comité, however, felt that the particular character of the Médoc's wine must be protected and preserved. In other words, it is better to produce a first-class Médoc than a second-class Saint-Émilion type, no matter how commercially attractive the latter may be. It further pointed out that

---

DAY 14   Médoc
Itinerary p. 26

Michelin Regional Map 71
Michelin Guide Vert *Côte de l'Atlantique*

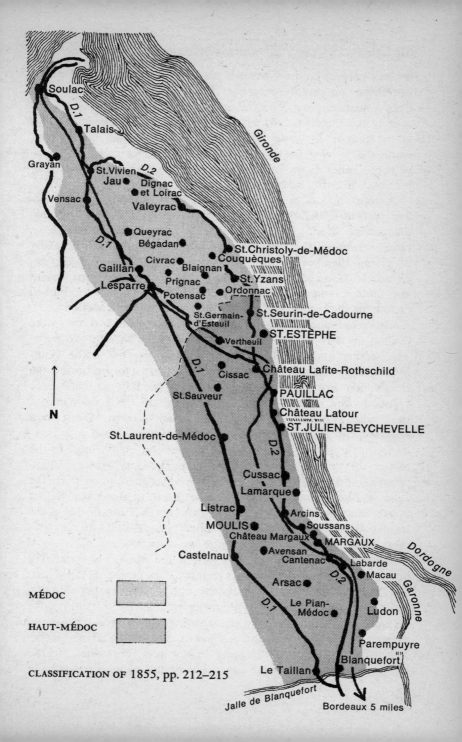

Soulac

D.1

Talais

Grayan

St.Vivien
Jau

Vensac

Dignac
et Loirac

Valeyrac

D.1

Queyrac
Bégadan

Civrac

Blaignan

St.Christoly-de-Médoc

Couquèques

Gaillan

Prignac

Lesparre

Potensac

St.Yzans

Ordonnac

St.Germain-
d'Esteuil

St.Seurin-de-Cadourne

Vertheuil

ST.ESTÈPHE

D.1

Cissac

Château Lafite-Rothschild

St.Sauveur

PAUILLAC

Château Latour

ST.JULIEN-BEYCHEVELLE

St.Laurent-de-Médoc

D.2

N

Cussac

Lamarque

Listrac

Arcins

MOULIS

Soussans

Château Margaux

MARGAUX

Castelnau

Avensan
Cantenac

Labarde

Macau

Arsac

D.2

Le Pian-
Médoc

Ludon

D.1

Parempuyre

Blanquefort

MÉDOC

HAUT-MÉDOC

Le Taillan

CLASSIFICATION OF 1855, pp. 212–215

Jalle de Blanquefort

Bordeaux 5 miles

Gironde

Dordogne

Garonne

D.2

seventy percent of the vineyards planted with Cabernet vines does not mean that seventy percent of the resultant wine will be made from Cabernet juice. The Cabernet is a shy bearer: seventy percent planted means only about sixty percent of the juice. This allows the small vintner plenty of leeway to soften his mixture, while still leaving the character of Médoc wines intact.

Three other types of grape used, though in very small proportions, are the Petit Verdot, the Malbec, and the Carmenère.

A good ratio of grapes for a fine Médoc would be about sixty-five percent Cabernet Sauvignon, fifteen percent Cabernet Franc, ten percent Merlot, and ten percent a mixture of the last three. Great vineyards that can impress on the consumer the necessity of giving their wines time to mature will use more Cabernet, especially Cabernet Sauvignon, as they shoot for more distant and more Olympian heights. Lesser growths, likely to be bibbed in four or five years, will use correspondingly more Merlot.

The geographical limits of the Médoc as a vineyard area were defined in 1911. Later on the region was divided into two parts. The section upriver (hence to the south) was called the Haut-Médoc, and that toward the Gironde's mouth (to the north) the Bas-Médoc. For a considerable time the growers in the Bas-Médoc brooded over what they considered a slur to the good name of their wine. For though Bas-Médoc meant Lower Médoc in a geographical sense, winegrowers are extremely sensitive to anything that might cast the remotest shadow on their wines. In the forties they managed to institute a change—or, as they felt, a reform—and so now there is the Haut-Médoc running from the Jalle de Blanquefort, about three miles north of Bordeaux, to just above Saint-Estèphe, thirty miles to the north. Beyond this is the former Bas-Médoc, now called simply the Médoc, running another twenty miles up the Atlantic coast to Soulac.

Despite the legal terminology, when the Médoc is spoken of in Bordeaux, it almost always refers to both the Haut-Médoc and the legal Médoc. In fact, the old dichotomy between the Haut-Médoc and the Bas-Médoc was not such an inaccurate one in the qualitative sense. By coincidence, all the great châteaux, as well as all the most famous towns, are in the Haut-Médoc. This is not to say that the other Médoc produces wines of little merit. It produces a good deal of very fine wine, especially in the communes on its southern border. Nevertheless, none can come close to matching the great Lafite, Margaux, Latour, and Mouton-Rothschild that lie on the other side of the line.

There are thus two classifications of regional wines: Médoc and Haut-Médoc, but ranked above these come six town wines of the Haut-Médoc: Saint-Estèphe, Pauillac, Saint-Julien, Moulis, Listrac, and Margaux. The viticultural region of each of these encompasses the name commune at its center and some of the better vineyards of the communes that surround it. If properly made, each wine is an archetype of the wines of the great individual vineyards of the commune. Saint-Estèphe is big, full, long-lived, the he-man of clarets; Pauillac is equally long-lived but more subtle and elegant; Saint-Julien is a little softer with a charming bouquet; Moulis and Listrac are agreeable but not the grandest of the Médocs; Margaux is soft, silky, subtle, with a flowery bouquet, the most feminine of the Haut-Médoc's wines.

Within these communes are about five hundred châteaux or *soi-disant* châteaux. Some, such as the magnificent Château Margaux, have both a superlative vineyard and a splendid château with classic façade; others may be little more than a farmhouse surrounded by vines. However, even the farmhouses are likely to have architectural charm. Southwestern France has not suffered the surge of population of most places, and there haven't been vast development and building. The houses are leftovers of a more leisurely and spacious time, and they show it. Many were built in the heyday of Bordeaux—during the seventeenth, eighteenth, and early nineteenth centuries—and have a purity of form that would shame more pretentious buildings elsewhere. Château or farm, they have been minutely classified, like so much else in France.

There are *crus paysans, crus artisans, crus bourgeois,* and *crus bourgeois supérieurs* for the non-noble growths. In between, corresponding to the semi-noble title of baronet, are the *crus exceptionnels.* Then five classified *grands crus* make up the Médoc's "house of lords": the fifth the barons, the fourth the viscounts, the third the earls, the second the marquesses, and the first the dukes.

The classification of the top sixty vineyards into five *grands crus* is based on the famous Classification of the Gironde of 1855, and this in turn was based on the prices the wines from these vineyards commanded during the first half of the nineteenth century and on the classifications of 1641, 1647, 1698, and 1767. The similarity between these classifications is striking, due, in part, to the fact that the makers of each new list took the previous one into account. But also the superiority of the soil tended to produce consistently excellent wines despite changes of ownership. Be that as it may, the Classification has been under steady attack for nearly a century. For, although the soil and site of the vineyards may be the basis for their greatness, hard work and premium vines can improve them, just as sloppiness, laziness, not replacing vines, skimping on machinery, cooperage, and fertilizer, failing to use enough insecticides or keep up a high standard of vinification—all can cause a vineyard of hallowed reputation to sink.

MÉDOC   CLASSIFICATION OF 1855

Premiers Grands Crus Classés:

Château Lafite-Rothschild	Pauillac
Château Margaux	Margaux
Château Latour	Pauillac
Château Mouton-Rothschild	Pauillac

Deuxièmes Grands Crus Classés:

Château Rausan-Ségla	Margaux
Château Rauzan-Gassies	Margaux
Château Léoville-Las Cases	Saint-Julien
Château Léoville-Poyferré	Saint-Julien
Château Léoville-Barton	Saint-Julien
Château Durfort-Vivens	Margaux
Château Gruaud-Larose	Saint-Julien
Château Lascombes	Margaux
Château Brane-Cantenac	Cantenac-Margaux
Château Pichon-Longueville-Baron	Pauillac
Château Pichon-Longueville-Lalande	Pauillac
Château Ducru-Beaucaillou	Saint-Julien
Château Cos-d'Estournel	Saint-Estèphe
Château Montrose	Saint-Estèphe

Nearly every wine lover feels that several vineyards were misplaced in the Classification of 1855, but few can agree as to which ones. Most vineyard owners, naturally enough, feel their vineyards are underrated, if anything, and certainly will not allow them to be ranked lower on the list. Therefore, the Classification stays frozen. Nobody seems to like it, but no agreement can be reached.

A few generalities may be made about it. The first great growths

---

Troisièmes Grands Crus Classés:

Château Kirwan	Cantenac-Margaux
Château d'Issan	Cantenac-Margaux
Château Lagrange	Saint-Julien
Château Langoa	Saint-Julien
Château Giscours	Labarde
Château Malescot-Saint-Exupéry	Margaux
Château Cantenac-Brown	Cantenac-Margaux
Château Boyd-Cantenac	Margaux
Château Palmer	Cantenac-Margaux
Château La Lagune	Ludon
Château Desmirail	Margaux
Château Calon-Ségur	Saint-Estèphe
Château Ferrière	Margaux
Château Marquis d'Alesme-Becker	Margaux

Quatrièmes Grands Crus Classés:

Château Saint-Pierre Sevaistre	Saint-Julien
Château Saint-Pierre-Bontemps	Saint-Julien
Château Talbot	Saint-Julien
Château Branaire-Ducru	Saint-Julien
Château Duhart-Milon	Pauillac
Château Pouget	Cantenac-Margaux
Château La Tour-Carnet	Saint-Laurent
Château Lafon-Rochet	Saint-Estèphe
Château Beychevelle	Saint-Julien
Château La Prieuré	Cantenac-Margaux
Château Marquis-de-Terme	Margaux

—the châteaux Lafite, Margaux, and Latour (and Château Haut-Brion, the Graves of such astonishing excellence that a place was made for it at the head of the Médoc list)—are still regarded as first-class. However, as everyone agreed, Château Mouton-Rothschild, declared a second growth in 1855, merited a position in the first echelon and it recently has been put there. In addition, such third, fourth, and fifth growths as Calon-Ségur, Palmer, Beychevelle, Talbot, Marquis-de-Terme, Mouton-Baron-Philippe, Lynch-Bages, Pontet-Canet, and Cantemerle should, in this writer's opinion, all be raised. They certainly warrant it in terms of the excellence they achieve and the price they command.

Whatever the shortcomings of the 1855 Classification, it is the keystone of the Médoc hierarchy, so it begins on p. 212.

The better-known of the *grands crus* châteaux will be discussed in detail in the following sections.

In my opinion the wines of Saint-Estèphe are ideally suited for game and beef, those of Pauillac for beef and lamb, those of

---

Cinquièmes Grands Crus Classés:

Château Pontet-Canet	Pauillac
Château Batailley	Pauillac
Château Haut-Batailley	Pauillac
Château Grand-Puy-Lacoste	Pauillac
Château Grand-Puy-Ducasse	Pauillac
Château Lynch-Bages	Pauillac
Château Lynch-Moussas	Pauillac
Château Dauzac	Labarde
Château Mouton Baron Philippe	Pauillac
Château Le Tertre	Arsac
Château Haut-Bages-Libéral	Pauillac
Château Pédesclaux	Pauillac
Château Belgrave	Saint-Laurent
Château Camensac	Saint-Laurent
Château Cos-Labory	Saint-Estèphe
Château Clerc-Milon-Mondon	Pauillac
Château Croizet-Bages	Pauillac
Château Cantemerle	Macau

Saint-Julien, Beychevelle, Moulis, Listrac, Cussac, and Saint-Laurent for beef, lamb, and roast fowl, and those of Margaux, Cantenac, Labarde, Macau, Ludon, and Arsac for roast beef, lamb, and roast fowl.

As for vintages to drink, the great growths of the Médoc take their time to develop and then last phenomenally long. For example, 1928 was a very hard year and only became ready in the late 1960s; it is splendid. 1961 and 1966 are superb years, some of the best of the century, but these top clarets should be left until the late 1970s to be drunk in their prime. 1970, '71, '72, '73, and '75 are all years to look forward to.

According to Brillat-Savarin, the destiny of nations depends on the manner in which they nourish themselves. Thus the sage of Belley brought cuisine into the realm of realpolitik a century and a half ago, and it is a provocative idea. Rare meat traditionally makes one combative; fish, brainy; and oysters, virile. What effects fowl and cheese have, or more importantly at this stage of our national existence, rice and soy beans, should provide think tanks such as the Rand Corporation with literally abundant food for thought.

The Flower Children maintain that alcohol stimulates outward activity, while their own more esoteric concoctions lead to a state of inner illumination. Although this may be debatable, no one would deny that the American social ethic is highly competitive and active. As rare meat and alcoholic beverages play an important part in our national nutrition, Brillat-Savarin's dictum would seem to have more than a grain of truth in it.

From the gourmet's point of view, however, the problem is hardly so philosophical. Which red meat with what alcoholic beverage is a question of personal taste, not national destiny. Beef is far and away the most popular of our rare meats, followed, if one includes "pink," by lamb. What goes best with them? It would be difficult to suggest more ideal beverages than the splendid red wines of the Médoc.

The Médoc, bordered on one side by the Atlantic and on the

other by the estuary of the Gironde, has its base line marked by the bustling port of Bordeaux. This extraordinary strip of land has had its reputation for producing fine red wines since the early Middle Ages. The famous—or infamous, depending on one's point of view—Classification of 1855, summarized in the preceding section, listed sixty-one of the entire region's finest châteaux, categorized into five great growths. It is in the Haut-Médoc—the southern half of the Médoc over all—that all these classified *grand crus* lie. This section and the one following discuss in turn a few of the more famous *grands crus*, first in the southern and then the northern halves of the Haut-Médoc.

For the adventurous wine lover wishing to explore the Médoc, Bordeaux itself is certainly the best base. In such excellent hotels as the Réserve and the Royal Gascogne, and such good restaurants as the Château Trompette and the Dubern, the sybarite may cosset his body and digestion to his heart's content. He should take advantage of the city, for although the Médoc is a viniferous paradise, it is a gastronomic Sahara—unless of course one has the good fortune to be invited to one of the great châteaux. But though the Médoc may not have many great public eateries, being right on Bordeaux's doorstep, one will nevertheless find some of the best provender in southwestern France: the oysters of Marennes, the eels of the Gironde, the *agneau pré-salé*. There is little danger of dying of starvation.

Taking Route Départementale D 1 out of Bordeaux in a north-westerly direction, one finds D 2E branching off to the right about five miles outside of town. This is the Route du Médoc. For forty miles it runs northward, threading its way like a string through pearls between some of the most noble vineyards in winedom.

The *grands crus* of the Haut-Médoc are geographically divided into two main groups. Southernmost is the one around the commune of Margaux, which includes such townships as Ludon, Macau, Labarde, Arsac, and Cantenac. There are twenty-three *grands crus* in this region, headed by the magnificent Château Margaux. These wines, the subject of this section, are famed for their delicacy, finesse, and bouquet.

For a dozen miles north of Margaux the soil is mainly alluvial loam, not the best for vines. Here there are no *grands crus* vineyards as the road winds through the villages of Arcins and Cussac.

But after Cussac it crosses a creek called the Chenal du Nord.
Once again the soil is crisscrossed by veins of gravel—good
vineyard country—and for fifteen miles the region on both sides
of the road is spangled with a galaxy of unsurpassable vineyards.
All but three fall in three communes lying cheek by jowl: Saint-
Julien-Beychevelle, Pauillac, and Saint-Estèphe. Within their boundaries are such outstanding growths as the châteaux Beychevelle,
Gruard-Larose, the three Léovilles, Talbot, the two Pichon-Lon-
guevilles, Calon-Ségur, and the Cos-d'Estournel. And leading
these noble wines are the peerless Lafite, Latour, and Mouton-
Rothschild.

Viniculturally, the Haut-Médoc begins about five miles north
of the Bordeaux city limits at a creek called the Jalle de Blanquefort, the border between the Médoc and Graves. First are a number of good little châteaux, some producing both red and white
wines—not *grands crus*, but the next best thing, *crus bourgeois
supérieurs*. In good years, these vineyards produce some very
agreeable wines, ones moreover that are quite moderately priced.
Among them are the Château Sénéjac, the Château de Parempuyre, and the fairy-tale Château d'Agassac; and farther north,
the Château Siran in Labarde, and a *cru exceptionnel*, the Château Angludet in Cantenac. Many feel that when a new classification of the Gironde can be arranged, these châteaux should be
included among the *grands crus*.

The wines of the southern Médoc, up as far as the town of
Macau twelve miles north of the Jalle de Blanquefort, have overtones of the nearby wines of Graves. That is to say they are prone
to be a little heavier and somewhat less distinct than the wines
that come from farther north. The difference, however, is marginal.

The southernmost commune of the Médoc that has a great
growth is Ludon, seven miles south of Margaux. It contains only
one, a third *cru classé* named Château La Lagune. The building
of the château itself is beautifully yet simply proportioned, and
is said to be the work of Victor Louis, the great eighteenth-
century architect who designed many of the most impressive
buildings of Bordeaux. It is surrounded by 125 acres of vineyards
planted primarily with Cabernet Sauvignon, followed by Merlot,
Cabernet Franc, and Petit Verdot. The wine is strong, solid, slow
to mature, soft, and scented. It seems to strike the mean between

a good Graves and a good Médoc. The château welcomes visitors. As it is only about ten miles outside of Bordeaux, even the most hurried traveler will find it easy to make the trip. Architecturally or viniferously, he won't regret it.

Directly to the north of Ludon is the village of Macau, famous for its artichokes and even more for an excellent vineyard, Château Cantemerle, one of the largest in the Margaux region. Cantemerle means the song of the blackbird, and the present building takes its name from a long-demolished fortress that served as a gigantic blackbird house in its post-military days. The wines of Cantemerle carry more than a hint of Graves. They are soft, solid, and round. Cantemerle was declared a fifth great growth in the Classification of 1855, but there is almost universal agreement that it should now be pegged higher.

The commune of Labarde has two great growths: Château Giscours, a third *cru,* and Château Dauzac, a fifth *cru.* Here the last traces of Graves disappear, and the wines take on the delicate, elegant characteristics of Margaux. Château Giscours is the smaller of the two. Until recently its reputation had slipped below its place in the 1855 list. However, since World War II there has been a concerted effort to improve and bring up to date all the aspects of vine growing and wine making. Because of this, Giscours is once again firmly in its niche as one of the better *grands crus.* Château Dauzac is right off the Macau-Labarde road. It produces about five thousand cases a year of good fifth growth, Margaux-type wine. A fifth growth, incidentally, is no insult. Only about ten percent of the Haut-Médoc's wines are listed in the Classification of 1855. To be among them is a very great honor.

About five miles inland from Macau and Labarde is the village of Arsac. In it is a fifth growth called Château Le Tertre. It is quite a large vineyard producing about ten thousand cases of delicate, light, and finely perfumed wine in an average year. Its bouquet is an intimation of that of the wines of Margaux and Cantenac.

Cantenac is one of the two great communes of the Margaux area, the other being Margaux itself. They are, in fact, inextricably intertwined, as Cantenac surrounds Margaux on two sides. The whole area is often referred to as Margaux-Cantenac. The wines are round, delicate, feminine, and velvety, with a distinctive bouquet that reaches its apotheosis in the wine of Château Margaux. They are thus ideal companions for lamb. Of the eighteen *grands crus* in the two communes, eight are more or less in Cantenac, and ten in Margaux.

Cantenac has one second growth, five third growths, and two fourth growths.

The second growth is Château Brane-Cantenac, named after a famous figure of nineteenth-century French viticulture, the Baron de Brane. Known as the Napoleon of Vines, he developed the vineyards of Mouton-Rothschild, which he then sold to concentrate on his vineyard in Cantenac. Today it produces about ten thousand cases of fine wine a year. Though perhaps not up to the reputation it had in the days of the Baron de Brane, the wine is long-lived and very agreeable.

Of the third growths, the palm, appropriately enough, should go to Château Palmer. It is one of the finest Margaux-Cantenac vineyards, and its reputation ranks it just under the Château Margaux itself. The vineyard is not only good, but generous, producing about ten thousand cases in an average year. The taste of the wine is archetypal of what a Margaux-Cantenac should be —soft, feminine, with great finesse and the astonishing bouquet that is the hallmark of all great wines of the region. Château Palmer would certainly be raised one rank higher if the Classification of 1855 were brought up to date. The name comes from one of Wellington's generals who entered Bordeaux with the invading English army in 1814. He liked it so much that he decided to stay, immortalizing his name by buying this splendid vineyard. Today it is owned by a consortium of British, French, and Dutch proprietors, and is easily recognized from the road by the huge banners of the three countries flapping from the château's rooftop.

A stone's throw from Château Palmer is another highly regarded third growth of Cantenac, the Château d'Issan, administered by Monsieur Emmanuel Cruse of the great Bordeaux shipping family. Though production is small, the quality of the wine more than makes up for it. Parts of the château date back five hundred years to the time of the English occupation. On the gate is written the motto: *Regum mensis arisque Deorum*—"For the tables of kings and the altars of the Gods"—a device that is repeated on Château d'Issan's labels.

Other nearby vineyards of considerable repute include the châteaux Boyd-Cantenac, Kirwan, Pouget, the Tudor-style Château Cantenac-Brown, and the Château Prieuré-Lichine. The last takes its name from the Benedictines, those renowned creators of other stimulating potables, who owned the property before the Revolution. *Prieuré* is the French for priory. All five vineyards produce very agreeable wines.

The word Margaux causes considerable confusion among neophyte wine lovers, as it stands for three things. One is an Appellation Contrôlée that covers the best parts of five communes—Margaux, Cantenac, Labarde, Soussans, and Arsac. Another is the name of the village at the center of this region that has no fewer than ten *grands crus classés*. The third is the name of the château that makes one of the finest red wines in the world.

The vineyard of Château Margaux was planted in the eighteenth century by a certain Monsieur de Fumel, military commander of Bordeaux under Louis XV. Its great merit was immediately apparent, so much so that by the middle of the nineteenth century it was awarded the supreme accolade of *premier grand cru,* an honor shared with only three other red wines of Bordeaux. After World War I its reputation fell off somewhat, but in the middle of the thirties it began to be acquired by a well-known Bordelais of wine affairs, Monsieur Ginestet. By the end of World War II he had full ownership of it, and he started lavishing on it the care and attention such a splendid vineyard deserves. It is now once again the *ne plus ultra* of red wines.

It is, of course, impossible to describe in words a great sensory experience, and the taste of a well-matured great vintage of Château Margaux is exactly that. Suffice it to say that it is velvety, elegant, fine, and with a powerful, almost perfumed bouquet that is unique. Opening a bottle will be an expensive but worthwhile affair.

There is also a white wine produced at Château Margaux called Pavillon Blanc, but it is not in the same category as the great red.

The château itself is a huge and impressive pile built at the beginning of the nineteenth century by the Marquis Douat de La Colonilla. It is vaguely in the Palladian style, with a theatrical grand staircase leading up to an Ionic portico. The present edifice is said to be built on the foundations of what was once one of the most powerful fortresses of Guyenne, property of King Edward III of England.

After Château Margaux come the four second growths of Margaux: Rausan-Ségla, Rauzan-Gassies, Durfort-Vivens, and Lascombes. Rausan-Ségla and Rauzan-Gassies were once part of the same vineyard, owned by a certain Pierre des Mesures de Rausan in the seventeenth century. Why one château chose a z instead of an s to spell the gentleman's name, I know not. It is one of those common eccentricities that outrage the neat and consistent. And in fact it mirrors the wine world. Every vineyard—no matter how similar in soil, grapes, and care—seems to have some little difference that sets it apart from its neighbors.

Rausan-Ségla is a fine old manor with a little over a hundred acres of vines. The vineyard is of the highest quality, second only to Château Margaux in the Margaux region. It was placed just below Mouton-Rothschild in the Classification of 1855, and although some might quarrel with this position today, it isn't far off the mark.

The neighboring Rauzan-Gassies has a rather less prepossessing building than that of Rausan-Ségla, but its vineyard is quite splendid. Production is about forty-five hundred cases per year, and the wine is also one of highest quality. Both Rausan and Rauzan are names to be watched for by the questing wine lover.

The last two second growths of Margaux are the châteaux Lascombes and Durfort-Vivens, both rather small, but both very good. Lascombes was acquired by a syndicate of American businessmen, and it is widely known and distributed in the United States. The Château Durfort-Vivens is owned by Monsieur Lucien Lurton, also owner of the nearby excellent Château Brane-Cantenac. It is a small vineyard, but a good one.

There are four third growths in the commune of Margaux, but only Château Malescot-Saint-Exupéry produces wine in quantity. The other three—Desmirail, Ferrière, and Marquis-d'Alesme-Becker—make under three thousand cases per year each, and so are seldom seen on the world market. Malescot-Saint-Exupéry may seem an unpronounceable and unrememberable name to the English speaking, but a good mnemonic is to think of Antoine de Saint-Exupéry, the French novelist, poet, and aviator who lost his life in the last war. The château was once the property of his family. It makes a lovely, fine wine, with the characteristic bouquet of all Margaux wines.

The Château Marquis-de-Terme is the only fourth growth in the commune of Margaux, and it should, in my opinion, be placed at least one rank higher. It is one of the finest, lightest, and most elegant of all the Margaux. About seventy-five hundred cases are produced during an average vintage year.

With the village of Margaux end the *grands crus* of southern Haut-Médoc, the great Margaux-Cantenac complex of vineyards. Their wines are generally described as subtle, fine, silky, and highly perfumed—all feminine attributes. The second great complex begins twelve miles to the north and encompasses over thirty superb growths of a quite different character than those of Margaux. It includes most notably the Haut-Médoc communes of Saint-Julien, Pauillac, and Saint-Estèphe, three towns lying side by side on the banks of the Gironde, twenty-five miles downriver from Bordeaux. The wines from these villages are virile and have great body and *sève,* the French expression that this time we might translate for a simile's sake as "muscle."

Orientals believe that the universe is a balance of the elements of yin and yang: one the eternal feminine, soft, pliable, and flexible; the other the essential masculine, elegant almost to the point of arrogance, assertive, definite, and strong. Neither can conquer, though each may try. Ideally, they should complement each other. The wines of the Haut-Médoc might be considered an ideal example of this male-female equilibrium. Like a perfect ballet couple, both partners have grace and beauty. Those of Margaux and Cantenac are languorous, exotic, and seductive: prima ballerinas. Those of Saint-Julien, Pauillac, and Saint-Estèphe have an elegance, power, and control of muscle that is spellbinding. They are the Nureyevs of the wine world.

Leaving Margaux by taking the Route du Médoc northward, one passes through the hamlets of Soussans, Arcins, and Cussac. None of these villages produces wines of *cru classé* quality, although they have a number of agreeable *crus bourgeois.* However, five miles to the west are Moulis and Listrac, two villages that have been honored with an Appellation Contrôlée. Wines from either are likely to be standard fare on French dining cars, and no other wine can beat their quality for the price.

There are no classified growths in either town, but there is one *cru exceptionnel* of international reputation, the Château Chasse-Spleen, halfway between Moulis and Arcins. The name means just what it would in English—the "spleen chaser." Spleen is, of course, an English word. It came into vogue in France after Baudelaire introduced it as the title of one of his poems in the middle of the last century. "*Je suis comme le roi d'un pays pluvieux,*" the poem begins—"I am like the king of a rainy country," —a good enough description of this wine of Moulis when the damps of autumn roll in off the Gironde.

There are twelve miles between the town limits of Margaux and the Chenal du Nord. The next fourteen miles contain no fewer than thirty-eight *grand cru* vineyards, the names of many of which are household words wherever the urbane congregate. The first township is Saint-Julien-Beychevelle, or Saint-Julien, as it is more commonly called. It is one of the five general areas allowed an Appellation Contrôlée of its own in the Médoc—the others being Margaux, Listrac, Moulis, and Saint-Estèphe. Of these, the regional wine of Saint-Julien is the most popular. Margaux may be the silkiest and most perfumed, Saint-Estèphe the most muscular, Moulis and Listrac the most moderately priced, but when it comes to the perfect synthesis of the region's bouquet, savor, body, and taste, a Saint-Julien comes close to filling the bill. It is the golden, or, in this case, the ruby mean.

Saint-Julien is one of the Haut-Médoc's smallest communes, but it contains five second growths, two third growths, and five fourth growths. On the right side of the road, immediately over the Saint-Julien town line, lies one of the Médoc's most beautiful châteaux, the Château Beychevelle. Though Beychevelle is only a fourth growth, nearly everyone agrees that if a new classification could be agreed upon, it would be elevated one, and perhaps even two, ranks. In the sixteenth century one of the château's proprietors was the Duc d'Épernon, favorite of the bizarre King Henri III. Henri, last of the House of Valois, drenched himself in perfume, wore monks' robes or ladies' dresses, and hid under beds during thunderstorms. Despite his eccentricities he was, for the savage times in which he reigned, a rather enlightened monarch. Épernon, one of his *mignons,* held the post of Grand Admiral of France. To salute the Admiral, ships going up and down the Gironde would dip their sails when they passed his castle. The French for "lowering the sails" is *baisser les voiles,* and this presumably was corrupted by time to Beychevelle. Whatever the origin of the name, the château produces one of the finest and most typical Saint-Juliens.

Across the road from Château Beychevelle is another fourth growth, Château Branaire-Ducru. Its owner worked steadily to bring the vineyard up to its former high repute. The first fruits of his labor started to mature in the late sixties and from their quality the oenophile should in the seventies be able to tell why Branaire-Ducru was considered one of the finest Médocs during the nineteenth century.

A little inland is Gruaud-Larose, a well-known second growth. It was a favorite of Thackeray's, and was so highly thought of by Charles XII that he elevated the vineyard and its owner to a barony. In the nineteenth century the estate was divided into two parts, Gruaud-Larose-Sarget and Gruaud-Larose-Faure, but was reunited in this century, and once again the wine appears under its classic name. Gruaud-Larose is not only a very good vineyard, it is also one of the Médoc's largest, producing about twenty thousand cases of wine per year.

Château Lagrange, a medium-sized vineyard, is a mile and a half northwest of Gruaud-Larose. It produces both white and red wines, but the red, classified a third growth, is certainly the better known of the two. The bottle is easily recognized by its rococo label, which shows the château flanked by two sixteenth-century soldiers holding banners with the date of the vintage.

About a mile and a half south of Saint-Julien, on the left side of the road, are two châteaux that have recently been reunited into a single estate, Château Saint-Pierre-Bontemps and Château Saint-Pierre-Sevaistre. Saint-Pierre-Bontemps has the agreeable meaning of Saint Peter of the Good Times. Despite the somewhat Rabelaisian connotation, the name was generated in a rather prosaic manner. A certain Monsieur Saint-Pierre left the estate to his son-in-law, Colonel Bontemps-Dubarry. As the name of Château Saint-Pierre-Bontemps-Dubarry would have demanded too much breath for anyone short of a mile runner, it was slightly abbreviated. It was a good choice, as both the name and the wine have been popular. The two estates together produce about ten thousand cases of sound, fourth-growth Saint-Julien.

Half a mile up the road toward Saint-Julien is the well-known Château Langoa, owned by H. R. Barton of Barton & Guestier, or as it is more familiarly known, B & G. The vineyard produces a very fine third-growth Saint-Julien that many feel should be elevated to the second rank.

To the east of Château Langoa begin the rolling acres of vines that make up one of the Médoc's most famous growths: Léoville. "I have never had a bad Léoville," said the late George Saintsbury, English literary figure and dean of wine critics, and there are few who would disagree with him. At one time Léoville was a single estate, but after the French Revolution it was split in three: Léoville-Lascases, Léoville-Poyferré, and Léoville-Barton. Together they run from south of Saint-Julien to the border of Pauillac.

Of the three Léovilles, Léoville-Barton is the smallest, with an annual production of some nine thousand cases. It is also the most southerly, lying directly across the road from Château Langoa. As both are owned by H. R. Barton, the pressing, vinification, storage, and bottling of the two wines are centralized at Langoa. Consequently, Léoville-Barton is not château-bottled, but since it is bottled by its proprietor and distributed by him through B & G, it comes down to the same thing.

Léoville-Poyferré has an annual production of twelve thousand cases, and Léoville-Lascases makes about sixteen thousand cases per year. All three Léovilles are second growths, and though they differ somewhat in taste, they are all generally considered the cream of the Saint-Juliens.

Two other well-known Saint-Juliens, some distance off the Route du Médoc, are the Château Ducru-Beaucaillou, a mile south of the town, and the Château Talbot, a mile west of it. Ducru-Beaucaillou was so improved by Madame Francis Borie during the decade of the sixties that it became one of the most appreciated of the second growths. The name comes from a former owner, a Monsieur Ducru, and the French for pretty pebble, *beau caillou*—probably a reference to the gravelly soil on which the vineyard lies.

Château Talbot is a well-known wine in England and America, to some extent because the Anglo-Saxon tongue finds little difficulty in handling the name, which comes from the last English commander of Guyenne, John Talbot, Earl of Shrewsbury. When well past the age of eighty, Talbot was defeated at Castillon in 1453. He is said to have died with his sword in his scabbard, for he had sworn never to raise it against the king of France, even though he was commander of the English army. Opinions about Talbot's prowess at arms differ. The present owners of Château Talbot call him the "Achilles of England." However, he is in fact best remembered for his defeats. First captured by Joan of Arc at Patay, he then lost Aquitania at Castillon. The English themselves probably best described him by naming a breed of hound after him.

The wine is a fine, full Saint-Julien. It would probably be raised a category on a new classification.

Directly inland from Saint-Julien lies the town of Saint-Laurent, with three *grand cru* vineyards. Leading them is the fourth-growth Château La Tour-Carnet, a vineyard famed in the annals of the Bordeaux wine trade since 1354. Even at that date its wines commanded leading prices. Since then the vineyard has been owned by Jean de Foix, grandfather of Henry IV, and Thibaud de Camin, brother-in-law of Michel de Montaigne. It currently produces about seven thousand cases of good red wine of the Saint-Julien type.

There are two fifth growths in Saint-Laurent: Château Camensac, which makes about seven thousand cases during an average year, and the better-known Château Belgrave, which produces about fifteen thousand cases. It is said that Belgrave Square in London was named after it. *Grave,* of course, is the local word for gravel, the best sort of soil for the Médoc's wines. Hence Belgrave might mean something like "lovely gravel," but that is my own guess.

Without much doubt, the commune of Pauillac produces as much great wine acre for acre as any town in the world. Only Vosne-Romanée, in distant Burgundy, can be held up in comparison. Of the sixty classified vineyards in the Médoc, eighteen are in Pauillac. Of the four finest wines of the Médoc, three are within its boundaries. The characteristics of a properly matured Pauillac are fullness, balance, a pronounced bouquet, and, above all, what can only be called elegance. These are the most aristocratic wines. They are also remarkably long-lived.

The town itself is the only one in the Haut-Médoc of any size, having a population of a little over five thousand. It is something of a port, with a long quay that fronts out on the Gironde. On one side of the quay is the usual hodgepodge of cafés, bars, and a few rustic restaurants where one can sit outside and watch the ships sailing to and from Bordeaux thirty miles upriver. It is an amusing place to pick up a little local color, and if one doesn't want anything too complicated, a pleasant meal. Local wines will, of course, be excellent.

The distance between Saint-Julien and Pauillac is about four miles. The first vineyard one sees on crossing the border between the two is off on the right-hand side. It is marked by a small dome-topped tower that seems to float like some bulky ship on a sea of vines. It is the legendary Château Latour, one of the three *premiers crus classés* of the Médoc, the highest rank attainable in the Classification of 1855.

The château was named after a long-demolished, high-turreted fortress that stood on the property five hundred years ago. During the war that ended in the French victory over Marshal Talbot at Castillon, the *sieur* who owned the château was an English sympathizer. When they lost, he fled. The new French governor ordered the tops of the castle's towers lopped off, saying that that was what he would do to the traitorous owner's head if he ever managed to lay his hands on him. Since that moment of bellicosity, Latour has been shrouded in the vines of peace. Before the French Revolution it was the property of the dean of the Médoc's wine families, the Ségurs, who also owned Château Lafite and Château Calon-Ségur. Under their tutelage the vineyard rose in reputation to the very top, a position it has held ever since.

The château had a change of management recently. In the sixties, new vines were planted, the wine being now nearly ninety percent Cabernet Sauvignon. Though the wines from the new planting have yet to fully mature, it is safe to assume that they will be splendid.

In character the Latours are sturdy, full, robust, dark in color

—in effect very masculine wines. When properly matured, they have a powerful bouquet and great finesse and live to a phenomenally old age. The vineyard produces about ten thousand cases in an average vintage year.

Bordering Château Latour to the north is one of the best-loved second growths, Château Pichon-Longueville, Comtesse de Lalande, and directly across the road its other half, the Château Pichon-Longueville-Baron. In the nineteenth century the two châteaux were part of the same estate. The original château and two-fifths of the vineyard make up the present Pichon-Longueville-Baron; Pichon-Longueville-Lalande retains the other three-fifths of the vineyard and another château. Both vineyards are splendid, as they are planted in the same gravelly soil that supports the neighboring Château Latour. Both wines need considerable time to reach their apogees—the Pichon-Comtesse perhaps a little less, as it has a slightly smaller proportion of the noble, but slow to mature, Cabernet Sauvignon. The Comtesse is thus a little fruitier and better when young, but both are sublime wines.

There are no other *grands crus* until the outskirts of Pauillac, where there are two fifth growths—Grand-Puy-Ducasse and Clerc-Milon-Mondon. Of the two, Grand-Puy-Ducasse is the more famous, as it is the seat of the Maison du Vin de Pauillac, where the Commanderie du Bontemps, the Médoc's answer to Burgundy's Confrérie des Chevaliers du Tastevin, has its headquarters.

West, southwest, and just north of Pauillac are a number of small fifth-growth châteaux: Grand-Puy-Lacoste, Batailley, Haut-Batailley, Haut-Bages-Libéral, Lynch-Moussas, Pédesclaux, Croizet-Bages, and Lynch-Bages. The last is by far the best known, with vineyard records that date back to the sixteenth century. It produces a lovely, typical Pauillac, and most wine lovers would agree that, like Frankie by Johnnie, it has been "done wrong" by the 1855 Classification.

About a mile north of Pauillac begins what must be to any true oenophile the *terra sancta* of winedom. In it are only five châteaux, but they make up in fame what they lack in quantity.

First is Château Mouton-Rothschild. Of all the injustices of the Classification of 1855, certainly the placing of Mouton as a second growth was the one that most needed correction. The wine is the peer of the three other growths of the Médoc, and in some years the best of all. In 1972 Mouton was elevated to be a Premier Cru, but in the century when it was only a second, it reveled in the injustice of its situation. Reflecting this was the motto Mouton took for itself: *"Premier ne puis, Second ne daigne, Mouton suis!"*— "First I cannot be, Second I do not condescend to, Mouton I am!"

The motto stemmed from that of the very proud and noble Rohan family, who flaunted *"Roi ne puis, Duc ne daigne, Rohan suis!"* as their device. The Rohans contributed a string of cardinals, generals, and even a few dukes to the Ancien Régime, but they are best remembered for their part in the famous "Scandal of the Diamond Necklace," an affair that rocked the throne on the eve of the Revolution by seeming to implicate Queen Marie Antoinette herself, if not in robbery, at least in an intrigue of the most damaging kind. Perhaps less known was an earlier necklace affair. Madame de Rohan was held up by a couple of highway robbers, one of whom tried to seize her necklace. To thwart him she clapped both hands over it, whereupon the brigand attacked her in an even more private place. "That won't do you any good, young man," the high-spirited lady cried. "If I drop my guard, you can get away with the necklace, but I know you can't run off with *that!*" At this point a guard appeared, disappointing the highwayman, and perhaps even the lady.

It is only fitting that Mouton should take the Rohan motto as its own. In the Médoc's necklace of vineyards, it is truly one of its brightest gems. Today Mouton is owned by Baron Philippe de Rothschild, descendant of Nathaniel de Rothschild, who bought it in 1853. Before that it was the property of the Napoleon of vines, Baron de Brane. Prior to him the vineyard was owned by a whole gallery of famous characters, including two of Henri III's *mignons,* the ducs de Joyeuse and Épernon, and Joan of Arc's companion in arms, Dunois, fondly known as "the Bastard of Orléans."

The quality of Mouton is in part based on the very high proportion of Cabernet Sauvignon used, over ninety percent. No vineyard in the Médoc uses more. The subsequent wine is hard and astringent when young; but given time to mature, it metamorphoses like a caterpillar to a butterfly into one of the most elegant, fine, beautifully balanced, manly wines of all.

Visitors to Mouton should not miss the wine museum, with its collection of vinous artifacts and art that goes back to Roman times.

Next door to Mouton-Rothschild is another vineyard owned by Philippe de Rothschild, Château Mouton-Baron-Philippe, formerly known as Mouton-d'Armailhacq. At one time the two Moutons were one vineyard, but one part became far better known than the other because of the efforts of the Baron de Brane. Mouton-Rothschild was classified a second growth in 1855 and Mouton-d'Armailhacq a fifth. However, Philippe de Rothschild bought Mouton-d'Armailhacq in the thirties, and since then has made a sustained effort to bring it up to the level of its more famous consort. He has planted very heavily in Cabernet Sauvignon, and uses the same methods of vinification and storage as at Mouton-Rothschild. The wine is splendid and will become more so as the new vines age, making its fifth-growth position still more unjust. Now most oenophiles would agree that Mouton-Baron-Philippe should be elevated one or possibly two categories.

Another vineyard that most feel is misplaced in the Classification of 1855 is the neighboring Château Pontet-Canet. This deservedly popular fifth growth is owned by the famous Bordeaux shipping firm of Cruse, and is one of the largest vineyards of the Médoc, with an average production of twenty thousand cases of wine per year. Pontet-Canet is not château-bottled, but as Cruse bottles all the wine and controls its distribution, it comes down to the same thing. The proprietor, bottler, and shipper being one and the same, the wine may safely stand on its and his reputation, and in this case both are good.

North of the Moutons is the fourth-growth Château Duhart-Milon, an excellent vineyard that makes about fifteen thousand cases of fine, typical Pauillac in an average year. Many feel that this vineyard should also be raised one rank.

On the northern border of Pauillac is Château Lafite, owned by another branch of the Rothschild family. Considered the first of the first great growths when it was classified in 1855, Lafite has ever since been at least in the very top echelon and often leading it. A great deal of its early fame was due to the Duc de Richelieu, the oenophile, aesthete, and libertine who did much to beautify Bordeaux. At eighty-five, after a lifetime of debauchery that would have exhausted a less exuberant man, he married a pretty widow. The king was amazed and asked him how he managed to do it. Richelieu attributed his vitality to Château Lafite, and with that it became the rage of Versailles.

The vineyard was bought in 1868 by Baron James de Rothschild for the then staggering sum of four and a half million francs. It has been passed on from father to son since, and is at present owned by Élie de Rothschild. The château is one of the prettiest in the Médoc, and has the additional attraction of containing one of the world's most distinguished cellars, with a collection of fine wines that includes every Lafite since 1797.

The wine itself is nearly impossible to describe. It has great *sève* when young, and slowly develops into the most elegant, subtle, full, and aristocratic of wines with a delicious bouquet. Only the very top wine of the estate is labeled Château Lafite. Wines from the second pressing or from vines not deemed up to first quality are sold as Carruades de Château Lafite. Even these are likely to be very good.

The town of Saint-Estèphe produces the sturdiest regional wines of the Médocs. They make excellent companions for roast beef and steak. Château Cos-Labory, an excellent small fifth growth bordering on Château Lafite and Château Cos-d'Estournel, is the first vineyard across the Pauillac-Saint-Estèphe line. Next to it, the spectacular Cos-d'Estournel boasts the most eccentric and amusing edifice in the Médoc, one that is faintly reminiscent of the odd, gold-domed Royal Pavilion at Brighton. It is a half Chinese, half Indian fantasy, with overtones of French medieval. This pagoda-roofed *bizarrerie* was built over a century and a half ago by Monsieur d'Estournelle, a merchant whose passion and trade were in the Far East. Whatever one may think of the château, few would deny that the wine is superb. It is a typical Saint-Estèphe, filled with *sève* when young, maturing into a full-bodied, lusty red wine with great charm and not a little elegance. It is one of the best of the second growths.

Another vineyard of Saint-Estèphe that has had a remarkable revival is the Château Lafon-Rochet. Classified a fourth growth in 1855, it all but disappeared during the next century. Recently, however, it has come into the hands of Monsieur Guy Tesseron, who has been working hard to bring the vineyard up to its former standards. The questing oenophile may soon have the pleasure of bibbing a long-forgotten star of Saint-Estèphe's galaxy. It is a wine that bears watching.

Château Montrose, a well-known second growth, is just south of Saint-Estèphe, almost on the banks of the Gironde. Called the "Latour of Saint-Estèphe," the wine is manly, slow to mature, long-lived, and full. The vineyard produces eight to ten thousand cases in a good vintage year.

The northernmost *grand cru* in the Médoc lies a little outside of Saint-Estèphe, near the road to Saint-Seurin. It is the third-growth Calon-Ségur, another vineyard most wine lovers feel should be elevated a rank. It not only produces a very fine wine, but it does so in large quantities, about fifteen thousand cases a year.

Calon comes from Calones, the old Roman name for Saint-Estèphe. In the eighteenth century, the vineyard became the property of the Marquis de Ségur, who also owned Latour and Lafite. His trinity of vineyards was considered the finest in the Bordelais. But Calon-Ségur doesn't have to rely on its noble past. It produces a gracious, full, *bouqueté* Saint-Estèphe, a wine that is thought by many to be one of the village's best.

With Calon-Ségur, the *grands crus* of the Haut-Médoc end. To the north lies the Médoc and beyond that the Atlantic. Although the Médoc produces a number of good little château wines and some sound regional wines, none can come up to the standards of the great Haut-Médocs.

The Haut-Médoc also produces a smattering of white wines, and even a few sparkling whites and rosés, but its real fame certainly rests on its superlative reds. It is there that the great Cabernet Sauvignon thrives as in no other place. What causes it—the climate, the gravelly soil, the river's damp air—may forever remain a mystery. But there it does produce some of the world's most *nuancé*, subtle, aristocratic, *bouqueté* red wines.

Saint-Émilion & Pomerol

Forty-five minutes east of Bordeaux, on an escarpment overlooking the valley of the Dordogne, lies Saint-Émilion, one of the most charming villages in France. It has all the attributes the adventurous tourist likes to find: an enchanting shrine and chapel with an ancient steeple towering over them, winding medieval streets, small restaurants, antique shops, and vineyards that produce memorable French red wines.

The village has a considerable history. The buildings of one of its best-known vineyards, Château Ausone, are supposedly built on the foundations of the villa of Ausonius, who was consul of Rome, tutor of the Emperor Gratian, and one of the greatest of the late Latin poets. After serving in the court of Valentinian and Gratian as it rambled over the empire, Ausonius retired to the Dordogne valley to spend his twilight years writing poetry and sipping the wines he loved so well.

In the eighth century, Aemilianus, a wandering holy man from the region of Vannes in Brittany, arrived. Within a short while he established a small monastery modeled on the discipline of the Benedictines. As both his and the monastery's reputation burgeoned, the town began to be called Saint-Aemilianus, or as it was pronounced in the Languedoc dialect, Saint-Émilion. Because of him the town developed a reputation as a hallowed place, and consequently in the following centuries became a way-stop for pilgrims en route to the shrine of Santiago de Compostela in northwestern Spain.

To explain the significance of this development, a small digression into medieval history is necessary. In the Middle Ages, Santiago, along with the Holy Sepulcher in Jerusalem, was considered one of the most important shrines in Christendom. The reasons were numerous, but among them certainly was the intense rivalry that existed between the French and Italian branches of the Church. This competition took several forms, one of which was the transferring by the French Pope, Clement V, of the papacy from Rome to Avignon in 1309, where it stayed for seventy years. For a short period there were even both an Italian and a French pope, the latter being denounced by the Italians as the antipope. And the Italians went even further. They branded many of the doctrines of the French, or Gallicans as they were then called, heretical.

The French on their part had little desire to have their pilgrims lured by the splendors of Italy on their journeys to the shrines of Rome and the Middle East. But how were they to avoid it? The perfect solution presented itself in the ninth century when a Spanish bishop discovered the tomb of Saint James the Apostle in the northwestern corner of Spain. Quickly agreeing with the Spanish that the newfound shrine was one of the first magnitude, the French declared it a pilgrimage worthy of any in Christendom. And to handle the flood of voyagers who shortly began trekking across France and northern Spain, a series of way stations and subsidiary shrines was set up.

RESTAURANT-HOTELS

Saint-Émilion (Gironde)	Hostellerie de Plaisance p. 26, p. 236
	Logis de la Cadène (pl. Marché-au-Bois; tel. 51.71.40—closed last 2 weeks of Oct.) p. 236
Libourne (Gironde)	*Hôtel Loubat p. 26, p. 245

RESTAURANTS

Saint-Jean-de-Blaignac (Gironde)	Auberge Saint-Jean p. 26
Saint-Émilion	Chez Germaine (pl. Clocher; tel. 51.70.88) p. 236

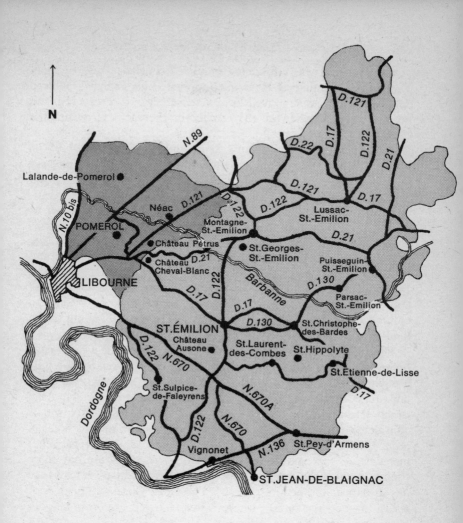

N

Lalande-de-Pomerol

N.89

N.10 bis

Néac   D.121   D.122

POMEROL   D.122   D.122

Château Pétrus   Montagne-St.-Emilion

D.21   St.Georges-St.-Emilion

Château   D.21   D.122
Cheval-Blanc

LIBOURNE   D.122

D.17

Barbanne

D.121

Lussac-St.-Emilion

D.21   D.17

Puisseguin-St.-Emilion

D.130

Parsac-St.-Emilion

ST.ÉMILION   D.130   D.17

Château   D.17   St.Christophe-
Ausone   des-Bardes

St.Laurent-   St.Hippolyte
des-Combes

D.122   N.670

St.Sulpice-   St.Etienne-de-Lisse
de-Faleyrens   D.17

N.670A

D.122   N.670

Vignonet   N.136   St.Pey-d'Armens

ST.JEAN-DE-BLAIGNAC

Dordogne

DAY 15
Itinerary p. 26

Saint-Émilion & Pomerol

Michelin Regional Map 75
Michelin Guide Vert *Côte de
l'Atlantique*

SAINT-ÉMILION

POMEROL

CLASSIFICATIONS p. 239, p. 245

Saint-Émilion was considered of such importance that Clement V, who was a native of Bordeaux, appointed his nephew, Gaillard de Lamothe-Pressac, doyen of its monastery. It prospered and grew, especially when in 1316 Lamothe-Pressac was awarded a cardinal's hat.

To this little bit of history Saint-Émilion owes much of its charm. Though the village has only slightly over three thousand inhabitants, it is dotted with convents, chapels, a hermitage, and even some catacombs. The main church faces out on an irregularly shaped, tree-shaded square called the place du Marché, as do the catacombs and the hermitage where Saint Émilion himself once lived. From the point of view of an architectural purist, the church may appear to be something of a disaster. Its façade and its flanking buildings are a mixture of Gothic, Romanesque, and Burgundian, a hodgepodge of styles. Yet the sum is enchanting and in fact quite majestic. Somehow its very variety seems to epitomize the extraordinarily civilized and cultivated feeling of the landscape on the banks of the Dordogne.

The church is not built up, but in. It is, in effect, a huge cave hollowed out of solid rock. And sitting directly on top of it is a square called the place du Clocher where there are two good and quite inexpensive restaurants. The Hostellerie de Plaisance, which has a garden and a lovely view overlooking the town, is considered by most people to be the best restaurant and hotel in Saint-Émilion. The host is Monsieur Loisel, and his *spécialités* include *foie gras* and *lamproie bordelaise*. As there are only nine rooms in the hotel, reservations had better be made in advance if you expect to spend the night. The Chez Germaine next door is also a good restaurant, where I have enjoyed *gratin de langoustines* and *entrecôte maître de chai*.

Another good little restaurant-hotel, this one down in the town, is the remarkably inexpensive Logis de la Cadène. The décor is rustic, but the service is agreeable and attentive. The specialties will probably include the by now familiar *lamproie bordelaise*, and there will be a hearty, inexpensive *prix fixe*.

It was during the English occupation of Aquitania that the wines of Saint-Émilion first became known to the outside world. The English admired them greatly, and large quantities were shipped from the nearby port of Libourne to England where many of them graced the king's table. But as with most things in heavy demand, there soon sprang up a brisk trade in ersatz Saint-Émilion. Consequently, in 1199, King John of England, the same monarch who was later forced by his barons to sign the Magna Charta, gave the town its charter, and with this in hand the town fathers took steps to guarantee the authenticity of their village's wine.

The upshot was that the first known laws of Appellation Contrôlée in France were put into effect under the English Plantagenet monarchs. Saint-Émilion and eight adjacent hamlets were the only ones allowed to supply wines carrying the name of Semilione*, as the English called the town. And in the days before château bottling had been invented, every cask had to be branded with a coat of arms and registered. It is interesting to note that the twentieth-century Appellation Contrôlée delimitations follow almost exactly the geographical outlines laid down by the edicts of the medieval English kings.

In 1453 John Talbot was defeated and killed at the battle of Castillon, five miles east of the town. It was a black day for English wine lovers when their "good dog, Talbot," as he was fondly known in street doggerel, caught an arrow in his throat, losing his life and the province in a single stroke. Local legend has it that the marshal called out his troops to hunt down a French army known to be loose in the neighborhood. Arriving in Saint-Émilion, his soldiers took advantage of the moment to do what troops in similar situations have always done—to "liberate" some of Semilione's liquid treasure. A little woozy from their morning's good fortune, the English army ambled toward Castillon. Then they did a very un-English thing. They sat down in the midday sun. Suddenly the French forces appeared from behind a nearby screen of trees. Talbot sounded the call to arms, but it was too late. Before his soldiers could pull themselves together, the French attacked. Talbot was killed, and his none-too-sober followers were put to rout. With that England's hopes of conquering France faded, and Aquitania fell into the arms of the French king.

Saint-Émilion, which had enjoyed a most favored status under the English as a wine-producing commune, now became one

* Probably also the ancestral root word for the grape varietal, the Sémillon, even though this is now grown elsewhere in Bordeaux.

among many, making a wine with a special flavor that was not particularly appreciated by the French, who were not used to it. Although Louis XIII is said to have praised it, and Louis XIV during one of his visits through the region sonorously pronounced it *"un doux nectar,"* neither monarch was known to drink hugely of it once he returned to Paris or Versailles. Kings, even by divine right, have to have something of the politician in them, and there is no better way of buttering up a constituency of *vignerons* than by praising their product. Saint-Émilion, both as a place and as a wine, became something of a rustic backwater, appreciated by the locals and a few cognoscenti, but ignored by the rank and file of international wine drinkers. As short a while ago as 1855, when the famous Classification of the Gironde was made, neither Saint-Émilion nor its neighbor Pomerol was mentioned, an inconceivable omission today.

Its rediscovery took place in the last half of the nineteenth century when the wines scored great successes in the Paris Expositions of 1867 and 1889. With that they came into vogue, and their popularity has been growing ever since. One reason is certainly the flavors of the wines themselves. They are often referred to as the "Burgundies of Bordeaux," and though this designation obviously is not entirely accurate, there is considerable truth in it. If somehow one could cross the wine of Saint-Estèphe in the Médoc with that of Pommard in Burgundy, the result would be something like a Saint-Émilion. Though a Saint-Émilion has the *sève* of a Médoc, it is fuller, rounder, more generous and vigorous, while at the same time it lacks a little of the Médoc's elegance and subtlety.

Another characteristic of Saint-Émilion wines that has added to their popularity is the way they mature. Though a great Saint-Émilion is likely to take as long if not longer than its Médoc counterpart to reach its acme, it is palatable far earlier. A young Médoc of any stature contains a high proportion of Cabernet Sauvignon, and this produces a wine that is initially hard, astringent, and tart. A young Saint-Émilion will not be great, but it won't be as mouth puckering as a young Médoc. And in this era when wines are consumed at an earlier and earlier age, that is a rather powerful consideration.

Until a few years ago, the wines of Saint-Émilion were classified in the most haphazard manner. The number of vineyards claiming to be *grands crus* was mind-boggling. Every tiny commune in the Saint-Émilionnais pleased itself and its proprietors with self-laudatory titles, a bit in the manner of those Central American republics whose armies contain no rank lower than colonel.

But in 1954 and 1955 the region of Saint-Émilion was classified in a manner that many think should serve as a model for the rest of the department of the Gironde. The rating at present has two top categories: *premiers grands crus classés* and *grands crus classés*. There are twelve vineyards, headed by Château Ausone

---

CRUS CLASSÉS OF SAINT-ÉMILION

Premiers Grands Crus Classés:

Châteaux "A"   Ausone
Cheval Blanc

Châteaux "B"   Beauséjour   La Gaffelière-Naudes
Belair   Magdelaine
Canon   Pavie
Clos-Fourtet   Trottevieille
Figeac

Grands Crus Classés "Châteaux":

L'Angélus   Corbin
L'Arrosée   Corbin-Michotte
Balestard-la-Tonnelle   Coutet
Bellevue   Croque-Michotte
Bergat   Curé-Bon
Cadet-Bon   Fonplégade
Cadet-Piola   Fonroque
Canon-la-Gaffelière   Franc-Mayne
Cap-de-Mourlin   Grand Barrail-Lamarzelle
Chapelle-Madeleine   Grand Corbin-Despagne
Chauvin   Grand Corbin-Pècres

Grand Mayne
Grand Pontet
Grandes Murailles
Guadet Saint-Julien
Jean Faure
Clos-des-Jacobins
La Carte
La Clotte
La Cluzière
La Couspaude
La Dominique
Clos La Madeleine
Larcis-Ducasse
Lamarzelle
Larmande
Laroze
Lasserre
La Tour-du-Pin-Figeac
La Tour-Figeac
Le Chatelet
Le Couvert
Le Prieuré
Mauvezin
Moulin-du-Cadet

Pavie-Decesse
Pavie-Macquin
Pavillon-Cadet
Petit-Faurie-de-Souchard
Petit-Faurie-de-Soutard
Ripeau
Sansonnet
Saint-Georges-Côte-Pavie
Clos-Saint-Martin
Soutard
Tertre-Daugay
Trimoulet
Trois Moulins
Troplong-Mondo
Villemaurine
Yon-Figeac

Some Grands Crus:

Capet-Guillier
De Ferrand
Haut-Sarpe
Lassegue
Montbousquet

---

and Château Cheval-Blanc, in the list of *premiers grands crus classés*. The *grands crus classés* number fifty-eight vineyards. After these top seventy classified growths come the *grands crus*, the *crus bourgeois*, and so forth to the total of several hundred growths.

The listing in the first two categories is quite static, as good vineyards in the hands of capable proprietors will usually consistently produce better wines than their lesser neighbors. However, there is a condition. Every vintage of Saint-Émilion is subjected to a blind tasting by a committee of experts to make sure that no matter what the wine is, it warrants its gradation.

This is a great improvement over some of the other systems of classification in the Bordelais where, come what may, the rank of a vineyard is rigidly fixed. Under such systems châteaux that have actually slipped into mediocrity keep their illustrious positions, and others that have elevated themselves remain frozen in the niche where they were placed over a hundred years ago.

By contrast, in Saint-Émilion a superlative *cru bourgeois* has the opportunity to rise to a rank commensurate with its true station, and a mishandled *grand cru classé* will soon be down with less exalted company. However, in practice the listing of Saint-Émilions tends to remain quite static, as the very existence of the safeguards keeps the *vigneron* on his toes. There is no profit to be made by letting the vineyard slip.

Beneath the château wines are the regional wines of Saint-Émilion and the villages and vineyard areas that surround it. The regional wine labeled Saint-Émilion must come either from the commune of that name, or from the seven hamlets that encircle it: Saint-Christophe-des-Bardes, Saint-Laurent-des-Combes, Saint-Hyppolyte, Saint-Étienne-de-Lisse, Saint-Pey-d'Armens, Saint-Sulpice-de-Faleyrens, and Vignonet.

Beyond this viticultural region are several villages and vineyard areas that are allowed to append the name of Saint-Émilion to their name. These are, in descending order of excellence: Saint-Georges-Saint-Émilion, Montagne-Saint-Émilion, Lussac-Saint-Émilion, Puisseguin-Saint-Émilion, and Parsac-Saint-Émilion, all lying to the northeast. To the west, and within the limits of the city of Libourne, is Sables-Saint-Émilion, a lowland area near the riverbank producing wines of modest quality. There are some very agreeable wines from these villages, especially from those first listed. Whatever they are, they will be a very good value.

As one may guess, the region of Saint-Émilion is large, by far the biggest producer of fine red wines in the Bordeaux area. All told nearly thirty million bottles are produced in a good vintage year. Generous, open, and sturdy, Saint-Émilions make ideal companions for red meat and game.

Saint-Émilion produces about seventy thousand cases of *premier grand cru classé* wine per year. Twenty thousand cases are made by two châteaux, Cheval-Blanc and Figeac, which, as they are on the Pomerol border, are almost extensions of the vineyards of Pomerol. Their wines are known as Graves-Saint-Émilion after the gravelly soil.

The other ten vineyards, headed by the magnificent Château Ausone, cover the rolling hills near the town itself and are known as Côtes-Saint-Émilion. Most of them are quite small, and all ten together produce only about fifty thousand cases during a good vintage year. Following is a short description of some of the *premier grand cru classé* châteaux.

Château Cheval-Blanc, first of the first great classified growths, is named after a famous inn that used to be on the property. Nowadays the vineyards produce ten thousand cases a year of what nearly everyone considers one of the very finest red Bordeaux —a rival of the first growths of the Médoc and Graves. The wine is soft, supple, and has a strong bouquet. In the winter of 1956 a frost destroyed a large quantity of the precious vines, but they are now all repaired, and so the supply of this splendid wine is no longer excessively limited. What there is, however, will be very expensive.

Next to Cheval-Blanc is Château Figeac, another large property producing some exquisite wines, with a character rather like that of its illustrious neighbor. Figeac produces not only good wine, but a considerable amount of it, the annual production in a good year being something around ten thousand cases.

On the brow of the hill overlooking the road on the left-hand side as one drives into Saint-Émilion is the other *premier des premiers grands crus classés*, the renowned Château Ausone. Unlike Cheval-Blanc, Ausone's production is very small, only about 2,500 cases a year. The château has the reputation of owning one of the finest vineyards in France. If the present château is indeed built on the ruins of Ausonius' villa, then its wines may well have been served to the Roman emperor. At any rate its history is ancient, as Roman tools, coins, and artifacts are constantly being dug up on the property. The cellars are hollowed out of the hill beside it, and there the wine is matured, rather than in the aboveground *chais* common to the Bordeaux region. This method of maturation, along with the fact that the vines grow on a hillside rather than on the flats like most other Bordelais vineyards, is given as the reason Côtes-Saint-Émilion are so similar in character to the wines of Burgundy.

Ausone is the property of Monsieur Jean Dubois-Challon, who also owns Château Belair, another *premier grand cru classé*, and the *grand cru classé* Chapelle-Madeleine. This trinity of vineyards is one of the best and most powerful collections on the north bank of the Dordogne. There are, incidentally, several châteaux called Belair in the Bordelais, but only this one is a *premier grand cru classé* of Saint-Émilion. The wary oenophile would be well advised to scrutinize the label carefully the next time he orders this wine. Chapelle-Madeleine has an annual production of about two thousand cases. "Full, soft, fine" is Mr. Frank Schoonmaker's description of the wine, and I can think of none better than that.

Another name that causes confusion unless one reads the label carefully—as there are several châteaux in Bordeaux similarly named—is Château Beauséjour. This property was divided into two smaller ones in 1869—one bearing one owner's name of Fagouet and producing approximately two thousand cases of wine a year, the other held by the Duffau-Lagarrosse family with an average production of about 2,500 cases per year.

In the bottom of the valley below Ausone is Château La Gaffelière-Naudes, owned by the Comte Malet-Roquefort. The name Gaffelière comes from the medieval word for a leprosarium, as the château was built on the site of an old leper colony. At present it produces only very good wine—about eight thousand cases of it per year.

Just to the east of La Gaffelière-Naudes is Château Pavie, a vineyard that produces the largest amount of fine Saint-Émilion. It averages fifteen thousand cases per year, and the wine is as excellent as it is copious.

The highly regarded Château Canon also lies rather close to the village. The manor itself is a delightful piece of architecture —a low, ivy-covered tower with a graceful eighteenth-century wing to balance it. Framing it are acres of green vines. The wines of Château Canon are a little like the building whose name they take—sturdy, long-lived, and graceful. The vineyards produce about 7,500 cases of wine per year.

Last, but certainly not least, is the excellent Château Trottevieille, a small vineyard that produces about three thousand cases of wine per year. It belongs to a member of the Borie family, which also owns Château Batailley, a well-known fifth growth in Pauillac.

Drinking wine two meals a day moderately—"surely the Good Lord didn't intend to restrict us to so little!" wrote the sixteenth-century philosopher and essayist Michel de Montaigne. Montaigne was born and lived most of his life at La Mothe-Montravel, a stone's throw from the Dordogne and the vineyards of Saint-Émilion and Pomerol. Surely their benevolent irrigation helped him conceive and write down his beautifully balanced thoughts. The countryside on the banks of the Dordogne seems the ideal counterpoint to Montaigne's *Essais*. There the works of man and nature blend harmoniously. The broad river, the picturesque châteaux, copses of trees, vineyards, fields, medieval villages, and delightful little restaurants seem a scene out of another age.

The commercial center of this part of the Dordogne valley is Libourne, a pretty and agreeable town of just over twenty thousand inhabitants. It lies at the intersection of the Dordogne and Isle rivers eighteen miles northeast of Bordeaux. It was built seven hundred years ago during the English occupation of Aquitania by their seneschal, Sir Roger de Leyburne, and the town was then named after him. It immediately became a shipping and trading point of considerable importance, a role it has enjoyed ever since; it is still the hub of the wine trade in the Dordogne valley.

Hugh Johnson, in his interesting book *Wine*, describes the town as "provincial" and being of "utter dullness." I must say that I disagree. It may not be a swinging metropolis, but it is a pleasant switch from the more frenetic centers of the twentieth century— a tree-shaded, sun-dappled, riverside town, scattered with medieval towers and buildings. At its center is a lovely arcaded sixteenth-century square, which is used once a week for a colorful outdoor market.

Better yet, Libourne has pleasant hotels and good restaurants. It is a good base from which to visit the surrounding vineyards.

Best known is the Hôtel Loubat, a comfortable *nid* not far from the railroad station. Its rooms are clean and moderately priced, and its restaurant has earned a star in the *Michelin*. The *spécialités* include *lamproie de la Dordogne, gratin de queues de langoustines,* and *ris de veau au foie gras,* and the wine list includes a good cross section of the best wines of the nearby vineyards of Pomerol and Saint-Émilion.

GRANDS CRUS OF POMEROL

Cru Exceptionnel:

Château Pétrus

Some Grands Crus:

Château Beauregard
Château Bourgneuf
Château Certan-le-May
Château Clinet
Château Clos-du-Clocher
Château Domaine de l'Eglise
Château l'Eglise-Clinet
Château Clos l'Eglise
Château l'Enclos
Château l'Évangile
Château Feytit-Clinet
Château Gazin
Château Gombaude-Guillot
Château Grate-Cap
Château Guillot
Château La Cabane
Château Le Caillou
Château La Commanderie
Château La Conseillante
Château La Croix
Château La Croix-de-Gay
Château La Croix-Saint-Georges

Château Lafleur
Château Lafleur-Pétrus
Château Lagrange
Château La Grave-Trigant-de-Boisset
Château La Pointe
Château Latour-Pomerol
Château La Violette
Château Le Gay
Château Mazeyres
Château Clos-Mazeyres
Château Moulinet
Château Nénin
Château Petit-Village
Château Plince
Château Clos-René
Château Rouget
Château De Sales
Château Taillefer
Château Trotanoy
Château Vieux-Château-Certan
Château Vraie-Croix-de-Gay

Libourne itself is not known as a wine-producing town, and this is somewhat unjust, as it does make quite a lot of wine, and much of it excellent. About a third of the wine called Pomerol lies within Libourne's borders, as does a goodly chunk of Saint-Émilion—Pomerol lying northeast and Saint-Émilion to the east.

The Pomerol villages include Pomerol itself and the sister villages of Lalande-de-Pomerol and Néac. Of the three, Pomerol is by far the most famous, and justifiably so. It was known in Roman times as a great fruit-growing center, hence the name, which derives from the Latin word for fruit, *pomum*, or perhaps from the goddess of fruit trees, Pomona. During the Middle Ages, Pomerol became a center for one of the greatest military orders of Christendom, the Knights of Saint John of Jerusalem, better known as the Knights Hospitalers, and they, undoubtedly inspired by Pomerol's muse, put down their swords and took up pruning hooks. The vineyards that were to make Pomerol renowned were most likely planted by them. Although Pomerol was started after the heyday of the English occupation, it gradually asserted itself as one of France's most pleasant wines. By the nineteenth century it was known everywhere, and Pomerol's reputation has been growing ever since.

In size Pomerol is actually the smallest of any wine-producing area in the Bordelais, but the wines hit an extraordinarily high average, one of the best in France. A good regional Pomerol from a reputable shipper or importer is about as safe a buy as one can hope to make among modestly priced wines. Whereas some areas, such as the Médoc, produce wines that range from the sublime to the nearly undrinkable, the red wines of Pomerol are almost always soft, generous, and very agreeable.

There are several reasons for this, but probably the most important is the types of grapes used. Pomerol, like all Bordeaux, is made of a combination of different grape varietals, the formula varying according to the taste and expertise of the vineyard owner. However, here as in Saint-Émilion, the emphasis is on the Merlot, a grape that produces good wine, but which yields excellent ones on the north bank of the Dordogne. Wines made from the Merlot mature relatively quickly. They are soft, with a velvety, full flavor and a deep color. They are what the French sometimes call "fat" wines, lacking perhaps the lean elegance of the better Médocs, but compensating for it by their warmth and vigor.

The countryside around Pomerol and the other communes on the northern shore of the Dordogne seem to reflect the character of their wines. In the Médoc, many of the great vineyards surround princely châteaux owned by the titled or wealthy. The resultant wines are like aristocrats—elegant, subtle, and fine. Pomerol, too, reflects its ecology. Here the châteaux are not so pretentious. Many of them are agreeable French country houses, good-looking, solid, and comfortable, whose owners live and work on the land. To be sure there are also a few ravishing little châteaux, such as the charming and beautifully proportioned Château Beauregard. But even in this case the owner lives in the château and personally guides the raising of the grapes and the vintaging of the wine. His wine, like most Pomerols, shows it. It is warm, soft, and generous. In short it is like a close friend. It has a personal feeling to it.

First of the Pomerols is certainly Château Pétrus, which is generally regarded as one of the top eight red wines of Bordeaux, with Lafite, Latour, Margaux, Mouton-Rothschild, Haut-Brion, Cheval-Blanc, and Ausone. Cost is in its own way a pretty accurate classification, and the price Pétrus commands certainly puts it at the top level of Bordeaux's pantheon of wines.

Petrus is the Latin word for Peter, and the château's label bears a portrait of the Saint with the key to the Pearly Gates in his hand. As those who were attentive in Sunday School may remember, *petros* was the Greek word for stone, and so when Jesus pointed to Peter and said, "Upon this rock I shall build my church," he was punning as well as being prophetic. The name is singularly apt for the château. Not only is the wine it produces divine, but the vineyard is gravelly and filled with small stones. The wine has a unique flavor that many associate with the taste of truffles, and which is said to be caused by a substratum of iron-laden earth. Whatever the reason there is no other wine like it. Generous, full, almost chewy with flavor, and having its unique bouquet, it well warrants its reputation as one of France's finest wines. Production, alas, is very small, something in the neighborhood of 2,500 cases a year, a factor that doesn't make the wine any cheaper.

The vineyard lies right on the border of Saint-Émilion, directly across the line from Château Cheval-Blanc. The former owner, Madame Edmond Loubat, was one of the legendary *grandes dames* of the wine world. Her meticulous care gave the property the reputation of being not only one of the finest, but one of the best-run vineyards in France. After her demise her niece, Madame Lacoste, and one of the most renowned proprietors and shippers of the Pomerol-Saint-Émilion region, Monsieur Moueix, kept up her tradition.

Other excellent Pomerols include the Château Certan and the Vieux-Château-Certan, the châteaux La Conseillante, l'Évangile, Beauregard, Clinet, Clos-de-l'Eglise Clinet, the châteaux Lafleur-Pétrus, Gazin, Lafleur, Latour-Pomerol—also a property that once belonged to the late Madame Edmond Loubat—the châteaux Nénin, Petit-Village, Plince, La Pointe, Trotanoy, and De Sales. These are all excellent, as are many others too small to mention.

In general Pomerol's vineyards are minuscule compared with the great estates on the other side of the Garonne and Gironde. Also the Appellation Contrôlée regulations governing the amount of wine allowed per acre of vines is the most restricted of any area in the Bordelais. For the wine lover this is a mixed blessing. It means that the wine of Pomerol will be of uncommon quality, but it also means that production will be small. On top of the official restrictions, the vineyards on the north shore of the Dordogne were ferociously hit by the freeze of February, 1956. Worst hit were the vineyards around Libourne. A great many of the vines were maimed, and some utterly destroyed. The result was a gradual shortage of wine that did not end until the vintage of 1964. All of this served for a while to keep Pomerol's and Saint-Émilion's prices unnaturally high.

Pomerols mature early for Bordeaux wines. Four years is enough for all but the top châteaux, and six will usually do them nicely.

Lalande-de-Pomerol and Néac, the two vineyard areas just to the north of Pomerol, are similar in soil characteristics and have exactly the same regulations governing the raising of grapes and vinification as Pomerol itself. Not surprisingly, the wines resemble Pomerols, though in general they are a little less complex and a little less subtle. Of the two, Lalande-de-Pomerol—with two rather well-known châteaux, La Commanderie and Bel Air—is usually given the palm over Néac. Whether quite up to Pomerol or not, both communes produce soft, warm, generous, quickly maturing red wines that are, *mirabile dictu*, remarkably inexpensive. And in this day of astronomically high wine prices this is no small blessing.

Pomerol, Lalande-de-Pomerol, and Néac come close to being Bordeaux's all-purpose red wines. They are ideal companions for beef as well as roast turkey, duck, and chicken. They are perhaps a little lusty for milk-fed veal, but with anything older they will serve admirably. For those who like red wine with their roast pork, Pomerol and its sisters will heighten its savor. And game, too, can well be squired by a few bottles of this agreeable wine. As the reader may guess, it is one of my favorite red wines. If he tries it, perhaps he will understand why.

Bordeaux

Lesser-Known Vineyards

The Greek Anacreon, whose lyrical poems extolled the delights of wine and love, is said to have strangled on a raisin—a sure warning to the wine lover to take his grapes in liquid form. We Americans have another reason to remember Anacreon. In the eighteenth century one of the favorite English drinking songs was called "To Anacreon in Heaven." Given a different set of words by Francis Scott Key, it emerged as "The Star-Spangled Banner." Anacreon's ironic demise was a little sad, but judging from the enthusiasm with which the poet wrote, he must have enjoyed the research for his works. What pleasure he would have taken in that vine-spangled corner of France, Bordeaux.

The preceding chapters have been dedicated to Bordeaux's more famous viticultural regions, but there is still more to be discovered in the smaller areas. Though their provender may not be as majestic as the top wines of the other regions, they are still sound wines, of remarkably good value because they are relatively unknown.

As we mentioned before, vineyards surround Bordeaux at every compass point. Starting due north, or at twelve o'clock, and going clockwise around the city seems as logical a way as any to organize our tour.

About twenty-five miles north of Bordeaux, on the east bank of the Gironde estuary facing out across the waters toward the Médoc, lies the old fortress town of Blaye. This rather pretty little village since ancient times has served as a river checkpoint to guard the rich cities up the Garonne and Dordogne. The most recent fortress was built on a hill between the river and the town by Vauban, Louis XIV's master engineer and military architect. Its imposing bulk still dominates both the town and the river up and down as far as the eye can see. It is no longer of any military value, and its barbicans and escarpments now only lure the occasional tourist coming up for the view or a pleasant place to have a picnic.

Behind Blaye is a large area named the Blayais, which makes up the northeastern boundary of the Bordelais. Just beyond it are the rolling vineyards of the Charente, whose wines provide the raw material for the king of *eau-de-vie,* Cognac. The Blayais produces a great deal of wine, mostly whites of no great consequence. There are some reds, however, that are pleasant and very cheap, and these are used frequently by the great Bordeaux shippers to make up their house-brand Bordeaux.

A little southeast of Blaye is Bourg, another small town girded by vineyards. In this case the region behind it is known as the Bourgeais. Smaller than the Blayais, it also generally produces better wines. The reds in particular are not to be sneered at. A properly matured Bourgeais from a good vineyard can be most agreeable—and a very good value. Not yet discovered by the American consumer or wine importer, the good red wines of Bourg would certainly go a long way toward satisfying the demand of the American wine lover for decent red wines at a moderate price.

Bourg lies close to the point of junction of the Gironde and the Dordogne. A little way up the Dordogne, just to the west of Saint-Émilion and Pomerol, are the Côtes-de-Fronsac and the Côtes-de-Canon-Fronsac. Of the two, the wines of Canon-Fronsac are superior, and the best of them, such as the wine of Château Canon itself, certainly bear watching. The region is improving, and some day may well join its neighbors of Pomerol and Saint-Émilion as the pearls of the Dordogne. About 350,000 cases of red Côtes-de-Fronsac and about 150,000 cases of Côtes-de-Canon-Fronsac are produced in a good vintage year. The best of these are somewhat similar to the wines of the neighboring Pomerol, but because they are not well known, they are considerably less expensive. Behind the Fronsadais, as the region is called, a good deal of thin, dry white wine is made to be distilled into brandy.

On the south bank of the Dordogne, opposite the Côtes-de-Fronsac, is the Graves de Vayres, a region that produces mostly white wines and a tiny amount of red. These wines should not be confused with those from Graves, a region twenty miles to the west on the other shore of the Garonne. Graves de Vayres are simply wines that come from grapes grown on the gravelly soil of Vayres. Though some of the Graves de Vayres is agreeable, it is not as high an appellation as Graves. Much of the wine is consumed in carafe *in situ,* though some is exported to the United States, and a considerable amount goes to Germany and Scandinavia.

One of the most recent of Bordeaux's Appellations Contrôlées is the Côtes de Castillon. These wines come from vineyards around the town on the north bank of the Dordogne, where the decisive battle of 1453 took place. The wine by law has to be red. In flavor it is somewhat akin to its better-known neighbor, Saint-Émilion.

Sainte-Foy-de-Bordeaux is the easternmost region of the Bordelais. Lying on the south bank of the Dordogne, it produces both red and white wines, though the former is made in minuscule quantities. Ninety-eight percent of Sainte-Foy's wines are white. They range from liqueur wines somewhat similar to Sauternes, though lacking its finesse, to so-called "dry" whites that are really semisweet. The liqueur wines are pleasant as dessert wines, and are remarkably inexpensive. In a good vintage year Sainte-Foy-de-Bordeaux produces about 500,000 cases.

The term Entre-Deux-Mers is apt to cause some confusion to the neophyte wine lover, as it refers to two things—one a geographical area and the other a viniferous area that does not correspond to the geographical one. The geographical area is delineated by the Dordogne to the north and the Garonne to the south and west. Entre-Deux-Mers, or "between the two seas," perhaps more accurately should be called "between the two waters," but the term is roughly descriptive, as the land lies in the fork formed by the confluence of the two rivers.

Technically, a number of viticultural regions fall within the geographical confines of Entre-Deux-Mers: Vayres, Sainte-Foy-de-Bordeaux, Saint-Macaire, Sainte-Croix-du-Mont, Loupiac, and the Premières Côtes de Bordeaux. Most of these regions proudly flaunt their own names instead of using the more general Entre-Deux-Mers. The vineyards of the viniferous Entre-Deux-Mers lie in the center part of the larger geographical area, the edges being allowed to call themselves by their own regional names.

Also, although both red and white wines are made in Entre-Deux-Mers, only the whites are allowed to carry the name. And, in fact, white wines are produced in very large quantities, close to a million cases in a good vintage year. Recently Bordeaux vintners began making wines tailored to fit current taste—that is to say dry, light white wines that are rather high in acidity, aiming at a type similar to Muscadet, the Breton wine from the mouth of the Loire. Though the resultant wines are certainly not great, they are admirable companions for seafood, and as such are very popular. Entre-Deux-Mers now produces this sort of wine. It often appears in spire-shaped bottles similar to the German and Alsatian ones, but the taste of course is not at all the same. Nevertheless the wine is very inexpensive and useful.

The limitations on the amount of wine permitted to be grown in Entre-Deux-Mers is 535 gallons per acre, putting it in the same class as plain Bordeaux white. By contrast, Graves is allowed only 428 gallons per acre.

The Premières Côtes de Bordeaux make up much of the western flank of Entre-Deux-Mers. They come from a narrow strip of land running twenty-five miles upriver on the east bank of the Garonne from a point just north of Bordeaux. Just opposite lie the regions of Graves and Sauternes. A great deal of wine is produced in the region—more than a million cases of white and 350,000 cases of red in a good vintage year.

The red wine can be very good indeed. Like its neighbor from across the river, Graves, it needs a little time to mature, but then it produces a good, sound claret. Coming from a reputable grower, shipper, or importer, it can be, if properly matured, one of the best wine buys from the Bordelais.

The whites too are very good. Until recently Premières Côtes de Bordeaux concentrated on producing sweet and semisweet liqueur wines somewhat akin on a lesser scale to those of Sauternes and Barsac from across the river. It now also produces rather dry and semidry white wines to cover the gamut of current tastes.

Sainte-Croix-du-Mont, Loupiac, and Saint-Macaire, three villages facing the vineyards of Sauternes and Barsac across the Garonne, have their own Appellation Contrôlée. The wines are of the same type as Sauternes and Barsac, lacking only their subtlety and finesse. Sainte-Croix-du-Mont and Loupiac are the better known of the three and have the higher appellation. Saint-Macaire is producing some dry and medium-dry white wines to satisfy the present market demands. The wines from all three villages must be white to carry their names.

Two towns that do not have a separate appellation, but which are equally well known, are Langoiran and Cadillac. The latter is a charming little village filled with medieval and Renaissance remains, among them the Château d'Épernon, at present being restored. It was built by one of King Henri III's favorite *mignons,* the Duc d'Épernon, Grand High Admiral of France and owner of one of the Médoc's most honored vineyards, the Château-Beychevelle.

Cadillac is, of course, the name of a well-known car, and indeed there is a connection between the village and the automobile. In 1701, a native of the region, Antoine de la Mothe Cadillac, colonial administrator of Canada, built a village and fort on the straits between Lake Huron and Lake Ontario to guard them. The French word for strait is *étroit,* and a village on it would be a *ville d'étroit,* which is how Detroit got its name. From there it was a short step to name a car in honor of the founder of the city.

Cadillac, a good liqueurish white wine, is a delicious companion for a sweet dessert. Served chilled, it is a pleasant apéritif.

Among the drier Premières Côtes de Bordeaux, Bordeaux-Haut-Benauge and Entre-Deux-Mers Haut-Benauge are two recent additions to the list of appellation wines of Bordeaux. The wines are white, quite dry, moderately priced, and good with seafood, pork, veal, and creamed fowl.

Bordeaux and Bordeaux Supérieur are red, white, or rosé wines that come from viticultural areas of the Gironde not more specifically defined, or from areas that for some reason are not allowed to bear their own names. This is not necessarily a sign that the wine is not up to snuff. Perfectly good red wines, for example, may be made in regions that allow only a white wine to carry their name. This red then has to call itself Bordeaux or Bordeaux Supérieur.

Of the two, Bordeaux Supérieur, obviously, is the higher classification, having had to pass more stringent controls of grape raising as well as vinification. Ordinary Bordeaux, for example, must come from vineyards producing not more than 535 gallons per acre, while Bordeaux Supérieur is limited to 428 gallons per acre. Huge amounts of these wines are produced: about fourteen million cases of Bordeaux Blanc and about three and a half million of Bordeaux Rouge in a good vintage year. In addition, about a million cases of Bordeaux Blanc Supérieur are made and two and a half million of Bordeaux Rouge Supérieur.

Though the amounts may be enormous, much of the wine can be quite good. However, as is the case with all regional wines where there is a great range in quality, look to the name and reputation of the shipper or importer. If his name is honorable and good, he will try to present the best bottle of wine for the price paid. To buy otherwise is just taking pot luck.

In summary, the Bordeaux region produces wines of nearly every flavor, color, and variety. In each category the best wines are at least equal to the greatest of their kind. Bordeaux also produces large quantities of good, sound, inexpensive table wines that again cover the full gamut of taste. These wines can provide the discriminating oenophile with pleasant companions for his table.

I have tried to cover as adequately as space would permit the salient points of Bordeaux wines. One last reminder should again be given: no wine tastes good unless it is properly matured. It is a crime to drink a great wine before its prime. So that you may avoid doing so, the chapter on vintages covers on pages 317–319 the position of Bordeaux bottled in the dozen or so years prior to the publication of this book and their prospects for the decade of the seventies.

Cognac

When Brillat-Savarin made his famous observation, "Tell me what you eat, and I will tell you what you are," he might well have said, "tell me what you eat or drink," for the drinking habits of men, nations, and cultures are apt to be just as indicative of what they are as the solid food they ingest.

For example, a reasonably accurate way of dividing the ancient cultures of the Mediterranean from the newer ones of northern Europe is by drinking habit. Mediterranean man has drunk wine since the dawn of history. He has used it for balm, nutriment, and conviviality. So attached to it has he become that it has even taken on religious significance. Every religion that stems from the Mediterranean's shores has used wine as an integral part of worship. The Hebrews and the Greeks, the Romans and the Christians, all have had rites in which wine played a part.

A further proof of the "Mediterraneanness" of wine jumps to the eye if one looks at an historical atlas. The high point of the Mediterranean tide was the Roman Empire. It seems no accident that the limits of viticulture and viticultural influence still trace the Empire's frontiers—the Rhine, the Moselle, and the Danube. Beyond that were the wild tribes of Germans, Slavs, and Celts; beer swillers all.

In the Middle Ages, it was a hallmark of culture for the nobility and clergy to keep up the practices of the great Mediterranean civilization, then at ebb. Latin was used for formal communications, while at the nobles' and monks' tables wine was served. The rough natives, reduced by their semicivilized masters to serfdom, continued to make do with beer.

Cognac

Michelin Regional Map 72
Michelin Guide Vert *Côte de l'Atlantique*

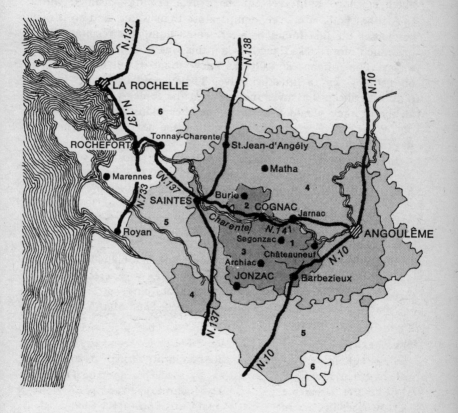

1   **Grande Champagne**
2   **Borderies**
3   **Petite Champagne**
4   **Fins Bois**
5   **Bons Bois**
6   **Bois Ordinaires**

Wine, of course, is the fermented juice of fruit—usually grapes. Beer, on the other hand, is fermented grain mash, flavored by hops. Even today the distinction between the two cultures is kept when it comes to hard spirits. Northern Europe and those areas influenced by its colonists drink whiskey—that is to say, a form of distilled beer. When a southern European has need for a little "high spirited" reinforcement, he drinks brandy—distilled wine.

Alcohol boils at a lower temperature than water, and so if one condenses the first fumes of a fermented liquid the resultant fluid has much more kick. Exactly when this was first observed is hard to say. The Romans and Greeks knew about it, but their method of distilling was a little primitive. They would boil wine in big pots with sheepskins over them. When the fumes ceased smelling alcoholic, they would take away the sheepskins and wring them out. What sort of hangover imbibers had the next morning, history has the kindness not to relate.

In the seventh and eighth centuries, the Moslem whirlwind swept across the Mediterranean world. The Prophet, of course, had specifically forbidden his followers to imbibe any form of

---

RESTAURANT-HOTELS

Angoulême (Charente)	*Hostellerie du Moulin du Main Brun (La Vigerie; tel. 2 at St.-Saturnin) p. 265
Saint-Martin-du-Faux (Haute-Vienne)	La Chapelle Saint-Martin p. 27

RESTAURANTS

Ile de la Reine, nr. Cognac (Charente)	Restaurant Robinson p. 265
Cierzac (Charente)	Le Moulin de Cierzac p. 27
La Rochelle (Charente-Maritime)	*Au Vieux Port (4, rue Chaine; tel. 28.23.41) p. 265

HOTEL

La Rochelle	Hôtel Champlain (20, rue Rambaud; tel. 28.59.98) p. 265

alcoholic drink, although they were allowed the comforts of kif, an Arabic form of marihuana. These sons of the desert considered wine sinful, dangerous, and debilitating—much the same attitude that Europeans took to the Arabs' form of pleasantry. *Chacun à son goût.*

However, though the Arabs were forbidden to drink alcohol, they did have other uses for it. When Arab houris prettied up for the evening to please their sheiks, they, like so many of their sisters before and since, spent a good deal of time hiding and highlighting certain features of their faces. One particular vogue, then as now, was to color and change the shape of the eyebrows, which they did by dissolving minute quantities of powdered anti- mony in a fluid distilled from wine. The word in Arabic for powder is *kuhl,* and so it and the fluid together were called by its name alone, the *kuhl*—in Arabic, *al-kuhl.* When Westerners first ran across it, they borrowed this name for the fluid alone, forgetting all about the antimony—hence our word alcohol.

The Arabs also greatly improved on the Greek and Roman methods of distillation. In fact, it was they who invented the pro- totype of the pot still, which is still sometimes called by its Arabic name, alembic. By the late Middle Ages alembics were known all over Europe. No self-respecting alchemist would have been with- out one. Therefore, it was only a question of time before some unknown benefactor turned his attention toward using the alembic to make potable alcohol.

Present-day distilling is done mainly by two kinds of stills: the old-fashioned pot still with its spiraling condenser rising from the top; and a nineteenth-century addition, the patent still. The most popular patent still is the Coffey still, named after its Irish inventor. The name is actually not too inappropriate when taken as its homophone, coffee: the still is in effect a huge percolator, or two of them, side by side—one to steam and one to condense—in which the alcohol is lured out of the wine or beer in much the same way that the essence is steamed from coffee. Though there are many advantages to the Coffey still, the old pot still continues to be used in the making of fine malt whiskeys, and in France in the making of that paragon of brandies, Cognac.

Nearly every region of France that grows the grape also produces some sort of grape brandy. Sometimes, as with the regal brandies of Cognac and Armagnac, it is distilled from wine made especially for the purpose. More often it is made from the dried-out skins of pressed grapes, which are sprinkled with water and sugar and encouraged to go through another fermentation, seeping whatever flavor they can from the grape residue. The result is a thin sort of wine that is then distilled to make grape brandy. The word for residue in French is *marc,* and brandy made from it is called by the same name.

Lately the French government, in an attempt to control France's rather frightening level of alcoholism, has been making vintners turn in all their pressings immediately after the juice has been pressed from them. No pressings; no marc. The consequence is the disappearance of the splendidly baroque machines of the itinerant *bouilleurs de cru.* These Rube Goldbergian contraptions looked like something between an old-fashioned steamroller and an 1820 locomotive. They would be trundled from farmyard to farmyard where the waiting marc would be heaped into them to have its alcohol steamed off. Until recently nearly every French vintner had his own particular batch of "white lightning" with which he regaled friends and family. A few years ago I rented a house with vineyard attached in Beaujolais. The *vigneron* in residence used to insist that I drink the "estate's" marc, and I still wince when I remember the next day's headache. Nevertheless, some marc, especially that of Burgundy, is carefully made. The best of it is a very good drink.

The best and best-known brandies of France come from two regions in the southwestern part of the country, Cognac and Armagnac. Of the two, Cognac is more elegant, finer, and more subtle. Armagnac is fuller, more evident; a warm-blooded son of the open air.

Though the population of Cognac is barely over twenty thousand, it certainly is one of the best-known towns in the world. Illustrating this is a story about the bishop of Angoulême, in whose diocese Cognac lies. A few years ago he went off to Rome for a meeting with his brother bishops. Quite naturally he introduced himself as the Bishop of Angoulême, but catching the look of disinterest in his brethren's eyes, he quickly reintroduced himself as the "Bishop of Cognac." At this there were lots of "aahs," and everyone came to ask him how things were going in his part of the world.

Arriving at Cognac, one finds that the place is hardly remarkable. It is a rather charming little provincial town on the banks of a lazily flowing stream, the Charente. The countryside around it consists of low, rolling hills covered with copses of trees and vineyards, with a scattering of châteaux and villages with streams flowing at their feet. The town is dedicated quite completely to the making of its famous elixir.

The history of Cognac as a beverage starts a half century after the death of François I with the accession of Henri IV in 1589. This benevolent Béarnais, *bon viveur,* gallant in love and war, and a cynic toward the doctrinaire, stopped the fury of a religious civil war by a simple diplomatic tactic. Leader and mainstay of one faction, he suddenly switched sides. The Protestants, his ex-followers, were flabbergasted; the Catholics, his sworn enemies, were nonplussed; and France, with a sigh of relief, collapsed into the arms of peace, something she had not known for forty years.

During the religious wars the area around the Charente had been a great Huguenot center. Near its mouth lay the Protestant stronghold of La Rochelle. As a result the entire area had become the battleground between opposing forces, its houses burned and pillaged, cattle slaughtered, and fields laid waste. But with the accession of Henri, the farmer returned to his fields, the artisan to his tools, and the banks of the river grew green with the vines of peace.

One effect of the religious wars, however, still remained. The Huguenots of the valley had come into close contact, militarily and economically, with their coreligionists in Holland. And the Dutch, perched on the chilly littoral of the North Sea, had for years reveled in the comforts of distilled, or, as they called it, "burned" wine. The Dutch word for "burned wine" was *brande-wijn,* and from this our word brandy derives.

The wine of the Charente was not considered great in itself, but it was discovered that when distilled it produced the finest of brandies. Ships were soon plying the Bay of Biscay and the Channel laden with precious *brandewijn* for the thirsty Hollanders. It wasn't long before the French, too, began to recognize the glories of this essence of wine. As their voyageurs and trappers penetrated Arctic North America, as their great explorers La Salle, Champlain, Bougainville, and La Pérouse wandered over the globe, this portable invigorator spread with them.

The process of making Cognac is complicated. The grape that is used has considerable influence over the character and quality of the subsequent brandy. In the Cognac region the only grapes allowed by law for brandy making are the Folle Blanche, the Saint-Émilion, the Colombard, the Blanc Ramé, the Jurançon Blanc, the Montils, the Sémillon, and the Sauvignon. In practice the vast majority of the wines are at present made from the Saint-Émilion, or, as it is called in Italy, the Trebbiano, in Algeria, the Ugni Blanc. In southern climes the Saint-Émilion produces full, rather ordinary white wines. In the more northern area of Cognac it makes a light, lean, hard, rather astringent wine, not very good for quaffing, but excellent for brandy making.

A great deal of calcium or chalk in the soil is usually beneficial for vines destined to produce white wines. The best vineyards of Champagne, Chablis, Montrachet, Pouilly-Fuissé, even those *albariza* vineyards in Jerez from which the finest Sherry comes—all have an abnormally high proportion of calcium or chalk. And so it is with Cognac. One of the terms defining excellence on a Cognac bottle's label is the area from which the grapes come, and these regions are ordered in almost exact proportion to the amount of calcium in their soil. The Cognac area is a rough bull's-eye. The very center is a small region around the town of Segonzac, bordered on the north by the river Charente, on whose banks sit the brandy-making towns of Cognac and Jarnac. The region is called the Grande Champagne—no relation to the sparkling wine made several hundred miles to the northeast. Cognacs made from wines of this region are called Grande Champagne or Fine Grande Champagne—*fine* being the French word for brandy. If properly made and matured, they set the standard for what the finest Cognac should be.

Embracing the area of Grande Champagne is a half-moon-shaped region to the south, called Petite Champagne. This, with another tiny area called Borderies, produces superb Cognacs that often rival those of the Grande Champagne itself. Then comes a ring called Fins Bois, which in its turn is encircled by Bons Bois.

Farther out, approaching the Atlantic coast, is the Bois Ordinaires, and on the coast itself, including the islands of Oleron and Ré, is the region called the Bois à Terroir. Each brandy coming from these different soils has its own special characteristic, and though some by themselves may not be especially pleasant, they can in small quantities be added to a blend to contribute a special savor.

Grande Champagne Cognacs are rarely seen on the market. The great brandy houses usually prefer to save their stocks to add elegance and delicacy to their blends. Often, however, one may see a Champagne Cognac—still expensive, but if produced by a good house, a very good brandy made of a mixture of Petite Champagne and Grande Champagne Cognacs.

All Cognac is distilled in old-fashioned pot stills made of burnished brick and copper. After the wine is fermented it is put into one of these kettles, under which an even fire is built. As the temperature rises, the alcohol begins to steam off and rises through the condenser where it cools and converts back into fluid.

Neither the beginning of the distillation, called the *tête,* or head, nor the end—the *queue,* or tail—is saved. Only the center is kept, the *coeur,* or heart. This first distillate is called the *brouillis,* or "mixed up stuff," an apt description, as the alcohol is still mixed with the wine.

The *coeur* of the *brouillis* is distilled again. Once again the *tête* and the *queue,* which have in them a number of unpleasant tasting and acting agents, are deleted. The heart of this second distillation is the *bonne chauffe*, or "good distillate." High in alcohol, white and clear like spring water, it is ready to be put into barrels and aged.

The aging of Cognac is another exact art. Cognac must be aged in barrels of oak that come from Limousin in central France. Though to the cursory observer oak trees may appear to be the same, this is not at all true. Oak, like vines, develops differently in dissimilar climates and soils—sometimes having more tannin, sometimes less, sometimes having fine, tight grains in the wood, sometimes larger, more absorbent ones. Oak casks are vital to the maturing of brandy, as the aging alcohol marries with the oak's tannin and other woody substances and is mellowed by them. Thus the sort of oak used helps to determine the type of brandy that will result, and for the flavoring and mellowing of Cognac, no other oak but that of the Limousin will do.

The brandy sits in the casks anywhere from three to fifty years, the marriage of raw alcohol and wood essences creating that glorious offspring that will soon be known as Cognac. Under ideal circumstances the brandy will rest until it has absorbed the proper amount of oxygen through the pores in the wood of its barrels. Conversely, a huge amount of alcohol evaporates into the atmosphere, a necessary loss if the Cognac is to develop properly.

After the ideal circumstances cited above, the brandy will be blended if necessary and bottled. From the moment it is in the bottle, Cognac no longer matures. Age in brandy is determined only by the length of time it stays in the cask, not how long ago it was made. Once in the bottle, it always remains the same.

Ideally, good Cognac should be from ten to forty years in wood. However, this presupposes the willingness on the part of the brandy maker to tie up a huge amount of capital in aging stocks. The economics of the world being what they are, few are willing to do this. Countless shortcuts have been invented, the most common of which are the addition of distilled water or weak brandy to get the Cognac to a proper ratio of alcohol to water, the use of caramel to give a young brandy color and to smooth out its roughness, and the maturation of brandy in oaken barrels used twice or more. All of this leads rather sadly to the debasing of one of mankind's noblest companions, especially if it is overdone.

Stars on a Cognac bottle mean very little, except that such a bottle by French law must be at least three years old—no great age. V.S.O.P. and Reserve must have at least four years, and V.V.O., V.V.S.O., V.V.S.O.P., X.O., Extra, Napoleon, *Vieille Réserve,* and *Vieux* must have been at least five years in wood before they may carry these names or initials. Five years is the age of the youngest brandy in the blend; usually there are several others of older age to lend taste, bouquet, and finesse.

Among the best Cognacs imported into the United States are, in my opinion: Bisquit "Extra"; Courvoisier Grand Fine Champagne; Courvoisier "Napoléon"; Delamain; Hennessy Grande Fine Champagne "Réserve"; Hennessy Grande Fine Champagne "Bras d'Or"; Hine "Triomphe"; Hine V.S.O.P.; Martell "Cordon

Bleu"; Martell "Cordon Argent"; Monnet "Anniversaire"; Otard V.S.O.P.; Polignac "Réserve" Fine Champagne; Rémy-Martin "Louis XIII"; Rémy-Martin "Lacet d'Or."

For the wandering gourmet Cognac itself has few gastronomic oases of note. There is one delightfully pretty little restaurant a short way upriver from the town on a tiny, wooded island, the Ile de la Reine. It is called Robinson after the well-known island inhabiter, Mr. Crusoe. One gets out to the island by a tiny cable ferryboat. The food is not extraordinary, but the ambience is delightful. It is all very Renoir-like and nineteenth century. Pointillistic light spatters down from the green carpet overhead onto the river. On its surface an occasional racing scull silently glides by, and opposite, shadowy forms on horseback post on a bridle path that follows the riverbank. The oysters at Robinson are delicious, coming from the nearby oyster beds of Marennes, among the finest in France. Needless to say, the brandy selection is superb.

However, a bit of well-timed traveling by car can get you to a luncheon or dinner of considerably grander style. Some thirty-four kilometers east of Cognac, on the road to Angoulême, is the quite regal Hostellerie du Moulin du Maine Brun at the tiny village of La Vigerie, boasting only one *Michelin* star, but nevertheless also the *Kléber* rating of *grande cuisine*. Or, one may head northward from Cognac for a ride of ninety-five kilometers to one of the most beautiful ports of France, La Rochelle. La Rochelle technically lies within the Cognac region, but it is not as noted for its brandy as it is for its sublime seafood. A splendid place to sample it is at the Vieux Port, right opposite the medieval tower at the harbor's mouth. A stone's throw from the restaurant is a fisherman's wharf with gaily painted trawlers bobbing on the tide, their nets hung up to dry. The port itself is enchanting, a great basin lined with sixteenth- and seventeenth-century buildings, its waters abustle with yachts and fishing boats as they make for its narrow, tower-guarded throat and the open sea. Au Vieux Port has earned one of the *Michelin*'s stars, and if one stops by to sample its piscatory provender, one will quickly see why. The host is Monsieur Epaillard and reservations are recommended.

To spend the night at La Rochelle, there is a very comfortable hotel complete with a pretty garden called the Champlain. It is named after Samuel de Champlain, explorer and French colonial

governor of Canada, who was a contemporary of our Pilgrim
fathers. He founded Quebec and laid the cornerstone of the French
American empire, leaving for us in the United States a souvenir
in the form of a lake he discovered, Lake Champlain, on the
border between New York State and Canada. He was born a few
miles from La Rochelle in the town of Brouage, and so is considered a native.

The Upper Loire

The Loire is the longest river in France, its banks overripe with château upon magnificent château. It was near this river that Eleanor of Aquitaine whiled away her twilight years, Joan of Arc fought her most decisive battle, Ronsard lived and wrote his immortal poems of love, and Balzac sharpened his insights on the motives, manners, and morals of the nineteenth-century French bourgeoisie.

Rivers have often been the spinal column of civilizations. The Yangtze and the Ganges, the Tigris-Euphrates and the Nile, the Tiber and the Danube, the Thames and the Loire have all produced cultures that flourished and overspilled their immediate valleys until the world around them was influenced by their artistry and ideas.

Each major river has a private personality that projects an image—not always a true one—on the public consciousness. The Mississippi invokes visions of stern-wheelers, jazz, and riverboat gamblers; the Danube is supposed to be blue, overhung with an aura of Tziganes, Kaffeeklatsches, zithers, and waltzes. The Loire, too, is a river of strong personality. Ask any informed person what he associates with the Loire; the answer will certainly be its châteaux, and then quite possibly its charming wines.

If any river can claim to be the river of France, the Loire certainly can. Its headwaters start far to the south in a low range of hills called the Cévennes, a scant eighty miles north of the Mediterranean. From there the Loire winds northwest through several of France's great medieval provinces: Languedoc, Lyon-

Upper Loire

Michelin Regional Maps 69, 65 & 64
Michelin Guide Vert *Châteaux de la Loire*

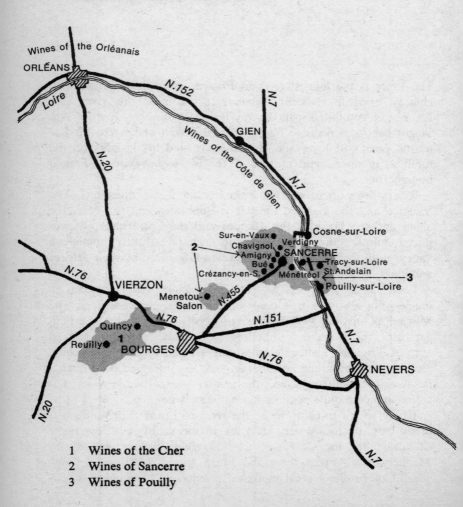

1   Wines of the Cher
2   Wines of Sancerre
3   Wines of Pouilly

nais, Bourbonnais, Burgundy, Nivernais, Berry, Orléanais, Touraine, Anjou, and Brittany. And its tributaries fan out to include Poitou, Angoumois, Limousin, Marche, Auvergne, Maine, and even Normandy. In the Middle Ages, when the bulk of heavy transport was moved by barges, this riverine net made the Loire valley the main highway of the country. Roanne, Nevers, Bourges, Orléans, Blois, Saumur, Angers, and Nantes were all medieval centers of considerable importance. And Tours, the Loire's most famous city, outshone Paris for several centuries as a center of culture and commerce.

Right after the collapse of the Roman Empire, Tours became a city of the first magnitude in the creation of the new entity that was to be known as France. Saint Martin of Tours became in effect France's first patron-saint, and Saint Gregory of Tours wrote France's first post-Roman history, a monumental work that gave the rambunctious Franks a sense of national identity and purpose. The valley of the Loire in fact became so well known as the cradle of the new French culture that it is still considered the place where the purest French is spoken. Today students wishing

---

RESTAURANT-HOTELS

Pouilly-sur-Loire (Nièvre)   *L'Espérance   p. 28, p. 274
                              Le Relais Fleuri (N. 7; tel. 1.28)
                                  p. 274
Sancerre (Cher)   Hôtel Point du Jour et Écu (10, rue
                                  St.-Martin; tel. 19)   p. 274

RESTAURANTS

Pouilly-sur-Loire   *Le Grand Cerf (tel. 61)
                              *Auberge Coq Hardi (N. 7; tel. 34)
                                  p. 274
                              *La Vieille Auberge (N. 7; tel. 55)
                                  p. 274
Bourges (Cher)   Restaurant Jacques Coeur   p. 27,
                                  p. 275

HOTEL

Bourges   Hôtel Central et Angleterre (1, pl.
                                  4-Pilliers; tel. 24.00.51)

to learn French at its most classical go to the Touraine, not to Paris.

But from the ninth century onward, the navigability of the river, the very feature that gave the Loire valley its pre-eminent position, began to work against it. Out of the north the Vikings appeared, and, using the Loire as a roadway into a rich interior they had not yet pillaged, rowed up in their dragon ships, robbing, burning, and raping as they went. Tours, though 150 miles from the sea, was sacked, and many of its most precious possessions, including the bones of Saint Martin himself, were moved inland.

For the same reason that Tours languished, its rival, Paris, began to flourish. Both were on major rivers; but whereas Tours sat peacefully on the shore of a straight, broad river, too wide to be defended, Paris squatted on an island citadel in the middle of a serpentine stream whose every bend was overshadowed by a fortress.

In 1154, Henry Plantagenet, count of Anjou and duke of Normandy, whose wife, the ubiquitous Eleanor of Aquitaine, was duchess of Gascony and Guyenne, became king of England. During the next three centuries, the Loire valley was in a state of continual warfare as the French tried to throw the Angevin-English out, and Henry's descendants attempted to lay claim to the whole of France. Vineyards and fields were trampled beneath the forces of Edward the Black Prince and the Constable du Guesclin. During that time, a number of English words were adopted by the people of western France. A kind of all-enveloping, protective bonnet designed to save young maidens from being seized and embraced against their wills was called a "kiss-me-not." And the English soldiers were known by the words they most frequently used—"les Goddams."

Angers was a focal point of the struggle. And probably the most decisive battle of the long wars was fought at another Loire city. It was at Orléans that Joan of Arc revived the demoralized French forces by raising its siege, and gave the English their first thorough drubbing. Ever after she was known as the Maid of Orléans.

In 1453, the English were finally crushed and the clouds of war rolled back. For the next century and a half, the Loire became one of the major centers of the Renaissance world. Drawn by its lovely countryside and pleasant climate, the French kings and their courts moved into the valley. Tearing down the gloomy *châteaux forts* with their thick walls, slit windows, dungeons, and oubliettes, they erected in their stead a scattering of fairy-tale palaces. The Loire's apogee came during the reign of the great François I, contemporary and rival of two other European monarchs of huge ambition, Henry VIII of England and Charles V of Germany and Spain.

Under François and his descendants, the Loire flourished as never before. The finest artists and craftsmen were imported to aid local artisans in the construction of a romantic dream. Airy châteaux and graceful palaces rose to glimmer in the waters of the Loire and its tributaries. Leonardo da Vinci was lured from Italy to work there. Benvenuto Cellini visited and sculpted. Catherine de Medici, wife of François' son Henri II, made her contributions to gastronomic history by bringing Florentine chefs versed in the classic cuisine—something the French had not been much interested in until then. She also brought the recipe for ice cream and a strange implement called a fork. The world's tables were never to be the same again. For the literary, too, it was a magical time to be alive. Joachim du Bellay, Rabelais, and the sublime Ronsard matched with wit and words their fellow artists' outpouring of paint and stone. Between them they did much to mold the French language into one of the most precise, elegant, subtle, and sensitive of this planet.

The only thing that could ruin this idyll was civil war, and in due course it came. In the sixteenth century the Protestant Reformation swept Europe, and France, like the rest of the continent, split in two as Huguenot and Catholic took up arms. The Loire valley became a cockpit of conflict. One of the greatest Protestant centers in France was Saumur, a city where a major reformist seminary was situated. Other places, including the well-known wine town of Sancerre, became Protestant citadels.

The result of the Reformation was twenty-five years of murderous warfare, ending finally when the benevolently cynical Henri IV promulgated the Edict of Nantes, which guaranteed religious freedom for all his subjects. However, in the last part of the seventeenth century, Louis XIV revoked the Edict, and with that nearly

400,000 Huguenots were forced to leave France. The Loire valley was hard hit, as many of its most industrious citizens fled to England, Germany, the Low Countries, and America.

With the religious wars, Paris and the new palaces around it such as Versailles began clearly to be the center of France. The Loire gradually declined into something of a rustic backwater. To be sure, there was a brief flurry of excitement when the river steamboat made its appearance in the 1830s. For a moment it seemed as if the Loire might regain its function as the nation's main artery. But shortly after the steamboat appeared, railroad lines began crisscrossing the country.

And so the Loire remains more or less as it was—a great, slow band of silver winding through a pastoral countryside, with elegant palaces gracing its bends and royal châteaux brooding benevolently over the riparian villages at their feet.

Gastronomically, the Loire has a plethora of specialties to offer. Touraine is known as the garden of France, and its fruits and vegetables have earned a reputation that makes them much sought after. From the mouth of the river at Le Croisic comes a host of *fruits de mer,* including some of the world's finest oysters. The waters of the Loire itself contain their own treasures—salmon, shad, eel, pike, trout, and carp. From Nantes comes what many believe to be the best duck of France, though Rouen might contest that. The forests are filled with birds and rabbits, and deer and wild boar besides. The lamb of Berry and Auvergne is widely renowned as is the *agneau pré-salé* from the mouth of the Loire. From Charolais comes fine beef. Cheeses are abundant: Cantal, Saint-Nectaire and bleu d'Auvergne from Auvergne; a somewhat Camembertlike cheese called the Olivet from Orléans; Sainte-Maure from Touraine; Nantais, a soft, fresh cream cheese from the mouth of the river; and probably most famous of all, Port-du-Salut, which originates from a Trappist monastery on the banks of the Mayenne, a tributary of the Loire.

The delightful wines of the Loire come from vineyards stretching for some three hundred miles along its flanks, and, as is normal for so large a region, they are as diverse as they are charming. The bulk are white wines, ranging from ultradry to medium sweet. But there are also reds, rosés, and sparkling wines.

The upper reaches of the Loire and its tributary the Cher produce good, full, dry white wines at Pouilly, Sancerre, Quincy, and Reuilly—all of which will be described in this chapter. The next chapter will concentrate on the wines of the center of the Loire valley: the reds, whites, and rosés of Anjou and Amboise; the reds of Bourgeuil and Chinon; the whites of Vouvray and Mont-louis; and the very good sparkling wine of Saumur. And the last chapter will be dedicated to Muscadet, a wine that comes from the mouth of the Loire near the city of Nantes.

In general, the wines of the Loire share several attractive attri-butes. They all have a clean, refreshing taste that makes them splendid for picnics and light luncheons, and they are moderately priced. Another characteristic is the rapidity with which they mature, and—the other side of the same coin—how quickly they decline. They are wines of youth—lissome, limpid, and charming. When they are young they are lovely, but they rarely age well.

The upper Loire, like the rest of the river, produces all sorts of wine, red as well as white. However, its fame lies in its excellent dry white wines, the best of which are made from a grape native to Bordeaux called the Sauvignon Blanc, but here named the Blanc-Fumé. There are four major vineyard areas where it is grown.

The first well-known region surrounds the prosaic-looking little village of Pouilly, just north of Nevers. The name causes con-siderable confusion because of its similarity to Pouilly-Fuissé, Pouilly-Loché, and Pouilly-Vinzelles, all in southern Burgundy. The wines in question are full dry whites, but there the resemblance stops. The best wines of Pouilly-sur-Loire are made from the Fumé grape and are called Pouilly-Fumé. Secondary wines are made from the Chasselas, and are named Pouilly-sur-Loire, after the village. The Burgundian Pouillys are made from Pinot-Chardonnay, which gives them a quite different flavor.

But why, if the Fumé seems to produce better wines, is the Chasselas grown at all? The Fumé thrives only on calcareous soil, whereas the Chasselas can be grown in clay and sand. The Chas-selas also produces more wine per acre than the Fumé, and so its wine is somewhat cheaper.

Pouilly-Fumé is an excellent dry white wine with an agreeable body and a bouquet that is reminiscent of the smell of gunflint. Pouilly-sur-Loire, the wine from the Chasselas, is a good wine with a somewhat heavier aftertaste. Both go well with all kinds of fish, as well as *blanquette de veau*, ham, pork, creamed fowl, sweetbreads, and brains.

Pouilly-sur-Loire may not be one of the loveliest towns, but it has many gastronomic attractions. Of its eighteen hundred inhabitants, the ones who aren't vintners must all be involved in the culinary arts, as, for a number of years seven or eight of its restaurants have been listed in the *Michelin* and in due course in the *Guide Kléber*. In 1971, *Michelin* awarded stars to no less than four out of seven.

In town is the Espérance, a restaurant with a view out over the river. Specialties are such delectables as *pâté de canard en croûte, sole soufflée Ali-Bab*, and *poulet sauté aux morilles*. A half kilometer south of town on Route Nationale 7 are two good restaurants. One, the Relais Fleuri, has a lovely garden overlooking the river. A stone's throw away is the Auberge Coq Hardi. Specialties include a sublime *truite au beurre blanc, poulet sauté au Pouilly,* and *crêpes Suzette* as they ought to be but usually are not. Another kilometer and a half on the same road is the Vieille Auberge, to which the *Guide Kléber* awarded the enticing description of "remarkable for all its simplicity" and recommended the *homard grillé à l'estragon*. (Be forewarned that this one may be closed for part of September and October.) All the restaurants carry a fine cross section of Pouilly's wines.

Downriver on the western shore opposite Pouilly is the region of Sancerre. Its name comes from the lovely medieval village that sits on a hilltop a few hundred yards from the river. The village has the placid and harmonious charm of winding streets, towers and ramparts, and even a Roman ruin. The comfortable, old-fashioned hotel Point du Jour et Écu has a restaurant with a rather remarkable décor: trompe-l'oeil painted-marble walls from the early nineteenth century. The food is good, with specialties including *canard farci* and *escargots au Sancerre,* and there are some comfortable rooms upstairs for those who choose to stay over.

The region of Sancerre produces two wines, a white made from the Blanc-Fumé, which is a close cousin of Pouilly-Fumé, and a very refreshing rosé made from the classic Burgundian red-wine grape, the Pinot Noir. Although the rosé is very good, it is produced in minuscule quantities. Consequently, when Sancerre is mentioned it almost invariably refers to the whites. Never a great wine in the sense of such white Burgundies as Montrachet and Corton-Charlemagne, Sancerre is certainly one of the most pleasant little wines, especially good in warm weather and with light luncheons. Fruity, dry enough, fresh, and with a kind of zest that makes one reach for another sip almost as soon as the glass has been put down, it is rightfully a great favorite in France. Lamentably, only about a hundred thousand cases are produced a year, and most of the wine is consumed in Paris before it can be exported.

Two hamlets that also produce white wines from the Blanc-Fumé grape lie about thirty-five miles west of Sancerre and Pouilly, near the delightful medieval city of Bourges. Their wines resemble those of Pouilly and Sancerre, which is not too surprising since the climate, the soil, and the grape are the same. These whites of Quincy and Reuilly are perhaps a little lighter and less *bouqueté* than those of Sancerre, and more markedly so than Pouilly-Fumé. Nevertheless they are very pleasant with fish and white meats, and serve well on picnics and summer luncheons.

Quincy is a sleepy little town on the river Cher, at this stage only a stream that drifts dreamily by the lovely seventeenth-century Château de Quincy. Both Quincy and Reuilly are too small to have any outstanding restaurants, but the touring gourmet is in no danger of starvation. In the nearby cathedral city of Bourges is the elegant Restaurant Jacques Coeur, named after an extraordinarily cultivated bourgeois of the Middle Ages whose palace at Bourges contained comforts on such a scale as to make even a twentieth-century sybarite envious.

Jacques Coeur was a self-made financial titan. From very humble origins, he succeeded in building up a commercial empire that spanned much of fifteenth-century Europe and the Middle East. Charles VII recognized his talents and put him in control of France's finances. He was a contemporary of Joan of Arc's, and like her he was to find that preferment, high rank, and success only excited the envy and hatred of those around him. Ultimately he was divested of his position, imprisoned, and finally exiled. But in his heyday he had the opportunity to build a palace that amply displayed his ingenuity and love of opulence. Apart from its magnificence, it had such modern oddities as heated bathrooms with hot water, and even houses for his carrier pigeons so that he could be in constant contact with all sections of his far-flung enterprises.

The restaurant named after him may not be quite as magnificent as his palace, but it is sumptuous enough. The food and service are good, and, as with all things of excellence, not especially cheap. The cellar of the Jacques Coeur contains a good selection of Quincy and Sancerre wines.

The Middle Loire

"For I was born and nourished in the garden of France; that is to say, Touraine," wrote François Rabelais. Although the author of *Gargantua and Pantagruel* was not especially known for his love of understatement, he did not exaggerate in this case. Touraine *is* a garden. Vegetables, shrubs, trees, grass, flowers, and vines shroud the gently rolling hills in a delicate green. Not only does this region seem a little more verdant than most others, but the vegetation blooms and ripens earlier. In Paris markets, the fruits and vegetables of Touraine are always a few weeks in advance of that of their neighbors.

The *douceur* of Touraine's climate is caused by the Gulf Stream, which sweeps down the western coast of France, carrying a river of warm, damp air. This warm air is usually rebuffed by the European continental land mass. But at the mouth of the Loire it finds an opening and lingers to caress the château-dappled banks of the river. The wine of Touraine and Anjou has the same quality as the landscape and the climate. It is soft, easy, gentle, and balanced. It may not be the greatest of French wines, but it is certainly one of the most agreeable. Even the neophyte wine bibber is struck by its *douceur.*

Touraine is named after a Celtic tribe of pre-Roman Gaul, the Turones, as is their ancient capital, Tours. The city lies on a peninsula formed by the Loire and its tributary the Cher. The vineyard country of Touraine begins about twenty miles upriver. In fact, two of the region's most romantic châteaux mark the boundary—Amboise on the Loire, and Chenonceaux on the Cher.

DAY 18
Itinerary p. 28

Middle Loire

Michelin Regional Maps 63 & 64
Michelin Guide Vert *Châteaux de la Loire*

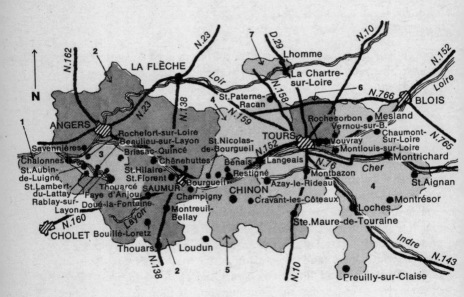

1 Coteaux du Layon
2 Anjou and Saumur
3 Coteaux de l'Aubance
4 Touraine
5 Bourgueil-Chinon
6 Vouvray
7 Coteaux du Loir

Chenonceaux, which many believe to be the most exquisite of all the châteaux, floats like a romantic dream on a series of arches over the river Cher. It is known as the "château of the six ladies" in honor of its most famous chatelaines during the five centuries after its construction. One of them was the beautiful Diane de Poitiers, the middle-aged mistress of the young king of France, Henri II, and, some believe, of his father, François I. While still in the prime of life, Henri was accidentally wounded in a joust and died shortly thereafter. His widow, Catherine de Medici, now had her moment of revenge. She moved Diane out of her comfortable *nid d'amour* into a château of meaner proportions, then took over Chenonceaux and carried on as a widow as she would have liked to have as a wife.

A few years later at Blois, a short way up the Loire from Amboise, Catherine's son, the clever and perverse Henri III, had his arch-rival, the duc de Guise, assassinated. When the king examined the work of his *mignons,* he exclaimed, "My God! How large he looks. He seems much bigger than when he was alive." Prophetic words. A few months later the king himself was to fall to an avenging assassin's blade. His widow, Louise of Lorraine, was in-

---

RESTAURANT-HOTELS

Chaumont-sur-Loire (Loir-et-Cher)	*Hostellerie du Château p. 28
Montbazon (Indre-et-Loire)	*Château d'Artigny p. 28
Langeais (Indre-et-Loire)	**Hôtel Hosten (2, rue Gambetta; tel. 55.82.12)
Chênehutte-les-Tuffeaux, nr. Saumur (Maine-et-Loire)	*Le Prieuré p. 29

RESTAURANTS

Tours (Indre-et-Loire)	***Barrier p. 28, p. 284
	*Restaurant Lyonnais (48, rue Nationale; tel. 05.66.84)
Angers (Maine-et-Loire)	*Le Vert d'Eau (11, blvd. Foch; tel. 88.42.74—closed Aug.)

consolable. Retiring to nearby Chenonceaux, she spent the remaining eleven years of her life in prayer and mourning.

Amboise, too, has its dramatic history. The builder of the present château was Charles VIII, who began it the year Columbus discovered America. Six years later, while hurrying to play a game of tennis, he banged his head on the lintel of a low doorway and died within a few hours. François I was brought up at Amboise. Like his contemporaries Charles V and Henry VIII, he was the very model of a Renaissance prince. He conversed easily with poets, astronomers, soldiers, architects, mathematicians, and musicians. It was he who did much to introduce the genius of fermenting Italy into France, including persuading Leonardo da Vinci to spend his last years at Amboise. The tomb of Leonardo is not in Italy, but at Amboise.

Probably the most somber event that took place at the château was the 1560 Huguenot plot to abduct the young king, François II, and his teen-age wife, Mary Queen of Scots, and to arrest the Duke de Guise and the Cardinal de Guise. The scheme was uncovered by the de Guise family, and its vengeance was ferocious. The château was filled with prisoners who were tortured, hanged, beheaded, or quartered in the courtyards, their dismembered bodies flung into the Loire. Shortly afterward the king himself died. With that the château seemed to fall under a curse, and it has not been used for much since.

Our interest in the Loire, however, isn't centered on its melodramatic history, but on its wines. The twin areas of Touraine and Anjou lie side by side, a one-hundred-mile strip of good vineyards around the cities of Tours and Angers. The vine-growing area is a large one, extending not only along the Loire, but also on the banks of its tributaries, the Cher, the Indre, the Vienne, the Aubance, the Layon, and the Loir. (The last should not be confused with the Loire. Le Loir is masculine and La Loire is feminine. It is perhaps apt that Le Loir is smaller and a tributary of La Loire.)

As is normal with so large an area and so diversified a soil, Touraine and Anjou produce many types of wine: sweet, semi-sweet, dry, and sparkling whites; flowery and subtle reds and rosés. Most of them share a common characteristic. Though sel-

dom grand, they are nearly always pleasant, and above all refreshing.

One of the great saints of early France was Martin of Tours,
and many vinous legends are associated with his name. He was
a native of Pannonia, a region that now lies between Austria and
Yugoslavia. When he left his native country, he carried with him
three vines: one in the bone of a bird, another in the bone of a
lion, the third in the bone of a donkey. Arriving in Tours, he
recognized the area as perfect vineyard country. He unsheathed
his vines and planted them; miraculously the next year each produced enough juice to make one bottle of wine. And so it is that
after one bottle a man sings like a bird; after the second, he has
the courage of a lion; after the third, he acts like an ass.

It is also said that Martin's donkey made a great contribution
to viticulture. Once when Saint Martin was visiting a *vigneron*,
he tethered his mount to some vines. When he returned, he discovered that the donkey had availed himself of the feast before him
and nibbled the leaves off all the vines he could reach. The *vigneron* was furious. But the next year, to everyone's surprise, the
munched-on vines produced more and better fruit than any of
their neighbors. Saint Martin's donkey had discovered pruning,
and ever since vines have been clipped after the *vendange*.

The vineyards of Touraine start on a line that runs from Amboise on the Loire to Chenonceaux on the Cher. With this as the
eastern boundary, the vineyard area extends downriver forty miles
to Bourgueil and Chinon, just above the city of Saumur. Technically Saumur is within the boundaries of the province of Anjou,
but the characteristics of its soil and wine are the same as those
of Touraine.

Grape types used in Anjou and Touraine are more or less the
same. The best white wines are usually made from a native of
the region, the Pineau de la Loire, or as it is most often called,
the Chenin Blanc. Reds and rosés are often made of the Cabernet
Franc, which was imported from Bordeaux during the seventeenth
century. It is locally called the Breton, not, as one might imagine,
after a native of the province of Brittany, but after an abbot
named Breton who was the secretary to the Cardinal de Richelieu.
The Cardinal had estates on the Loire, and to improve them, he

ordered his secretary to import Bordeaux vines and have them planted. They throve, and local *vignerons* soon began planting them too, naming the vines after the man who they thought had introduced them. And so the good Abbé Breton's name is perpetuated in viticultural history just for obeying orders.

Far and away the best-known wine of Touraine comes from Vouvray and the seven surrounding villages: Chançay, Noizay, Parçay-Meslay, Reugny, Rochecorbon, Sainte-Radegonde, and Vernou, all lying on the north bank of the Loire, a stone's throw upriver from Tours. All are entitled to the appellation of Vouvray. Vines have been cultivated here for well over a thousand years and have been favorites of such appreciative *fins becs* as Henri IV, who went so far as to have a vineyard in Vouvray just to supply the needs of his table.

And few would quarrel with his taste. Vouvray is a delightful wine, if a somewhat inconsistent one. It is always white, and by law must be made of the Chenin Blanc or the Menu-Pineau. Like the wines of Alsace, Vouvray fluctuates radically depending on the weather. Great, sunny years usually produce flowery, rather heavy, and somewhat sweet wines; moderate years, wines that are light, refreshing, and pleasantly dry; off years, wines that are prone to be somewhat acid. A good deal of *pétillant* Vouvray is produced, *pétillant* being a wine that isn't quite sparkling but leaves a tingle on the palate. Sparkling wine is also made in the Vouvray region.

A few hundred yards from the Loire is a low line of bluffs tracing what must have been the river's high-water mark in some previous geological epoch. Nowadays they serve man, not the river. Tunneled in them is a warren of caves where the Vouvray vintners bottle and store their wines. Bottling is done early, and the wine is aged in glass rather than in wood. Although the great sweet Vouvrays have considerable staying power, the other lighter, and, to my taste, more pleasant ones should be bibbed when the blush of youth is still on them. Four years brings them to their fruity and refreshing peak.

The vineyard region of Montlouis is directly across the river from Vouvray on the peninsula formed by the confluence of the Cher and the Loire. The vineyards entitled to this appellation are near the towns of Montlouis itself, Husseau, Lussault, just downriver from Amboise, and Saint-Martin-le-Beau, a short way from Chenonceaux. The wines are all white and greatly resemble Vouvrays. They are made from the same grape varietals, bottled early, and aged in glass. Among the lesser wines there is sometimes a *goût de terroir*—taste of the soil—but the better ones are virtually undistinguishable from average Vouvrays. Because Montlouis is not well known, the wines are cheaper.

About thirty miles downriver from Tours, near the junction of the Loire and another of its tributaries, the Vienne, stands the medieval town of Chinon. It is a dramatic village with the escarpment of the hill above it crowned by the huge, somber ruin of a château. This fortress was the scene of one of the most important acts of French history. It was one of the last holdouts of Charles VII. The English had driven him from almost all his domains, when news arrived that a young dairymaid from Lorraine had heard voices that had told her to throw the English out of France and have Charles formally crowned at Reims, the traditional anointing place of France's kings. So sure of this was she that she had left her home and was walking across France to persuade Charles of his and her destiny. Charles didn't like the sound of this one bit. Whatever the gullible populace thought, he knew the English were tough. As for Joan of Arc, for that was the girl's name, she sounded rather demented. To avoid her, and also test her, he disguised himself as a courtier and had someone else play the part of king. Joan entered, immediately singled him out from the crowd around him, and hectored him on his cowardice. Flabbergasted by her miraculous way of finding him, he agreed to supply her with armor and a horse to go to Orléans to combat "les Goddams." Thus began the career of the Maid of Orléans and the re-creation of the kingdom of France.

Chinon produces red and rosé wines from the Breton or Cabernet Franc and the Cabernet Sauvignon, and white wines from the Chenin Blanc. The reputation of the whites is rather overshadowed by the wines of Vouvray and Montlouis, but the reds and rosés have a fine standing. The reds in particular have been singled out for some rather original praise by Jules Romains, who said, *"C'est un vin pour intellectuels."* The wine is delicate and thoughtful. It doesn't assert itself vigorously; yet, properly aged, which is about four years, its subtlety, velvety taste, and violet-hinting bouquet provoke memory and thought. It is not a wine to go with game or lusty red steaks. Rather, it complements a delicate *gigot*, or, perhaps best, veal.

Directly across the Loire from the French atomic center at Avoine-Chinon lie the villages of Bourgueil and its neighbor, Saint-Nicolas. The region produces reds and rosés from the same grapes used at nearby Chinon. The wines are similar, but a Bourgueil can be harder and thus take more time to mature. A good Bourgueil demands about five or six years and will last fifteen. It too goes well with lamb and lightly flavored meat and fowl.

Touraine-Amboise, Touraine-Azay-le-Rideau, and Touraine-Mesland produce all the different types of wine. However, Azay and Amboise are most reputed for their whites, whereas Mesland is becoming much appreciated for a rather fruity rosé made from the Gamay Noir *à jus blanc,* the same grape that makes the amiable red wines of Beaujolais.

The visitor would be very well advised to make Tours a stop on his itinerary. There is the restaurant Chez Barrier. For years it was known as one of the very finest restaurants in France, and it was a pleasure to note that the *Michelin,* in 1968, at last recognized it and gave it the supreme accolade of three stars. *Kléber* followed suit with the maximum recommendation of *première table de France.* The outside of the restaurant is not too prepossessing, but the food is spectacular. Listed as specialties have been *écrevisses au Vouvray, darioles de ris de veau, suprême de poularde à la tourangelle,* and *soufflé glacé aux framboises.* The wine list, of course, shows the best of the region's harvest, and one may safely put oneself in the hands of the sommelier. Reservations should certainly be made in advance.

The name Anjou stems from the ancient Gallic state of the Andes. The Romans recognized it as an entity, and when the Franks came to France they established it as a countship under the direction of a count. Counts, generally speaking, ran frontier provinces for the crown, and because of the danger of their position were given considerable local autonomy. The frontier in this case was Brittany, where the British and Gallic Celts brooded over being thrust onto a peninsula by the new invaders.

When Henry, count of Anjou, became king of England in the twelfth century, he founded the Plantagenet or Angevin line—Angevin meaning from Angers, the capital city of Anjou. With that, the wines of the region were exported in large quantities to England, where they earned a devoted following. The Dutch also became very fond of them, possibly because Anjou a little later on was a great Protestant center, and the Dutch liked trading with their coreligionists. Royalty seems to have had a penchant for Anjou's wines. Charlemagne is said to have owned vineyards there. François I and Louis XIV enjoyed the wines, and Louis XV bibbed them with Madame de Pompadour at his *petits soupers*. An English monarch famed as an elegant sybarite was Edward VII, and his favorite wines came from Parnay.

The region of Anjou produces light reds and rosés, sparkling as well as still white wines, elegant dessert wines, and some very pleasant medium-dry white wines that seem preordained to go along on a summer picnic.

Starting at the border of Touraine, the first city of Anjou is the old Protestant center of Saumur. Nowadays it also has a certain reputation as the home of France's cavalry school. In 1940, when France seemed completely beaten by the onrushing hordes of panzers, the young cavalry students left their classrooms and set up a defense that held up the Wehrmacht for a few days. The cavalry school was all but wiped out and the Wehrmacht soon swept on. Yet, in France's blackest hour this brave try did send a little thrill of pride through a demoralized people, allowing them to warm themselves in the glow of their compatriots' honor. The Resistance was born soon after, and it is possible that it owed some measure of its considerable success to the *beau geste* of the doomed young cavalry students of Saumur.

Saumur produces wine of nearly every variety. After Champagne, it is France's best sparkling-wine region. A bottle of sparkling Saumur, though perhaps lacking some of Champagne's extraordinary elegance and finesse, is excellent nonetheless. In France, of course, it is forbidden to call a wine that does not come from that region Champagne, and so a Saumur must still call itself Saumur. A good brut sparkling Saumur is an excellent apéritif before lunch, and a splendid potation to end a supper. And it has one pleasant advantage over Champagne: its price.

Saumur also produces considerable quantities of other white wines very much like the Vouvrays of Touraine. This is not surprising, as the soil and the grapes are similar. Reds and rosés are also made, usually from the Breton or Cabernet Franc grape. Not generally extraordinary, they can be surprisingly fine in a good vintage year.

The Coteaux de l'Aubance is a region named after the river that flows into the Loire near Angers. It is known for its whites and rosés, the former of which are developing a considerable reputation as good light luncheon wines. The area was overlooked in the nineteenth century, as vogue then demanded wines that were full, sweet, and flowery, and the Aubance area didn't have the right kind of soil to produce them. However, taste changes, and now the Aubance, which does make a pleasant medium-dry white wine, is in favor. The rosés should not be overlooked either. Both they and the whites are good values.

The Coteaux du Layon is the region next to the Aubance down the Loire and is also named for the river that it straddles, the Layon. Without much doubt it produces the finest wines of this section of the Loire valley. Its whites range from medium-dry to liqueur wines that are only slightly below those of Sauternes. The greatest of these—and they are very fine wines indeed—come from Quarts de Chaume and Bonnezeaux. The grapes are picked in much the same way as for Sauternes and *Beerenauslesen*, that is, after a fungus named the *Botrytis cinerea* has dried the grape to an almost raisinlike state. The resultant wine is honeyed, bursting with bouquet, and thick with natural glycerin. It is the essence of grape flavor, and for those who like to terminate their meals with a sweet, it makes the ideal liquid dessert.

The rosés of the Coteaux du Layon carry one of two names referring to the type of grapes used for the wine. Cabernet rosé is likely to be a very pleasant bottle of wine. A label without the word Cabernet, however, indicates that the wine was probably made from a grape type named Groslot, which I suppose must have its admirers, but I am not among them.

Coteaux de la Loire is the name given to the viticultural region on the north bank of the river opposite the mouth of the Layon. The city of Angers lies just to the north of it. It is famed for two white wines. One is a very pretty dessert wine, which resembles its neighbor across the river on the Layon. There are also a number of dry, white wines, made from the melon grape, that are similar to the Nantais Muscadets—excellent companions for the Loire's fishy denizens as well as *fruits de mer*.

The Lower Loire

Between Newfoundland and the coast of Europe flows a three-thousand-mile span of iron-colored water, pushed by currents and prevailing westerlies. Its unending waves sweep in long gray ranks toward Europe's shores. About a hundred miles off the coast of France the torrent of water is suddenly braked by a steeply rising undersea shelf. There it piles up. The result is a turmoil of brine called the Bay of Biscay, known for centuries as one of the most treacherous bodies of water. In the days of sail, mariners would try to cross it quickly lest they be overwhelmed in one of its sudden violent storms.

The south of the bay is bounded by Spain, the east by the ancient Roman province of Aquitania, and the north by Brittany, a rocky, irregular finger that prods out into the Atlantic. The Loire flows through the southern part of Brittany before ending in the storm-tossed waters of the Atlantic.

Brittany is in many ways the least French of France's provinces. The rest of the country was populated by such German tribes as the Franks and the Burgundians who interbred with Gallo-Romans. But Brittany's inhabitants came, as the name suggests, from the British Isles.

In the fifth century, the Roman legions, garrisoning what is now England, were recalled to defend their homeland against the hordes of barbarians pouring through the Alps. The Britons, who had grown soft in the four hundred years of *pax Romana,* were left to fend for themselves. Shortly after, marauding bands of Saxons, Angles, Jutes, and Danes landed. Bit by bit they drove the native Celts back into the hills of Wales, Scotland, and Cornwall. Many of the Celts took to their ships and sailed westward to Ireland, or southwestward to the stony promontory jutting out from the coast of France, Armorica. So many landed there that the peninsula was renamed Brittany, "land of the Britons." The Celts of Brittany kept in close contact with their British cousins across the Channel, so much so that many of their legends were held in common, each appropriating them as their own. According to the Bretons, for example, King Arthur and his round table were Bretons, as were Tristram, Isolde, and Merlin. Tintagel Castle was situated not in Cornwall, as the British believe, but on the north coast of Brittany, near Brest. And even today, when Bretons find themselves with a surplus of vegetables they can't get rid of in France, they hop in their boats and take them to their Welsh cousins up the Bristol Channel. There is no language barrier. The bargaining is done in Celtic.

For ten centuries the Bretons lived in virtual isolation from the rest of France. Facing the sea as they did, they became preeminently maritime. During the dark ages, Breton fishermen swept far out into the Atlantic and by the twelfth century were fishing off Newfoundland. Thus, three centuries before America was discovered, the fact that there was land on the other side of the Atlantic was common knowledge in Brittany. In fact, one of

---

HOTEL-RESTAURANTS
  Nantes (Loire-Atlantique)

*Hôtel Central & Rôtisserie
    Crémaillère   p. 29, p. 294
*Hôtel Duchesse Anne (3, pl.
    Duchesse-Anne; tel. 74.30.29)
    p. 294

RESTAURANTS
  Ancenis (Loire-Atlantique)

La Chaumière (20, rue Rayer; tel.
    1.29—closed late Sept. & early
    Oct.)

  Basse-Goulaine, nr. Nantes
    (Loire-Atlantique)

*Restaurant du Parc   p. 29
*Mon Rêve (tel. 10)

Lower Loire

Michelin Regional Maps 63 & 67
Michelin Guide Vert *Bretagne*

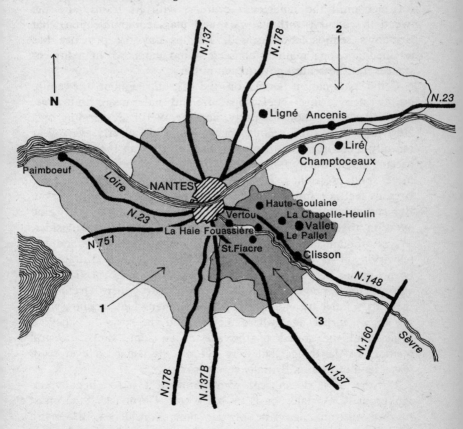

1   Muscadet des Coteaux de la Loire
2   Muscadet Sèvres-et-Maine
3   Coteaux d'Ancenis

Columbus' most convincing arguments when he presented his project to the courts of Portugal and Spain was the testimony of Breton fishermen.

In the sixteenth century, Brittany was incorporated into the kingdom of France, but kept many of the privileges of a separate domain. Its ports quickly became the home of the French navy and merchant marine, and it soon found itself involved in rough rivalry with the island kingdom across the Channel. Even so, it was not until the nineteenth century, with its trains, and the twentieth century, with its wars and mass communication, that Brittany's semi-isolation ceased. To this day the province has retained a strong regional character—too much so, in many instances, for the central government in Paris.

Celtic nationalism seems on the rise throughout the entire northwestern fringe of Europe. Ireland has made itself free. Scotland has a nationalist party, and the Welsh are forming one. Now the Bretons too seem to be boiling a bit. Nearly every year recently there have been riots and barricades, with French officials peering out of their prefectures through a hail of vegetables and more solid projectiles. Part of this ferment is due to what the Bretons feel is a mishandling of their agricultural overproduction. But certainly much of it is also caused by the well-known Celtic aversion to being governed by anyone, least of all an outsider.

And though the centralizing state, the automobile, and the television set have made inroads into Breton culture, Brittany has by no means become an integral part of France as yet. The land still remains strangely different. It is a country where Druids still seem to wander by moonlight, where dolmens and menhirs whisper of an earlier age, where the fog and the surf, the smell of brine, and the sound of the sea evoke some dim, ancestral memory of the things that were before time began. If ever there was a land of Merlin, Brittany surely is it.

But the magic doesn't end with the mood. Gastronomically and viniferously, Brittany casts a spell too. Curnonsky, the most revered gastronomic critic of our time, considered Brittany a Lucullan jewel. And after one visits the area, it is hard to disagree with his verdict. Its artichokes, round and big, are regarded as the finest in France. Its *agneau pré-salé* is considered by many gourmets to produce the tastiest *gigots* in the world. Butter abounds. Brittany, moreover, is the home of that delicate rolled-up pancake, the crêpe, which the Bretons use as others do the sandwich. In effect, it is a hot, tubular sandwich stuffed with a host of tasty fillings. Dessert crêpes are made of wheat flour, and are served either with a stuffing of jam, sugar, and cream, or, as in the case of the familiar crêpes Suzette, with orange rind and Grand Marnier. Main-course crêpes are usually made of buckwheat flour and are filled with ham, eggs, cheese, or tomatoes, or a mixture *de la maison*. In Paris, Breton *crêperies* have become a fixture, displaying their hot griddles called *galetières*, their bowls of batter and stuffings, and their stocky Bretons armed with their *raclettes*—batter spreaders that look like small rakes without teeth.

But without doubt Brittany is most famous for its *fruits de mer*. Armorica, the ancient name for the province, meant "land of the sea," and the ocean has repaid the compliment by pouring its bounty of shellfish into Brittany's larder. Its lobsters are the best in France—some think the peers of our own Maine lobsters. Its delicious oysters of Cancale and the tiny gray shrimps bring tears of anticipation to the eyes of any true crustacean lover. As for the clams and the *moules marinière*, it's worth a trip to Brittany just to taste them.

It seems almost divine Providence that Brittany's *fruits des vignobles* should provide the ideal wine to go with its *fruits de mer*. The areas producing each lie cheek by jowl. The Loire, as we mentioned earlier, ends its long trip by running through southern Brittany. At the mouth of the river is the pretty little fishing village of Le Croisic, a town well known for the excellence of its *portugaise* oysters, its lobster fleet, and a fish auction where a display of the sea's treasures are scrutinized by the big Paris buyers, who then have them packed in ice and shipped off to the capital. It is an attractive village, its quays lined with seventeenth- and eighteenth-century houses, many of which were built by the Duc d'Aiguillon, minister of Louis XV and governor of Brittany. About forty miles upriver from this piscatorial paradise, around Brittany's largest city, Nantes, lie vineyards that in the past few years have earned a large international following, the producers of Muscadet.

Only Chablis can rival Muscadet as the perfect companion for oysters. And although the best Chablis may be far grander, Muscadet wines are a very good value. The wine is a pale yellow, perhaps slightly green-tinged, dry, with a fruity bouquet and that touch of acidity necessary to complement shellfish or any fish served with *beurre blanc*. This acidity, like the lemon so often served with these dishes, enhances their flavor and counterbalances any possible tendency toward heaviness.

The wine from around Nantes has been known for centuries. Abélard, who was a native of the region, is said to have sipped it with Héloïse, and Rabelais praised it in 1530. But although local boosters may gloss over the fact, there is little likelihood that current Muscadet bears much relationship to the wines of the Middle Ages, because in 1709 a ferocious frost struck the mouth of the Loire, destroying the vineyards outright. The local *vignerons,* in order to avoid a repetition of this disaster, scouted far and wide to find a vine suited for their climatic conditions. One they tried was the Melon de Bourgogne, or as it is sometimes called, the Gamay Blanc, a grape grown in Burgundy, but not as a wine grape. There it is used to make *verjus,* a slightly fermented green grape juice which is a basis for many Burgundian sauces and for the mustard of Dijon.

The grape throve at the mouth of the Loire, where it was rechristened the Muscadet. The wine it produced proved an ideal companion for freshwater fish such as salmon, carp, and eel, as well as for the seafood that lay beyond Le Croisic. It had several interesting characteristics. It seemed to do best on the north side of hills, rather than on the customary southeastern side. When the grape was picked before it was completely ripe, the wine had a fine fresh bouquet as well as a characteristic touch of acidity. This, rather than high sugar and alcohol content, was what a Muscadet lover looked for, and in this century when the laws of Appellation Contrôlée were written, Muscadet was the *only* wine with a *maximum* alcoholic limit beyond which it could not go without losing its name.

During the nineteenth century, the vogue was for pungent, thick, and honeyed white wines. Consequently Muscadet, whose characteristics are quite the opposite, was unknown beyond a circle of local admirers. In the late twenties tastes began to change, and it was then that a group of Muscadet growers invited some of the best-known sommeliers of Paris to sample the relatively unknown wines. They accepted the invitation and were impressed. They began suggesting Muscadet to their Paris clientele as an excellent white wine to go with fish and shellfish. Since then the rise of Muscadet has been phenomenal, paralleled only by that of Beaujolais. And though the two wines are different in color, in many ways they share the same attributes. They are both fruity and refreshing, which seems to be the current taste. They both mature quickly and should be drunk young. Muscadet should be drunk at anywhere from one to three years. After that it loses its blossom quickly.

The grapes are often picked when they are slightly underripe in order to guarantee the requisite acidity. The wines are fermented in barrels and sometimes bottled immediately after the fermentation has stopped. The precise moment is a very fine line to tread, and often one will have a bottle of Muscadet that is slightly sparkling, or *perlé* as the French say. Such wines tingle the palate and are quite delicious.

There are three Muscadet appellations. In ascending order of excellence, they are: Muscadet, Muscadet des Coteaux de la Loire, and Muscadet de Sèvre-et-Maine. A wine carrying the name of either of the last two will be made to a slightly higher standard of vinification than the first.

The region of Sèvre-et-Maine lies directly across the river from Nantes, and its wines have the reputation of being fruitier with a little more bouquet than those from the Coteaux de la Loire. Most simple Muscadets come from villages just below the southern edge of the region classified as Sèvre-et-Maine.

The wines from the Coteaux de la Loire come from over a score of communes on both banks running from Nantes to a point thirty-five miles upriver to the east. The Loire here is lazy and wide, a broad, slow-moving deluge that drifts by verdant islands and vineyard-clad banks. Certainly one of the most spectacular views of it may be found in the little hilltop town of Champtoceaux, from whose castle and battlements one can see the river for twenty miles in each direction. All around is a green carpet of vines laden with future Muscadet.

The wines of the Coteaux de la Loire are harder, a little greener, and more acid than those of Sèvre-et-Maine. This makes them perhaps more ideal companions for oysters and clams, whereas those of Sèvre-et-Maine serve better with seafood in general, freshwater fish and veal, pork, cold fowl, and ham. Picnics, too, are admirably graced by a bottle of Sèvre-et-Maine.

Apart from Muscadet, the *vin du pays* from the region at the mouth of the Loire is another white wine made from the Folle Blanche grape, better known as the Gros Plant. Like the Muscadet, this wine is named after the vine—the Gros Plant or sometimes the Gros Plant du Pays Nantais. The Gros Plant is in many respects a younger, less sophisticated brother of the Muscadet. It is coarser, less *nuancé,* and less interesting. Nevertheless, it is a perfectly good quaffing wine to accompany seafood, and is the one usually served in carafe in all the local restaurants. It is not bottled under an Appellation Contrôlée label, but under the government seal of V.D.Q.S., which stands for Vin Délimité de Qualité Supèrieure. This is not to be sniffed at. Although Appellation Contrôlée usually signifies wines that aspire to the highest standards, a V.D.Q.S. ticket on a bottle is a legal guarantee of origin. If the area so guaranteed happens to produce good wines, then the bottle is likely to be a pleasure, and an inexpensive one at that. In 'short, if one wants an uncomplicated, dry white wine to wash down the region's *fruits de mer,* a bottle of Gros Plant du Pays Nantais is just the thing.

For a good place to bed and batten, Nantes, a city of over a quarter of a million inhabitants, offers a number of friendly oases. The city itself is worth a visit. It has a fine cathedral and an impressive *château fort* that sits in the center of the city with powerful self-assurance. It was begun in the fifteenth century by Duke François II of Brittany. The specialties of Nantes include its famous duckling, smaller and more succulent, most gourmets feel, than its rival, the duck of Rouen, all sorts of seafood, and fish such as salmon and pike.

There are two good hotels in Nantes, the Central Hôtel, which has one of Nantes' finest restaurants, the Rôtisserie Crémaillère, and the Duchesse Anne, named after the duchess of Brittany whose complicated marriages finally incorporated the province into the kingdom of France. Both hotels have been bestowed with one of the *Michelin*'s stars, and both serve a good cross section of regional specialties. Their wine lists, of course, have a number of splendid examples of Muscadet, and also some good Gros Plant if the visitor would like to experiment.

Normandy & Its Calvados

DAY 20
Itinerary p. 29

Michelin Regional Map 54
Michelin Guide Vert *Normandie*

With the Loire, the wine tour of France, strictly speaking, comes to an end. But speaking strictly isn't much fun, especially when there is one of France's loveliest provinces left to see, one moreover that produces a brandy (albeit made from apples) that is known to the ends of the earth.

The verdant duchy of Normandy is nestled up against the English Channel. It was named after the Northmen, or Vikings, who in the ninth century stormed out of the northern seas in their longboats, plundering and murdering wherever they landed. Their energy was prodigious. They romped down the western coast of Europe and probed into the Mediterranean as far as Byzantium. They swept across the North Atlantic, settling in Iceland, Greenland, and Newfoundland, and quite possibly extending their explorations as far as Minnesota and Florida. France was of course a mere stone's throw to them, and so their dragon ships were perpetually off her coast, nosing into the rivers for towns to sack.

The king of France soon saw that there was little he could do to stop them, so he decided to join them. He offered them the rich land on both shores of the Seine's mouth as their own (a region they had so thoroughly pillaged and demoralized that it was no loss anyway), on the condition that they settle down and become faithful vassals of the French crown. This was a dangerous game, inviting the lion into the parlor and expecting him to become a good tabby cat. It didn't work. The Norse accepted the land with alacrity, took the title of duke of Normandy for their chief, entrenched themselves, and then spent a large part of the next six centuries trying to make off with the rest of the French kingdom. They came very close to succeeding. By the twelfth century the dukes of Normandy owned England, Ireland, and Wales, and two-thirds of France too. The bloodiest part of French medieval history is the story of how the French kings just barely succeeded in keeping their obstreperous houseguests from throwing them out of their own home.

Since then Normandy has usually been at peace. There was a flurry of war in the sixteenth century when the Huguenot forces of Henri IV won two decisive battles there. Three and a half centuries later, in June, 1944, the Anglo-American armies landed on Normandy's shores and spent a hideous two months trying to force their way through Norman hedgerows, long parapets of earth covered by trees and shrubbery that line the roads and fields. In peacetime they seem charming, separating each field into its own enclosed little kingdom. But to an attacking army they are a nightmare, as they make perfect natural defenses.

Now Normandy is once again a land of peace and plenty. Her landscape is idyllic. Half-timbered thatched farms surrounded by ducks and geese, browsing cattle, and apple orchards are everywhere. Small brooks tumble down the lightly wooded hills and through the placid fields and orchards on their way to their

---

RESTAURANT-HOTELS

Bagnoles-de-l'Orne (Orne)	*Hôtel Bois-Joli p. 29
Honfleur (Calvados)	*Ferme Saint-Siméon p. 29, p. 299

RESTAURANTS

Lisieux (Calvados)	*Restaurant du Parc (21, blvd. H.-Fournet; tel. 62.08.11)
Pont-l'Evêque (Calvados)	*Hostellerie de l'Aigle d'Or (68, rue Vaucelles; tel. 1.41) p. 299

rendezvous with the nearby English Channel. Everywhere the sea lends its tang of salt to the air.

From Normandy's cattle she gets her famous cream and butter, and even more renowned cheeses, such as Camembert, Pont-l'Évêque, and Livarot. From the orchards come Norman pears and apples, cider that many believe to be the world's best, and certainly what is its most famous product, applejack, or Calvados.

Calvados is named after a department in the heart of the province. Its northern boundary is on the Channel, running from the mouth of the Seine to the base of the Cotentin peninsula about sixty miles to the west. The shape of the department is roughly that of a rectangle thirty miles deep. In it lie such famous medieval towns as Bayeux, Caen, and Lisieux.

As any reader of Simenon knows, "un 'tit Calva" is the *digestif par excellence* of the French middle classes. Inspector Maigret could scarcely have solved a single case without a few glasses to stir his sensitivities. As a pick-me-up it is almost the perfect drink. It has the lovely, fresh aroma of apples, and a good swallow is guaranteed to make one breathe deeply. Americans these days have a habit of complaining about how expensive France has become. This is only true if one insists on toping and eating what one is used to back home. Calvados is a good example of the happy alternative. A normal Calvados, the kind truck drivers finish a meal with at little *routier* restaurants, is astonishingly cheap. As a nightcap, or as a little something to settle the evening's vittles, it is splendid. In fact, in Normandy, a land of heroic eaters, it is called a *trou normand*—or "Norman hole-maker." The reason is that a little Calvados is often served midway in the gargantuan Norman repasts. There is a pause after the first five courses in which a glass or two of Calvados is tossed down to help things settle. The Norman hole having been made, serious eating can begin anew.

There are, according to French law, twelve different types of Calvados, eleven of which are named for valleys or *pays* where they are made, the twelfth being just plain Calvados. Which is the best is of course a matter of considerable dispute among Normans. I happen to like them all. However, the region that has the greatest reputation is the Calvados from the Pays d'Auge, a strip of land in the eastern part of Calvados, south of Deauville and Trouville. It lies between two small rivers, the Dives and the Touques, a land that also provides extraordinary cheese, as Camembert, Pont-l'Évêque, and Livarot. The soil of the Pays d'Auge is very rich in chalk, which may explain why the cheeses have a special flavor, and may also be the reason that the apples for the Calvados are considered so fine. Just as white wine seems to thrive in calcareous soil, so, apparently, does cider, the chalk lending the fruit a little hardness to carry its flavor over into the brandy.

The making of the best Calvados is rigidly controlled by law. There are specially permitted ways to mash and press the fruit. Fermentation must last at least one month, and no chemicals are allowed to speed it up. The resultant cider must reach four percent alcohol and contain no more than two and a half grams of volatile acid per liter. No sugar may be added to raise the alcoholic percentage, and the cider must have the general character of being *une boisson saine et loyale*. This cider must be distilled in old-fashioned pot stills. As in Cognac, the heads and tails are thrown away, and the brandy as it leaves the still must contain no more than seventy-two percent alcohol, the other twenty-eight percent being made up of natural fluid, containing apple flavor. Calvados must be presented to the public at between eighty and one hundred proof.

The best Calvados is then aged in oaken casks, sometimes with hazelnut shells thrown in. Aged Calvados, like Cognac and Armagnac, has a golden hue from the wood. However, most run-of-the-mill Calvados is not aged, and it is as clear and innocent-looking as spring water. The resemblance ends there. It is strong stuff, and not to be imbibed in large quantities unless one has a good stock of aspirins at bedside to cope with the hour of awakening. Nevertheless, aged or otherwise, Calvados in limited quantities is a good, stimulating brew. It annihilates minor *aigues*, warms the blood, picks up the heart and appetite, dismisses petty fears, and leaves the mouth tasting as fragrant as an orchard. There's nothing wrong with that.

Calvados imported into the United States include Bellows Vallée d'Auge, Calvados "Arc de Triomphe" of Boulard, and Calvados "La Normande" and Grande Fine of Busnel.

Visiting Normandy is one of the greatest pleasures of touring

France, and the cuisine, with its magnificent beef and lamb, its game, its superb shellfish and Channel sole, and above all its cheeses and its luxurious cream, is something that will make any weight-watcher weep in frustration. Probably the most charming spot from which one may explore the Pays d'Auge is the ravishing little fishing village of Honfleur, just to the west of the mouth of the Seine. It has a port filled with fishing boats, Viking churches of the early Middle Ages, half-timbered hotels and restaurants that are clean, comfortable, and gastronomically memorable. Some are spectacular in style, food, and price. Others are just plain good and inexpensive. All are charming.

Most impressive because of its site, its ancient house, its *grand confort,* and its fine cuisine is the Ferme Saint-Siméon at the edge of Honfleur on the road to Trouville. The host is Monsieur Goulet and his specialties include *matelote honfleuraise, coquilles Saint-Jacques meunière,* and *poulet Saint-Siméon.* Near the center of town on the lovely place Sainte-Catherine is the small but pretty Auberge de la Lieutenance. Its cuisine is fine and its prices reasonable. Close by is another pleasant hotel, the Hostellerie Lechat, also on the place Sainte-Catherine.

Eight miles south of Honfleur is the famous cheese center of Pont-l'Evêque. It is also the home of one of the most famous Calvados distilleries, that of Père Magloire, which welcomes visitors. There are some fine restaurants in Pont-l'Evêque, the finest probably being the Hostellerie de l'Aigle d'Or. It is a lovely stage-coach inn dating back to the sixteenth century. The proprietress is Madame Castelain and the specialties are *cassolette de moules*, *crème aux herbes, médaillon de porcelet,* and *carré d'agneau.* Needless to say, the cheese tray—the other cheese villages of Camembert and Livarot being only a stone's throw away—is excellent.

The Lesser Vineyards

In previous chapters we have wandered through all the major vineyard regions of France that produce wines of superior quality: Burgundy, Bordeaux, the Rhône, the Loire, Alsace, and Champagne. However, in a country so dedicated to Bacchus there are a number of small, scattered areas that make some wines of considerable distinction. Because of their size, these are likely to be overlooked, and it is a pity, for many of them are unique and in their own ways excellent. These vineyards, scattered though they may be, nevertheless fall in two clear sections of the grand circle of the wine tour of France. One is the Franche-Comté, the ancient province between Burgundy and the Swiss frontier. The other is the long rambling trip across the south of France, from the mouth of the Rhône westward all the way to the Basque country before one heads north to the great complex of Bordeaux.

Franche-Comté was for two centuries under Spanish rule. The mountain range running through it is the Jura, a northwestern outrider of the Alps. On its slopes are the vineyards of Arbois, Château-Chalons, and L'Étoile. Arbois is the most famous of the three wines and comes from around the village of the same name. At its center is a fifteenth-century arcaded *place* that could have been plucked right out of a town in Castile—not surprisingly, as Arbois was a possession of the Spanish crown for centuries. It is a pretty square, but is scarred by a motley hodgepodge of electrical wires and old posters announcing sales and the impending arrival of pop groups—not at all in harmony with the feeling of the place. However, on the square is the tasting center of the wines of Arbois, where one may sample the local vintages. It is a shame that André Malraux, who did so much to repair and clean the historical monuments of Paris, did not extend his horizons to this pretty town, famed as the site of many of Louis Pasteur's most important experiments. If its façades and architecture were treated with the reverence they deserve, Arbois would be one of the loveliest villages of France.

The wines of the Jura come in all three colors: red, white, and rosé. Though the red is not particularly noteworthy when compared to its Burgundian neighbors, some of the rosés are quite good. However, the wines for which the area is best known are the whites, in particular the Vin de Paille and the Vin Jaune. The Vin de Paille—wine of straw—is a liqueur wine made from overripe grapes that have been left out to dry on straw mats. Actually, at this point it is something of a historical curio. Taste for sweet wine has faded, making all the effort expended in producing Vin de Paille no longer economically worthwhile. It has all but disappeared.

Vin Jaune, which is an entirely different kind of wine, is still going strong, however. It has a distinctively Sherry-like flavor, somewhat similar to a light *amontillado*. The grapes are not picked until very late in the season, which means that the sugar content —the element that determines how much alcohol the resultant wine will have—is high. After the grapes are pressed, the wine is put into old casks, unlike most of the other wines of France, which are stored either in new barrels or completely refurbished ones. The *flor*—or yeast—in the old barrels spreads quickly and forms a film on top of the wine. This word *flor* is actually the Spanish word for yeast, and it is speculated that this special type of yeast, one which gives a distinctive flavor and can live in wines of high alcoholic degree, was brought from Spain in the sixteenth century.

Another similarity is that in Spain the solera system works on much the same principle as the Arbois reutilization of old casks. In a solera, new wine is added to old, filtering down through the lees of previous vintages until it picks up the character of the wines previously in the solera. In Arbois, the essence of the old wine remains in the cask, and the new wine, which is allowed to sit in the cask untouched for several years, picks up its quality as it matures. The result, not surprisingly, has the haunting memory of a light *vino de jerez* or a *montilla*.

Arbois is a pleasant stopping-off place when one is driving from Paris to Switzerland. Midway between Dijon and either Lausanne or Geneva, it is freckled with agreeable restaurants and comfortable hotels. Most famous is the Hôtel de Paris, owned by Monsieur and Madame Jeunet. It has been awarded a *Michelin* star. The restaurant is attractive, rustic in décor, and the *spécialités,* which include a pike soufflé and *coq aux morilles et vin jaune,* are delicious. The wine cellar is amply provided with the best local produce, and there are a number of comfortable rooms. Other pleasant oases are Les Messageries and the Rôtisserie de la Balance.

Seyssel is an odd little town straddling the Rhône downriver from Geneva. It is joined by a suspension bridge; half of the village is in the department of Ain, the other in Savoie. Ten miles south is Brillat-Savarin's birthplace, Belley, with its excellent Hôtel Pernollet. The hills around Seyssel produce a good dry light wine to accompany the superb fish of Lake Annecy and Lake Geneva. Made from the Roussette grape, the wine is a great local favorite, so much so that not much gets exported except to Switzerland. A good sparkling wine that ranks along with sparkling Saumur as one of the best French sparkling wines outside of Champagne is also made at Seyssel.

The provinces of the south and southwest of France may not produce the finest wines of the land, but they produce a great deal of it and some well worth knowing of, as has been noted. Furthermore, a zigzag trek westward from the Riviera to Saint-Jean-de-Luz on the Atlantic is as various and fascinating an itinerary as any sightseeing motorist could wish. Saint-Jean or the inland Basque village of Ascain are excellent places to pause for a few days at the end of the trip before going on to Bordeaux.

Provence produces a number of wines, none of them superb but many of them refreshing and hearty—perfect accompaniments to the Mediterranean's *fruits de mer* and pungent cuisine. The reds are high in alcohol and have a soft but pronounced flavor; the rosés are sprightly and refreshing; the whites, while not especially subtle or grand, go down remarkably easily if imbibed in the warm sun of their native region.

The most famous regions are Bandol and Cassis, two pleasant little ports lying on the *calanques* between Toulon and Marseille. Cassis in particular is a lovely little town nestled at the mouth of a cliff, with a tiny harbor crowded with yachts and fishing boats. Right on the port are several good restaurants, among them El Sol, Chez Gilbert, and Chez Nino. As Cassis is only fifteen miles from Marseille and a tourist town as well, it is a good idea to make a reservation on Sundays, holidays, and during the summer season.

The word midday in all Latinate languages is synonymous with south, presumably because in the northern hemisphere the sun at its noon apogee marks that direction. The midi in France consists of the *départements* that sweep in a southwesterly quarter circle from the mouth of the Rhône to the Spanish frontier north of Barcelona. It is to wine what the Midwest wheat belt is to grain. There are miles of vineyards spewing forth almost a billion gallons of wine a year. Needless to say, quality is not generally emphasized in the region. It is the land of the *gros rouge*, which the French workman downs by the liter. However, there are also some better than average wines. Best known are the reds, whites, and rosés of Corbières that come from a massif lying just north of the Pyrenees near Perpignan. Narbonne, known in Roman times as the center of Gallic wine making, also produces a well-known wine, Minervois, which may be red, white, or rosé. Both carry the official Vins Délimités de Qualité Supèrieure seal. In both instances the robust red is the best wine, and at the price one pays for it, a very good value.

There are several dessert or liqueur wines from the region too, most of which are fortified and made from subvarietals of the

Muscat or Muscatel grape. Among these are the Muscat de Beaumes de Venise, northwest of Avignon; the Muscat de Lunel, which is between Nîmes and Montpellier; the Muscat de Saint-Jean-de-Minervois, about thirty miles inland from Montpellier near Lodève; the Muscats de Frontignan and Mireval, near the coast between Montpellier and Béziers; and the Muscat de Rivesaltes, just north of Perpignan. Probably the best as well as the best known is the Muscat de Frontignan.

The Muscat grape, which reaches its acme of excellence around Frontignan, dates probably from the time of the Crusades. Frontignan is very close to Aigues-Mortes, the gloomy little town that was France's only outlet into the Mediterranean during the thirteenth century. It was constructed by Louis IX, better known as Saint Louis, as the center of French operations during their fight to gain control of the Holy Land. Consequently it became an important center of Middle Eastern trade, as merchants, sea captains, commissaries, and crusaders passed through the town.

After the collapse of the Roman Empire, Northern Europe had been more or less cut off from the luxuries of the highly developed civilizations at the Mediterranean's eastern end. But with the return of the crusaders, it suddenly became aware of a host of exotic methods, materials, and plants that did much to add dimension to the primitiveness of its culture. Algebra, arithmetic, astronomy, astrology, chemistry, Arabic numerals, cotton, silk, taffeta, damask, strange spices and herbs, the damask rose, the lily, the carnation, and the tulip, the orange and lemon, and many new kinds of vines—all became known at about this time.

The Syrah and the Muscat were probably among the new vines brought in. The Muscat, named after a port on the eastern coast of Arabia, has since spread to nearly every warm area where grapes grow. Known variously as Moscatel, Moscato, Muscadelle, and so forth—there are a dozen varieties—it produces wines that range from excellent to mediocre. In California it makes a medium dry white wine with an odd, flowery flavor and bouquet that, though it marries well with a sweet wine, is not to my taste in a drier, lighter one. From the Muscat-doré-de-Frontignan, a special subvarietal, comes an excellent, sweet, liqueur white wine. The grapes are left on the vine to overripen, their stalks pinched a while before they are picked to interrupt the flow of sap from the vine. They thus dehydrate partially, so that the resultant juice is viscous, thick, and honeyed. Some of the wine is fortified, some not. In either case it is high in alcohol, pungent with Muscat flavor, and of course sweet, making it an excellent accompaniment for pastries and other sweet desserts.

Frontignan itself is not a very prepossessing village. A scant thirteen miles away, however, is the lovely old town of Montpellier with its hotel, the Résidence des Violettes. It is comfortable and pretty, with a good cuisine and a wine cellar of fine local vintages. Situated away from the center of town, this hotel is a member of the Relais de Campagne, an organization that has selected some of the loveliest old châteaux and manors in France and made them into hotels of charm and taste.

Closer to the center of town is another fine hotel, the Métropole. Though not as picturesque as the Violettes, it has an excellent cuisine. Moreover it is around the corner from Montpellier's best restaurant, Les Frères Runel. *Spécialités* include *grive au foie gras, gratin de sole et de langouste*, and *langouste grillée cardinal*. It has a fine collection of regional wines. Furthermore, the *Guide Kléber* has awarded the restaurant the crown of *grande cuisine*. It is closed from the middle of August until late September.

Two other sweet wines come from Banyuls and Maury, near Perpignan by the Spanish border. These are made from the Grenache grape, are fortified, and have a russet color. They have a somewhat oxidized taste, known among winetasters as *rancio*, a characteristic shared by Madeira and Marsala. Both Banyuls and Maury are very pleasant as dessert wines.

Blanquette de Limoux, a sweetish sort of sparkling white wine, is made near the restored medieval city of Carcassonne, between Narbonne and Toulouse. A somewhat similar still wine from the same region is called simply Vin de Blanquette. Both are made from the Mauzac grape, with a small admixture of Clairette Blanche. Though Blanquette de Limoux seems to be greatly admired locally, if one may mix one's winey metaphors, it is not my cup of tea.

Gaillac and Gaillac Mousseux, white wines rather like those of Limoux, come from around the town of Gaillac on the river Tarn between Albi and Toulouse. The main grape used is the same Mauzac. A large quantity is made into sparkling wine, or, as it is known in French, *vin mousseux*. It has very little to commend it except its price.

From the steep vineyards on the slopes of the foothills of the Pyrenees near Pau in southwestern France come the golden colored Jurançon wines. Pau, once the capital of the province of Béarn, is famous as the birthplace of Henri IV. It is said that immediately at birth he had his lips rubbed with garlic and wine, surely the most rapid introduction to the delights of gastronomy recorded. The wine in all probability was a Jurançon. Made from the Gros and Petit Manseng and Courbu grapes, with a small admixture of Lauzet and Camaralet, the wine is sweet and spicy with an odd flavor reminiscent of cinnamon. The grapes are picked late and thus are overripe and filled with sugar. The wine, too, goes well with any pastry or sweet dessert.

Probably the most agreeable place to stay in Pau is the Hôtel de France et Restaurant Crémaillère on the corner of place Royale and the boulevard des Pyrénées. It has a fine view of the Pyrenees on one side and a lovely old square with plenty of room to park on the other, plus the added advantage of being near the center of town. The specialties include *confit d'oie, truffes au champagne,* and *crêpes paloises.*

Irouléguy is a Basque wine from the slopes of the Pyrenees, a few miles behind the picturesque fishing village of Saint-Jean-de-Luz on the Bay of Biscay. The white wine can be a very agreeable companion to the Bay's piscatory produce. The red, however, is usually rather hard and acid.

Bergerac is a provincial little town fifty-five miles east of Bordeaux on the banks of the Dordogne River. Famous for its connection with Rostand's *Cyrano*, it also has a certain reputation as a secondary wine center. Bergerac does produce some red wines but they are not great. Harsh and hard when young, they never develop the grace and elegance of a Bordeaux.

Bergerac's most famous wine, however, is Monbazillac, which in good years has a fair resemblance to a minor Sauternes. Using Sémillon, Sauvignon, and Muscadelle grapes, it is made in the same way as Sauternes: the grapes are allowed to stay on the vines late into the autumn until a fungus, the *Botrytis cinerea,* forms on the skin. This fungus devours the waterproofing element of the skin of the grape, letting the water out, but leaving the thick, honeyed essence of the grape within. The grapes shrivel and reach the point of *pourriture noble* before they are picked and pressed. They develop a dehydrated essence—sweet, thick, and powerful of bouquet. Monbazillac lacks the subtlety and nuance of a great Sauternes. However, it is pleasant enough with a sweet dessert and for this reason is used as an inexpensive stand-in for Sauternes among the French middle classes.

Bergerac is in the Périgord, the center of world truffledom and also the area from which comes the finest *pâté de foie gras*, although Alsace might dispute that. The best hotel is the Hôtel de Bordeaux, which has a rather good cuisine, featuring, of course, a *foie gras truffé*. If one follows the customs of the country, this should be washed down with a cool bottle of Monbazillac. Other *spécialités* include *lièvre royale* and a number of good local cheeses.

RESTAURANT-HOTELS

Dole (Jura)	*Grand Hôtel Chandioux (pl. Grévy; tel. 72.03.25)
Arbois (Jura)	*Hôtel de Paris (9, rue de l'Hôtel-de-Ville; tel. 29) p. 302
	Les Messageries (2, rue Courcelles; tel. 1.03) p. 302
Montpellier (Hérault)	Résidence des Violettes (113, av. Lodève; tel. 92.97.00) p. 305
	Hôtel Métropole (3, Clos-René; tel. 72.50.96) p. 305
Belley (Ain)	*Hôtel Pernollet (9, pl. Victoire; tel. 2.43) p. 302
Bergerac (Dordogne)	Hôtel de Bordeaux (38, pl. Gambetta; tel. 57.11.61) p. 307
Pau (Pyrénées-Atlantiques)	Hôtel de France & Restaurant Crémaillère (blvd. des Pyrénées; tel. 27.86.62) p. 306
Ascain (Pyrénées-Atlantiques)	*Hôtel Etchola (tel. 54.00.08)

RESTAURANTS

Arbois (Jura)	Rôtisserie de la Balance (47, rue Courcelles; tel. 70) p. 302
Cassis (Bouches-du-Rhône)	El Sol (quai Baux; tel. 08.76.10) p. 303
	Chez Gilbert (19, quai Baux; tel. 08.71.36) p. 303
	Chez Nino (1, quai Barthélémy; tel. 08.74.32) p. 303
Montpellier (Hérault)	*Les Frères Runel (27, rue Maguelone; tel. 72.63.82— closed mid-Aug. to late Sept.) p. 305
Pau (Pyrénées-Atlantiques)	*Restaurant Pierre (16, rue L.-Barthou; tel. 27.76.86)
Bergerac (Dordogne)	*Le Cyrano (2, blvd. Montaigne; tel. 57.02.76)

HOTEL

Cassis	Les Roches Blanches (rte. Port Miou; tel. 08.79.30)

Vintages 1964-1975

Over four centuries ago, the Renaissance poet Joachim du Bellay wrote, *"Heureux qui, comme Ulysse, a fait un beau voyage."* It is, we hope, a fitting epitaph for this last chapter on the wines of France. But as we end our tour, we note that bits of information are still to be discussed: a summary of the past dozen vintages, and a few general tips on how to choose good, sound, inexpensive wines.

A few cautionary words should always preface notes on vintages, and vintage charts in particular. Within any given year and place there is always a multitude of factors that can cause wide differences in bottles. A dishonest or inept wine maker can ruin the finest of vintages, just as an inspired one can produce good bottles in what is generally considered a sorry year. There are other elements, too. Spot weather conditions, such as local hailstorms and frosts, can single out vineyards, or even parts of them, for destruction. Proper fertilization and careful pruning of bad grapes and dead foliage can often allow a small quantity of good wine to be made in years of generally bad weather. On top of this comes a host of other variables: the pressing the wine was made from; the care the wine was given after it was bottled; the temperature when it was shipped; the conditions of storage when the bottle arrived in the United States. These last three are the responsibilities of the shipper or importer. If his reputation is good, he will do the best he can to treat his wine in the best manner possible. But if he elects to cut corners financially, banking on the reputation of some great vineyard to return him a maximum profit whether he takes care of the wine or not, then even the grandest and best made wine from the most memorable vintage will be lacking. All these variables are, of course, impossible to encompass within a vintage chart's rigid frame. Nevertheless, a chart has its uses. It is a large-scale map of winedom's varied domains, which does give an idea of the general lay of the land. And a rough map is, after all, better than no map at all.

Although the great vineyards and best-known subregions of every wine area have been discussed at length, this framework hasn't allowed us much chance to speak of the ways to find good, regular drinking wine of moderate price.

WINE CONDITIONS IN 1976

The best vineyards of France are superb, but their area, strictly controlled by law, is very small. All the *grand cru* vineyards of Burgundy lumped together would barely cover a single small California vineyard. This means that in *normal* times these wines will always be expensive, varying according to the size and quality of the vintage and the economic potential of the market.

At the moment, the wine world is living in the aftermath of a most *abnormal* time. Consequently the astute wine lover looking for estate bottlings of a respectable grower or searching for wines from a reputable shipper or importer may with a bit of luck and perseverance pick up some fine bargains. The reasons for this are several.

One is that since 1969 there have been an extraordinary number of fine vintages, many not only splendid in quality but large in quantity besides. A lot of good wine available holds prices down.

Another was the phenomenal wine bubble of the early 1970s, when wine was bought feverishly by every speculator who saw in it an instant fortune. The more they bought, the more prices were pushed up; the more prices went up, the more this convinced them that they had found a hot way to make a killing. It was a bad time for the real wine lover, as he watched his favorite vintages swept up and away in a price tornado of speculative buying.

But tornados are apt to end in a bump, and this was no exception. First came the rise in oil prices, which meant that much of the world's surplus wealth passed into the hands of the sons of the Prophet, and he had forbidden them to touch alcohol. Along with the oil squeeze came the recession. Between the two, the bubble of overconfidence was pricked, driving many of the would-be financial wizards to jettison their stocks of wines both good and bad at what they could get for them, which was usually a lot less than they had paid. The result was great confusion in the wine market. Instant fortunes evaporated, heads rolled, and prices tumbled. The wine-loving consumer is still living to some extent in the aftermath of this happy event.

It is a condition, of course, that cannot last. With hard times receding, more and more people both here and abroad once again can afford to drink their favorite vintages, and with this increase in demand, overstocked inventories are shrinking to normal.

Additionally, the vintage of 1975, though a good one everywhere except in central Burgundy, where drenching autumn rains came down just at picking time, has also been everywhere a small one, which will further cut down on backlogs. There are already signs at the vineyard level, particularly in the Rhône and Loire valleys, whose wines French restauranteurs can use to replace nonexistent 1975 regional Burgundies, that prices are rising as demand overtakes supply. In short, times are becoming normal again, and with that, wine prices will start going up.

For anyone who can afford it, right now would seem a fine time to lay down a good cellar. Of course, in general it is the great named vineyards that command the highest prices. However, these wines are really not meant for everyday consumption. In this latter category the oenophile has reasonable grounds for future optimism.

The reasons for this are also several. During the great wine bubble a great many vineyards were planted, some by serious wine makers in good viticultural regions. It takes four years for a vine to produce wines, seven before it really produces fully and well, and so many of these vineyards will soon be coming on stream. Also, during the past few decades, there has been considerable upgrading of techniques in both the growing of grapes and the actual making of wine. The effect of this has been much more marked on the production of good, sound table wines than it has been on the great *grands crus* vineyards. These latter have, in order to sustain their reputations, nearly always used the finest of grape types and lavished intense care upon them. Thus it is now those areas that were once considered marginal that should be of considerable interest to the thirsty oenophile questing for a good, inexpensive wine to irrigate his supper. These are the regions that can produce, and will continue to make, wines of merit at reasonable prices, if the wine maker is knowledgeable and has invested in the best grape varieties, fertilizers, presses, barrels, and so forth.

In choosing wine from a broad area, it is always difficult to single out good bottles. For though some wines will be excellent, others made by disinterested *vignerons* will not be up to par. Again, look to the name of the shipper or the importer. It is his business to know what is going on in these regions, and if his reputation is good, he will try to keep it so by producing the best bottle he can.

A good bottle of regional Burgundy from a top shipper or importer is apt to give more pleasure than, let us say, a Chassagne-Montrachet from an unknown source. The reason is simple. In Burgundy there are a lot of nooks and crannies which are too small to be classified with some local appellation but which nonetheless produce fine wines. Conversely, though a town such as Chassagne-Montrachet generally produces wines of considerable distinction and thus may be higher up on the Burgundian hierarchical ladder, there are corners of the village that produce wines of middling merit. Yet wines from these nondescript corners still, if they pass certain governmental standards, may call themselves by the town name. Thus the best shipper's "Burgundy" will overlap a mediocre town wine, as his best town wines will overlap wines from individual vineyards that have not been excellently maintained.

For this reason a top regional wine from a renowned shipper may be more expensive than a poor town wine from what is technically a higher appellation. However, if the shipper's or importer's reputation is topnotch, it will almost certainly be a better bargain. And with today's improved wine-making techniques, it may well be a very fine wine to boot.

A Few Observations on the Past Dozen Vintages, from 1964 to 1975.

BORDEAUX RED

The red wines of Bordeaux are split into two main groups, those from the Médoc and Graves southwest of the Garonne and Gironde rivers, and those from Saint-Emilion and Pomerol on the northern bank of the Dordogne. In the Médoc and Graves, the predominant fine-wine grape is the Cabernet Sauvignon. In Saint-Émilion and Pomerol it is the Merlot. Although climatically there is usually not much difference between the two regions, as they are only about twenty-five miles apart, the two grapes sometimes react in different ways to the year's weather, so it seems necessary to treat the two separately on the vintage chart.

1964: An irregular year, but in many instances a great one. The problem in this case was an autumnal downpour. In the regions of Saint-Émilion and Pomerol, the earlier-ripening Merlot had already been picked, so the wines are generally excellent, though a bit soft. They should be consumed now, as they probably will not get any better.

The Médoc and Graves were not so well favored. Those châteaux which had the good fortune to pick early produced some memorable wines. Those that picked during the downpour produced wines that were mediocre. Trust your shipper or importer here. If he is a good one, he will have chosen to import the châteaux that picked early. 60–90 E.

1965: A mediocre year that is by now generally over the hill. 50–65.

1966: A very fine wine, comparable in many ways to the grand vintage of 1961. These wines were heavy in tannin, hence slow to mature, so they should last through the 1980s. 99 S.

1967: A very fine year, perhaps a bit better in Saint-Émilion and Pomerol than in the Médoc and Graves. Not quite so hard as the '66s, these wines should be excellent from now on. 90–95.

1968: In general, 1968 was not an outstanding year, and even those wines that were good were very light and delicate. If any are still about, they should be consumed now. 40–65 E.

1969: A sound year in Bordeaux, but not a great one, though puffery at the time of the *vendange* made it seem so. 80.

1970: A very fine and large vintage, producing wines that matured well and quickly. These wines should be good to drink from now on. 95.

1971: Another very fine year, smaller in quantity than 1970, which produced wines that should be at their best in the *grands crus* in the 1980s. 90 S.

1972: This was the year when the wine bubble grew to an irrational size. The vintage was an excellent one, and quite copious. Growers and speculators from as far afield as Japan and Hong Kong caught the fever, and prices skyrocketed. Merchants are still trying to flog these excellent but vastly overpriced wines for something like what they paid for them, but the hope has dimmed. 85.

1973: A good vintage, and a huge one. The fall of 1973 saw the oil crisis, the beginnings of the recession, the publicizing of the Bordeaux wine-scandal trials, and the advent of a fine-in-quality and grand-in-size vintage. Prices tumbled as so much good wine came in that there was no room to store it. Several well-known vineyards simply declassified their wines voluntarily and sold them under regional names to alleviate their storage problems. Prices of *grands crus* châteaux roughly halved the opening prices of the two previous years. 85.

1974: This was a useful year, good without being great. However, the recession continued, and the bottom appeared to have dropped out of the Bordeaux market. Prices dropped to a third of what they had been two and three years earlier, and still there were precious few buyers to be found. Bordeaux cellars were brim-filled with unsold fine wines. 65.

1975: With the exception of a devastating hailstorm which struck the lesser towns Moulis, Arcins and Blanquefort, in the Médoc, and a few villages across the river in the region of Blaye, the vintage of 1975 was an excellent one, though small in quantity. The small size came as a great relief to the Bordelais growers, as it gave some respite from the overproduction of the phenomenal past seven years. Of these, six were outstanding vintages and one useful, a glut that helped keep the wine market depressed. With this year, many wine growers hoped that the market would bottom, and a new, higher equilibrium could be found. 90 S.

THE WHITE WINES OF BORDEAUX

The white wines of Bordeaux are similar to the reds in that their vintages must be considered in two parts. This has nothing to do with the grape type or the site of the vineyards, but rather with the climate of the late autumn—that is to say *when* the grapes are picked. Grapes to make dry wines are picked early, before they become overripe and too full of sugar. They do not demand overabundant sunshine and may be picked early in the autumn. The great sweet liqueur wines of Sauternes and Barsac, on the other hand, are best made from grapes of a hot summer, and a long warm autumn, as they are picked late, after the *pourriture noble* has had a chance to help them dehydrate. Thus a moderately warm summer is all that is needed for dry whites, one that extends up till mid-September, whereas the liqueur wines need a hot summer, and more, a dry warm autumn up until November when the last picking takes place. As the requirements differ, the same year can produce excellent white wines but poor sweet ones. Thus the two types are put in separate categories on the vintage chart.

1964: A splendid year right up till picking time, when rain began to fall, and fall, and fall. Graves picked early were fine. Sauternes and Barsacs were virtually nonexistent. 85–40.

1965: A mediocre year, all of whose wines are well past whatever small prime they once had. 40.

1966: Good dry whites, but poor to irregular in Sauternes and Barsacs. 85–60.

1967: A fine year for both dry and liqueur wines. 85–90.

1968: Passé. 40.

1969: A fine year in Graves, and in Sauternes and Barsacs. 85.

1970: A superb year in Sauternes and Barsacs, and excellent in Graves too. 95–90.

1971: Fine vintage both in Graves and Sauternes/Barsacs. 95.

1972: Good dry whites; mediocre liqueur wines. 80–60.

1973: Useful dry whites; mediocre liqueur wines. 75–60.

1974: Useful dry whites; poor liqueur wines. 70–40.

1975: Good dry whites, excellent Sauternes and Barsacs. 85–90.

THE RED WINES OF BURGUNDY—CÔTE D'OR

1964: An excellent large vintage which produced beautifully balanced wines that matured quickly. 95 E.

1965: A very wet year in Burgundy, which produced few wines of merit. 30.

1966: An excellent year, which produced beautifully balanced red wines. A large vintage too. 90 E.

1967: A year that produced light red wines of considerable merit. 80.

1968: Generally a miserable year. 30.

1969: A marvelous year, akin in some respects to the magnificent 1961s. Hardy and long-lived, the wines should be superb for many years to come. 99 S.

1970: A fine wine, full, fresh, and quickly maturing. Should be drunk before the 1969s. 85 E.

1971: An excellent year. 90 S.

1972: A very interesting year, producing fine wines that are still rather closed. They should take a bit more time to mature and then should last for a long while after that. 85 S.

1973: A superb, very large vintage. Having matured with astonishing rapidity, these wines are delicious. Fine wines to drink from now on, before starting on the '71s and '69s. 95 E.

1974: A very mixed year. It started off well but was in large part ruined by rains just before and during picking. 50–70.

1975: In the Côte d'Or, the crop appeared to be destined to be very small but good, until torrential autumn rains ruined even this small prospect. A few very great vineyards may try to make some wine this year by selective choice of individual grapes, but in general the year is literally a washout. Beaujolais, which ordinarily produces a quickly maturing wine in large quantities, also was atypical. It produced a very small crop, surprisingly high in tannin, which means that these wines will take a while to mature and then last for some time.

WHITE BURGUNDY

Although all of Burgundy has more or less the same sort of climate, there is such a large geographical spread in the white-wine regions—from Chablis, a short way south of Champagne, to Pouilly-Fuissé, on the northern border of Beaujolais—that spot weather conditions can make a considerable difference.

1964: A big fat wine that matured quickly. If any is left, it should be bibed soon, for it certainly will not improve. 85.

1965: Best forgotten. 30.

1966: A superlative year in white wines that came as close to perfection as I know. Properly cared for, these wines should be lovely to drink right now. 100.

1967: A small vintage because of hailstorms and spring frost, but what there was, was nicely balanced and very good. 85.

1968: Oh, dear! 30.

1969: A year that produced very fine, big, long-lasting whites, but in small quantity. 90 S.

1970: Full, fruity, quickly maturing. Fine wines that should be consumed soon. 85 E.

1971: A very fine year. 90.

1972: Generally a not very good year, with a few exceptions of those wine makers who had the courage to delay picking till late October—a risky business that in this case worked, as there was an Indian Summer. 65.

1973: The greatest recent year: fine, full wines and a lot of them. 95.

1974: A wet autumn produced wines that were irregular; quality is mediocre to good. 50–70.

1975: The Côte d'Or had an appalling autumn with torrential rains, which lowered the quality of the whites considerably. Pouilly-Fuissé was struck badly by hailstorms, so it produced a tiny crop. Chablis, on the other hand, escaped the vagaries of weather and produced very good wines, but in moderate quantities. 50–85.

RHÔNE

1964: A good year, but not as spectacular as the rest of France. 80.

1965: Another good year, better than the rest of France. 80.

1966: An excellent year. 90.

1967: Perhaps the best year in the past dozen. 95.

1968: Mediocre. 65.

1969: Very good year, making wines to keep. 85 S.

1970: A fine, full, fruity vintage. 90 E.

1971: An excellent vintage. 90.

1972: Not quite up to '71, but very good just the same. 85.

1973: A large vintage and a good one. 80.

1974: A good year. 80.

1975: A hot summer followed by a rainy autumn has as its result a year that is quite irregular. There was some rottenness in grapes in many areas at the time of picking. Depending on the grower and wine maker, if the best grapes are used to make the wine, it should be quite good; if not, it will be mediocre. In any case, the vintage was small, and prices are beginning to rise. 60–75.

ALSACE

1964: A great big year, full in body and aroma, which produced wines of extraordinary weight and flavor. 95.

1965: A poor year. 50.

1966: An excellent year. 90.

1967: A very good year. 80.

1968: Thin, lean wines of no consequence. 30.

1969: Excellent year. 90.

1970: Excellent year. 90.

1971: Excellent year. 90.

1972: Good year. 70.

1973: Very good year. 85.

1974: Useful. 70.

1975: A very rainy summer followed by a dry Indian summer has caused a mixed situation in Alsace. Those who risked picking late will have a good, small vintage. Otherwise it is mediocre. 60–80.

THE LOIRE

The wine regions of the Loire stretch from Muscadet at its mouth to Pouilly-Fumé and Sancerre, which share more or less the same climate and temperature as Burgundy. In fact, geographically they are far closer to Burgundy than they are to Muscadet regions. Additionally, the Loire makes many types of wines—dry whites, liqueur whites, and reds and rosés—and as each has its particular needs of climate which may differ quite radically from its neighbors, a vintage chart of the Loire is even more difficult to make than one of some other viticultural region. As a general rule, however, white and rosé Loires are wines of youth and should be drunk young.

1964: A fine year, but now passé for white wines and rosé. 50–80.

1965: A year to be forgotten. 40.

1966: A grand year in its time, the reds are still memorable. 95.

1967: A fine useful year, the reds of which are still good. 85.

1968: Not to be looked for. 40.

1969: Superb from one end of the Loire to the other. 95.

1970: An excellent year throughout. 90.

1971: Another excellent year. 90.

1972: A very good, useful year. 70.

1973: A superb year in the liqueur wines of Anjou, also the reds, rosés, and wines from the upper Loire—that is to say, Pouilly-Fumé and Sancerre—but not as good for the wines of Muscadet, dry wines with a certain amount of acidity which do not thrive on the same climate as the ones mentioned before. 90–75.

1974: An irregular year depending on the region. 50–75.

1975: A good vintage but a small one, with prices beginning to rise, as Loire wines are standard Parisian restaurant fare. 85.

	1964	1965	1966	1967	196:
CHAMPAGNE	Vint.	NV	Vint.	NV	NV
BORDEAUX Red (*Médoc & Graves*)	60-90E	50-65	99S	90	40-6!
BORDEAUX Red (*Pomerol & Saint-Emilion*)	95E	50-60	95S	95	40
BORDEAUX Dry White (*Graves, etc.*)	85	40	85	85	40
BORDEAUX Liqueur White (*Sauternes & Barsac*)	40	40	60	90	40
BURGUNDY Red (*Côte d'Or*)	95E	30	90E	80	30
BURGUNDY White (*Côte d'Or*)	85	30	100	85	30
BEAUJOLAIS	80-90	30	85-90	90	50-7
CHABLIS	80	30	95	85	40
RHONE	80	80	90	95	65
ALSACE	95	50	90	85	30
LOWER LOIRE (*Muscadet*)	80	40	90	85	40
CENTRAL LOIRE (*Anjou & Touraine*)	80	40	90	75	40
UPPER LOIRE (*Sancerre & Pouilly-Fumé*)	90	40	95	85	30

Key:	below 50	very poor	80 to 89	very goo
	50 to 59	poor	90 to 99	excellen
	60 to 69	passable	100	superb
	70 to 79	good		

1964–1975

1969	1970	1971	1972	1973	1974	1975
Vint.	Vint.	Vint.	NV	Vint.	NV	Vint.
80	95	90	85	85	65	90S
80	95	90S	85	85	75	90
85	90	95	80	75	70	85
85	95	95	60	60	40	90
99S	85E	90S	85S	95E	50-70	30-65
90S	85E	90	65	90	50-70	50
90S	90E	90	85	80	75	60-85
90	85	90	70	90	80	85
85	90	90	85	75	75	80
90	90	90	70	85	70	60-80
95	90	90	70	75	75	85
95	90	90	70	90	60	85
90	90	90	70	90	50-75	85

R   red only
NV   nonvintage
S   slow maturing
E   early maturing

INDEX

Index

About the Author

FREDERICK S. WILDMAN, JR., was born in New York City and taken on his first tour to French vineyards at the age of six by his father, the distinguished wine importer.

After serving in the Army, he joined the family firm and thereafter made some one hundred trips to vineyard areas of Europe, America, and Africa. He was wine correspondent for *Gourmet Magazine* from 1965 to 1969, and now lives with his wife and children in a Moorish "mas" in the mountains south of Granada, Spain.